ANTIRACISM INC.

Fig. 1. Hieronymus Bosch, *Ship of Fools* (1490–1500)

First published in 2019 by punctum books, Earth, Milky Way.
https://punctumbooks.com

ISBN-13: 978-1-950192-23-6 (print)
ISBN-13: 978-1-950192-24-3 (ePDF)

DOI: 10.21983/P3.0250.1.00

LCCN: 2019937769
Library of Congress Cataloging Data is available from the Library of Congress

Editorial Team: Chip Badley, Lexxus Edison Coffey, Molly Guillermo, Carmen Guzman, and Jessica Reincke
Cover Design: Carmen Guzman and Vincent W.J. van Gerven Oei
Book Design: Vincent W.J. van Gerven Oei
Cover Image: Detail from Manuel Arenas. "Artificial Breathing" (2010 installation). Courtesy of the Mattress Factory.
Index: Sherri Barnes

HIC SVNT MONSTRA

AntiRacism Inc.

Why the Way
We Talk about
Racial Justice Matters

Edited by Felice Blake, Paula Ioanide,
and Alison Reed

Contents

Part IV — Racial Justice Praxis

Acknowledgments

The *Antiracism Inc.* program, sponsored by the UCSB English Department's American Cultures & Global Contexts Center and the UC Humanities Research Institute, sought to transform how we do the work we do. One of the most delightful aspects of such a foundation is that we had the incredible opportunity to spend time learning together with a wonderful group of generous and committed people.

We are grateful for the fellowship of the Antiracism Inc. working group and radical poets/pedagogues: George Lipsitz, Paula Ioanide, Nick Mitchell, Chandan Reddy, Daniel Ho-Sang, Swati Rana, Aisha Finch, Barbara Tomlinson, Sarah Haley, Sunaina Maira, Shana L. Redmond, Kevin Fellezs, Glenn Adams, Lalaie Ameeriar, Daniel "Fritz" Silber-Baker, Gregory Mitchell, Colin Ehara, Ebony P. Donnley, Dubian Ade, Dahlak Brathwaite, David Scott, former Director Felice Blake, and then graduate fellows Alison Reed and Roberta Wolfson. In our collective project, we have witnessed transformations both subtle and startlingly beautiful, reinvigorating our belief that the ongoing work of building alternative worlds goes at the speed of relationships.

Members of the SB Coalition for Justice, particularly Sunny Lim, Sonya Baker, Danielle Stevens, Michelle Mercer, and Katie Maynard shared valuable organizing lessons. Thank you to the Shawn Greenwood Working Group members of Ithaca, New York—James Ricks, Gino Bush (1942–2018), Shawnae Milton,

Kayla Young, Clare Grady, Aislyn Colgan, Mario Martone, and Paula Ioanide—for sharing vital lessons learned through localized struggles against racist policing. To Californians United for a Responsible Budget (CURB), particularly Diana Zuñiga, thank you for instigating and inspiring new coalitions against prison expansion. Members of the Coalition for Sustainable Communities—particularly Ashley Kiria Baker and Corinne Bancroft—we are grateful for the opportunity to bring our work to Santa Barbara's Earth Day: jails are toxic! We learned so much from People Organizing for the Defense and Equal Rights of SB Youth (PODER), with deepest appreciation to Gaby Hernandez, Marissa Garcia, Savanah Maya, and Kathy Swift for sharing your wisdom and light with us.

The *Antiracism Inc./Works* program series held many events over the course of three years. We would also like to thank the students of Black Sexual Politics 2013, Antiracism and the Problem of Colorblindness 2014, and Antiracism Inc.: Intersections 2014 for their participation in the syllabi emerging from the program series and to the graduate fellows, Drs. Alison Reed and Roberta Wolfson, for co-teaching these courses. The course "The Poetics of Struggle" during Spring and Fall 2014 provided students and campus community members the opportunity to work with brilliant artist-in-residence Daniel Silber-Baker. We are grateful to the Interdisciplinary Humanities Center, UCSB's English Department, and the UC Institute for Research in the Arts for supporting this course.

The ANTIRACISM INC./WORKS program held a reading series for which we are grateful for the generosity of time and engagement from Drs. George Lipsitz, Paula Ioanide, Alison Reed, Amanda Phillips, and Nick Mitchell. We also express our gratitude for contributors to our film series, including Drs. George Levi-Gayle, Kum-Kum Bhavnani, Leah Fry, and Xavier Livermon.

Thank you to the Letters and Science Council of Deans for funding for the *Antiracism Inc.: Intersections Conference,* and to our presenters Drs. Marlon Bailey, Sarah Haley, C. Riley Snorton, and Ashon Crawley for adding critical insights to an evolving conversation.

All of our public gatherings were filmed by Emanuel Garcia. Excerpts can be seen at:

https://www.youtube.com/watch?v=aAEruQ_eT3U
https://www.youtube.com/watch?v=Lf9H4t6beN8

Thank you also to Tiye Baldwin who designed the *Antiracism Inc.* and *Antiracism Inc./Works* logos. It was a pleasure to work with you and we are truly thankful for your enthusiasm and creativity.

We would also like to thank Alison Reed's Graduate Research Assistant at Old Dominion University, Meghan Morris, for her careful editorial assistance as the work neared completion.

Thank you to everyone who participated in the *Antiracism Writes* program, especially Ismael Huerta and the students of Dos Pueblos High School, San Marcos High School, and La Cumbre Junior High School. We are so grateful for their hospitality and collaboration.

Finally, we are immensely grateful for all the love and labor put into this project by punctum books co-director Eileen Joy. She saw the significance of this project early on, and carried it all the way to the finish line. Thank you to punctum's co-director Vincent W.J. van Gerven Oei for his infinite patience through many drafts and changes as well as the book's design! The collaborative spirit of this project was continued in the production phase through the remarkable editing, design and layout work of UCSB students Molly Guillermo, Lexxus Edison Coffey, Jessica Reincke, and Carmen Guzman (who designed our beautiful cover). We thank Sherri Barnes for completing the index and Chip Badley for copy-editing support.

This project is dedicated to all visionary workers.

Antiracism Incorporated

Felice Blake and Paula Ioanide

This collection traces the complex ways people along the political spectrum appropriate, incorporate, misuse, and neutralize antiracist discourses to perpetuate injustice. It also examines the ways that people committed to the struggle for racial justice continue to organize in the context of such appropriations. *Antiracism Inc.: Why the Way We Talk about Racial Justice Matters* reveals how antiracist claims can be used to propagate racial injustices, and what we can do about it.

Current rhetoric on race claims to embrace principles of racial equality, anti-discrimination and diversity; yet old and new forms of racial violence, exploitation and discrimination persist. Although racial justice and decolonization movements developed critical language about the relationship between race and power, social actors across the political spectrum weaponize such rhetoric as a counterrevolutionary maneuver against ongoing liberation struggles. For example, in his attack on the Mexican American/La Raza Studies program in the Tucson Unified School District, Tom Horne (R), Arizona Superintendent of Public Instruction, repeatedly invoked Martin Luther King Jr. to argue for the state's ban on ethnic studies programs.[1] In a 2007 "Open Letter to the Citizens of Tucson," Horne writes:

---

1 *Precious Knowledge*, dir. Ari Luis Palos (Dos Vatos Productions, 2011).

DOI: 10.21983/P3.0250.1.02   17

> In the summer of 1963, having recently graduated from high school, I participated in the civil rights march on Washington, in which Martin Luther King stated that he wanted his children to be judged by the content of their character rather than the color of their skin. That has been a fundamental principal [*sic*] for me my entire life, and Ethnic Studies teaches the opposite.[2]

Horne misuses King's aspirational vision toward a colorblind society to deny the ongoing presence of group-based racial discrimination. Appropriating King's moral authority, Horne declares himself the champion of antiracism. In a gross neutralization of King's radical visions for racial justice, Horne mimics antiracist claims to reproduce racial oppression. As the struggle over Tucson students' ethnic studies education intensified, Horne claimed that the predominantly Latinx student activists who were fighting to save the La Raza Studies Program were "Bull Connors because they're resegregating" and that "we are the ones standing up for civil rights."[3] Martin Luther King Jr. must have been turning in his grave listening to Horne's outlandish claims!

Horne, who helped author the now infamous Arizona SB2281 law that attempted to ban Ethnic Studies classes in the state's public schools,[4] used more than rhetoric to shift public perceptions about race, resistance, and education. On 3 May

---

2   Tom Horne, "An Open Letter to Citizens of Tucson," June 11 2007, http://www.faculty.umb.edu/lawrence_blum/courses/CCT627_10/readings/horne_open_letter_tucson.pdf.

3   Gary Grado, "Horne: Tucson District Violates Ethnic Studies Ban," *Arizona Capitol Times,* January 3, 2011, http://www.azcapitoltimes.com/news/2011/01/03/horne-to-find-tucson-in-violation-of-ethnic-studies-law/.

4   In August 2017, federal Judge A. Wallace Tashima found that Arizona's SB2281 violated students' constitutional rights and that the state showed discriminatory intent in passing and implementing the law. See: Julie Depenbrock, "Federal Judge Finds Racism Behind Arizona Law Banning Ethnic Studies," *National Public Radio,* August 22, 2017, https://www.npr.org/sections/ed/2017/08/22/545402866/federal-judge-finds-racism-behind-arizona-law-banning-ethnic-studies.

2011, Tucson's school district headquarters became a militarized zone. In response to student activists' 26 April 2011 takeover of the school board meeting, the state unleashed 100 police officers in riot gear, a helicopter squad, patrols, K9 bomb-sniffing units, and rooftop snipers in 90-degree weather during the school board's meeting. Though we may scoff at Horne's shameless appropriations of antiracist discourse, because his words can deploy an astonishing level of militarized force against Brown school children, it is incumbent upon us to understand antiracist appropriations as violent acts in both rhetoric and practice.

The struggle over Ethnic Studies in Tucson, Arizona illustrates the questions and problems this collection seeks to address. Ask someone, "What is the antidote to racism?" Their response is likely to be: antiracism. But if a state representative like Tom Horne claims to be antiracist *and* activists struggling to preserve Ethnic Studies also claim to be antiracist, what is the distinction between them? Horne illustrates what we define in this collection as "Antiracism, Inc." He uses discourses originally created by freedom movements to undermine the very outcomes that those struggles produced and continue to struggle for. Ethnic, queer, and feminist studies programs in educational settings owe their very existence to mass mobilizations led by people of color. Stealing and appropriating the language of antiracism, Horne and others like him reveal their organizing tactics of incorporation and appropriation in the war against people of color and any program that empowers them. Education becomes a primary site for staging a battle over how people of color can and should exist.

Rhetorically, Horne's tactic thinly veils his support for systemic racism through his discursive performance as a Martin-Luther-King-loving antiracist. Materially, antiracist appropriators, which include militarized state agents, reinforce their message of opposition through the law and the threat of death. The remarkable mobilization of power in Tuscon, Arizona in response to a high school Ethnic Studies program signals just how insecure the security state is about the legitimacy of its own claims to power.

The state's response is also indicative of just how powerful the knowledge rooted in indigenous and La Raza studies can be. Indeed, the cultivation and use of this powerful knowledge are what distinguish the activists who defended the Ethnic Studies program in Tucson as examples of what we call "antiracism works." Distinct from the rule of law and the threat of death that guide antiracist incorporation to sustain the racial order, these young students and teachers in Tucson produced an empowering program that responded to the needs of predominantly Latinx aggrieved communities. The Ethnic Studies program they created was oriented *against* white domination and *towards* the active engagement with the epistemologies, methods, and histories stemming from radical movements by people of color. Antiracism worked for these educators, students, and community members because they developed coherence between the words and outcomes they produced. In a context of systemic discrimination where communities are regularly under siege by border patrol and police forces, the Mexican American/La Raza Studies program gave students frameworks for understanding their conditions and the legitimation to envision alternative ways of being and being together in this world.

Antiracism Inc.: Why the Way We Talk about Racial Justice Matters therefore examines the appropriation, incorporation, and neutralization of antiracist discourses as a unique technology to advance racism. How did Dr. Martin Luther King Jr.'s radical platform for challenging the racism, militarism, and materialism triad get sanitized into nationalistic projects of selective remembrance? Who could have imagined that the language of mid-twentieth century freedom movements would one day be used to argue that colorblindness is the solution to systemic racism? If power has co-opted, sanitized, and otherwise incorporated antiracist discourse and strategies, how do ongoing struggles for justice build on movement legacies and imagine new possibilities for collective social life? How do we contest a state that capitalizes on the mass detainment and deportation of non-white immigrants while claiming to celebrate diversity and multiculturalism? How do you fight against racist injustice when the perpetrators of injustice claim to be antiracist?

We examine antiracist incorporation as a unique modality of racism. Incorporation and appropriation tactics attempt to neutralize powerful, counterhegemonic discourses that can dismantle the status quo. From Reconstruction-era struggles for free public education for all southern children, to the Black Panthers' Free Breakfast Program in the 1960s and 70s, to the ongoing struggle for Ethnic Studies programs across the country in the 2000s, these mobilizations seek to feed the people physically and intellectually *and* to radically transform society. Rather than looking at resistance only in dialectical relationship with incorporation however, our collection engages with the analysis of what Cedric Robinson calls "racial regimes." As we know, "racial regimes are unrelentingly hostile to their exhibition," but this is because they "do possess history, that is, discernible origins and mechanisms of assembly."[5] In other words, racial regimes depend upon projecting themselves as the only logical terms of creating, maintaining, and experiencing order. This collection interrogates how current antiracist incorporations help construct the present racial regime and why our unique perspectives on this peculiar method of advancing racism is necessary for renewing racial justice praxis.

We see the unrelenting hostility that accompanies the revelation of a racial regime's "mechanisms of assembly" in contemporary US foreign policy approaches, expanding carceral logics, routinized sexual abuse, increasing surveillance, and other systems of coercion. At the same time, this is also a highly defensive moment for white Americans due to increased public debates about cultural appropriation, yet we still witness "black-" and "brownface" spectacles as well as tokenized forms of racial inclusion. What's more, Black culture, especially music, has now come to represent US popular culture. How can all of this be

---

5   Cedric Robinson, *Forgeries of Memory and Meaning: Blacks and the Regimes of American Theatre and Film Before World War II* (Chapel Hill: University of North Carolina Press, 2007), xii.

true simultaneously?[6] As stated above, antiracist incorporation seeks to neutralize counterhegemonic discourses, practices, and movements. But it does so through the hyper- or coercive visibility of people of color. Gendered, racist, and sexual violence occurs in tandem with antiracist appropriation and incorporation *as multipronged modes of neutralization*. Indeed, antiracist incorporation becomes a privileged modality precisely because it has become impossible to dismiss the popularity, visibility, and radical imagination associated with people of color.

While related to colorblind, multicultural, and diversity discourses, the deployment of antiracist incorporation as a strategy for advancing neoliberal and neoconservative agendas is a unique phenomenon that requires careful interrogation and analysis. Colorblindness, multiculturalism, and diversity discourses deny, conceal, and minimize the persistence of systemic racism. Antiracist incorporation openly articulates the problem of racism and racial justice in order to reinterpret their meanings. A popular method of reinterpretation is to disregard group-based discrimination by limiting definitions of racism to individual sentiments of racial animus. For example, conservatives critique protesters like Colin Kaepernick for highlighting patterns of systematic police violence against people of color by saying that stereotyping an entire group of people (i.e., white police officers) is racist. Incredibly, conservatives perform themselves as the authentic antiracists because they champion individualism over group-based stereotypes. Further, they deem Kaepernick unpatriotic precisely because he refuses to adhere to the terms of his purported inclusion into the national body (i.e. remaining silent on matters of systemic racism).

People in power also declare themselves antiracist in order to rewrite history and re-conceal the racial regime. For example, declaring that "we all have implicit bias," as Hillary Clinton did during the 2016 US presidential debates, does the minimal work of recognizing the existence of racism at the interpersonal

---

6   Ibid., 281.

level.[7] This acknowledgement, however, is generally made with the ulterior motive of exonerating those who state it. In other words, the antiracist appropriator recognizes racism in order to establish her moral credentials as someone who opposes it. Even still, such universalizing claims about implicit bias normalize racism as an unfortunate facet of human psychology while erasing the material conditions aggrieved communities continue to face. Racism is thus reduced to a matter of uncomfortable but personal internal tensions. Antiracist appropriators are primarily concerned with deciphering who is a racist and who is not, rather than working to dismantle racism's socially shared institutional and affective structures. What we call antiracist appropriation encompasses the ways that seemingly benign discursive practices can reproduce terribly violent outcomes. Antiracist appropriation perpetuates racism and bamboozles the critiques of racial domination.

Antiracism Inc.: Why the Way We Talk about Racial Justice Matters also considers new ways of struggling toward racial justice. The collection focuses on people and methods who do not seek inclusion in the hierarchical pecking orders of gendered racial capitalism. We focus on aggrieved communities who have always had to negotiate state violence and the appropriative moves of co-optation, but who also spend their energies on building the worlds they envision. They seek to transform social structures and establish a new social warrant guided by what W.E.B. Du Bois called "abolition democracy."[8] This warrant privileges people over profits, environmental sanctity, and ecological harmony. It reshapes social relations away from the violence and

7 "Clinton on Implicit Bias in Policing," *Washington Post*, September 26, 2016, http://www.washingtonpost.com/video/politics/clinton-on-implicit-bias-in-policing/2016/09/26/46e1e88c-8441-11e6-b57d-dd49277af02f_video.html. Democratic presidential nominee Hillary Clinton said implicit bias in policing can have "fatal consequences." http://www.washingtonpost.com/video/politics/clinton-on-implicit-bias-in-policing/2016/09/26/46e1e88c-8441-11e6-b57d-dd49277af02f_video.html.

8 W.E.B. Du Bois, *Black Reconstruction in America: 1860–1880* (New York: Free Press, 1998), 184.

alienation inherent to gendered racial capitalism, and towards the well-being of the commons.[9] It establishes methodologies that permanently strive toward "freedom dreams" without imposing monolithic or authoritative definitions of resistance.[10] As such, it never presumes a shared definition of resistance from the outset, but compels us to develop radical imaginaries within the shifting context of dominant power.

For example, we have witnessed the mass galvanization of people across the US to challenge racist policing against Black people in the Movement for Black Lives. We are witnessing new struggles for immigrants' rights in the Undocumented and Unafraid movement. We are watching the protection of indigenous land and resources as water protectors fight oil pipelines and the catastrophic logic of neoliberal desperation for profits and new markets. The Standing Rock and Idle No More movements are recent mobilizations of a centuries-long force opposing the genocidal project of human and natural exploitation.[11] Because power seeks to neutralize revolutionary action through incorporation as much as elimination, these freedom dreams, as well as the language used to articulate them, are constantly transformed through the critical and creative interventions stemming from the active engagement in liberation struggles.

Why the Way We Work Matters

> *Americans have learned that the tremendous changes we now need and yearn for in our daily lives and in the*

---

9   Clyde Adrian Woods, "Les Misérables of New Orleans: Trap Economics and the Asset Stripping Blues, Part 1," *American Quarterly* 61, no. 3 (2009): 769–96; Clyde Adrian Woods, "Do You Know What It Means to Miss New Orleans? Katrina, Trap Economics, and the Rebirth of the Blues," *American Quarterly* 57, no. 4 (2005): 1005–18; Stefano Harney and Fred Moten, *The Undercommons: Fugitive Planning & Black Study* (New York: Autonomedia, 2013).

10 Robin D.G. Kelley, *Freedom Dreams* (Boston: Beacon Press, 2003).

11 Nick Estes, *Our History Is the Future: Standing Rock Versus the Dakota Access Pipeline, and the Long Tradition of Indigenous Resistance* (New York: Verso, 2019).

*direction of our country cannot come from those in power
or from putting pressure on those in power. We ourselves
have to foreshadow or prefigure them from the ground up.*
— Grace Lee Boggs[12]

Antiracism Inc.: Why the Way We Talk about Racial Justice Matters began in the fall of 2012 as a series developed across three years of thematic programming at UC Santa Barbara's American Cultures & Global Contexts Center (ACGCC) under the directorship of Dr. Felice Blake. We thought critically about the university in the context of antiracist appropriations and worked practically to draw resources and cultural capital from the institution towards addressing the needs of aggrieved communities. Housed within the English Department of UCSB, Antiracism Inc. programming privileged collaborative and non-hierarchical modalities among scholars, activists, poets, and artists in order to engender radical decolonizing methodologies as well as decolonizing discourses. While this collection could not contain all of the work we accomplished during our three years of meetings, we are excited to invite our readers into critical and creative engagement. As Grace Lee Boggs and other radical actors have argued, we can't simply remain oppositional to power or seek incorporation into its structure. Rather, we must change social relations from the ground up, working toward the shared vision of an inter-dependent mutuality that fosters collective well-being and sustenance.[13]

The Antiracism Inc. program and collective created methods of working, learning, and being together toward a vision of radical social transformation that simultaneously negotiates domination and exceeds its epistemological and ontological paradigms. We wanted to model a way of producing knowledge that

---

12 Cited in Robin D.G. Kelley, "Thinking Dialectically: What Grace Lee Boggs Taught Me," *Praxis Center*, October 13m, 2015, http://www.kzoo.edu/praxis/ thinking-dialectically. Original source: Grace Lee Boggs, *The Next American Revolution: Sustainable Activism for the 21st Century* (Berkeley: University of California Press, 2012), xiv.

13 See, e.g., Boggs, *The Next American Revolution*.

is uncommon in academic domains that privilege individualist production — one that was at once creative, intellectually rigorous, and dialogic. We sought to foster openness, develop relationships, engage in improvisation, and emphasize process over product. Such methods have long been central to the organizing modes of the Black Radical Tradition. While the immediate demands of organizing and scholarly work may sometimes cast art aside, the space to imagine opens up new ways of thinking and being, allowing for "an ethics of co-creation."[14]

Our version of interdisciplinarity followed the concept of "accompaniment" about which Barbara Tomlinson and George Lipsitz write in relation to Archbishop Oscar Romero who mobilized for justice in El Salvador during the 1970s.[15] We borrowed from each other where the other left off. We participated in workshops where renowned scholars were asked to silently gaze into the eyes of poets and students for five long minutes. We experienced the sharing and development of knowledge in many forms. We formed ciphers in which scholars were moved to break out of their conventional presentation styles and to spit poetry. Activists, artists, and academics broke bread collectively, not as an afterthought to our meetings, but as an extension of the work. We understood that thinking and being together in our messiness, fallibility, breakdowns, and breakthroughs within and beyond institutional spaces were necessary for building trust and affective joy. As Robin D.G. Kelley's *Freedom Dreams* reminds us:

> Struggle is par for the course when our dreams go into action. But unless we have the space to imagine and a vision of what it

---

14 Daniel Fischlin, Ajay Heble, and George Lipsitz, *The Fierce Urgency of Now: Improvisation, Rights and the Ethics of Cocreation* (Durham: Duke University Press, 2013).

15 Barbara Tomlinson and George Lipsitz, "American Studies as Accompaniment," *American Quarterly* 65, no. 1 (2013): 1–30, https://doi.org/10.1353/aq.2013.0009.

means fully to realize our humanity, all the protests and demonstrations in the world won't bring about our liberation.[16]

Initially, the Antiracism Inc. program engaged in a collective process of identifying how the radical visions of mid-twentieth century freedom movements have been co-opted, misused, or neutralized through incorporative strategies. In doing this work, we realized that the post-Civil Rights shift toward incorporating antiracist discourses rather than Jim Crow exclusion (at least rhetorically) was tactically necessary precisely because previous freedom movements succeeded in rendering overt forms of racial exclusion morally illegitimate. In short, power made concessions by opening the opportunity structure to non-white men, and adapting its public discourse on race and racism in response to people's remarkable organizing power.

Yet, as Lipsitz reminded us during one of the Antiracism Inc. anti-conferences, today's success can become tomorrow's failure. No victory is permanent. Currently, radical racial justice movements face the enormous challenge of fighting the resurgence of overt forms of racism in the neo-fascist era of Trump, *and* the covert forms embedded in neoliberal institutional policies that endorse sanitized and de-radicalized forms of antiracism, diversity, multiculturalism, and colorblindness. As Grace Lee Boggs cautions in the epigraph above, in order to avoid the exhaustion of oppositional politics, radical racial justice movements must also trust in their abilities to create the worlds they want to build, rather than believing that those in power will cede the resources, spaces, and tactics necessary for such transformation.

Take, for example, the regularity with which police kill Black and Brown people only to be exonerated by the state with impunity. In 2015, the police reportedly killed over one thousand people. Charges were brought against eighteen officers only. No

---

16 Kelley, *Freedom Dreams*, 198.

officers were ever convicted that year.[17] Between 2005 and April 2017, 80 officers had been arrested on murder or manslaughter charges for on-duty shootings. During that 12-year span, 35% were convicted, while the rest were pending or not convicted, according to work by Philip Stinson, an associate professor of criminal justice at Bowling Green State University in Ohio.[18] A movement that limits itself to seeking "justice" via the state's procedures will undoubtedly lead to cynicism, despair, and defeat. As Jelani Cobb commented on Twitter following the exoneration of Jeronimo Yanez, the police officer who killed Philando Castile, "Let's drop the pretenses and stop bothering to put police on trial for needlessly shooting black people. It would be more honest that way."[19] By contrast, grassroots movements that seek to create forms of community protection and restorative justice beyond the purview of the state neither expect nor seek restoration exclusively from the state. Instead, they recognize oppressed people's grievances and situate them within the long history of radical struggle. Such movements engage in transformative processes that seek to heal the underlying causes of violence.

For example, the Safe OUTside the System (SOS) Collective, an anti-violence program led by and for lesbian, gay, bisexual, two-spirit, trans, and gender non-conforming (LGBTSTGNC) people of color (POC) in Central Brooklyn, New York, creates community-based safety without relying on the police. Over their ten years of organizing, the Collective found that this is hard work! Coordinators Tasha Amezcua, Ejeris Dixon, and Che J. Rene Long state in their remarkable essay in *TruthOut*,

---

17 Matt Ferner, "Here's How Many Cops Got Convicted Of Murder Last Year For On-Duty Shootings," *Huffington Post*, January 13, 2016, http://www.huffingtonpost.com/entry/police-shooting-convictions_us_5695968ce4b086bc1cd5d0da.

18 Madison Park, "Police Shootings: Trial, Convictions Rare for Officers" *CNN*, October 3, 2018, https://www.cnn.com/2017/05/18/us/police-involved-shooting-cases/index.html.

19 Jelani Cobb, Twitter post, June 16, 2017, 2:04pm, https://twitter.com/jelani9/status/875821378401837056.

the lessons, struggles, and sustained work of co-creating community safety requires multi-pronged approaches to the complex problems that people in their community face. The SOS Collective integrates cultural work in its organizing strategies while assessing LGBTSTGNC people of color's vulnerability to both police abuse and interpersonal violence. Within the context of Brooklyn's gentrification, the Collective also fosters strong interpersonal relationships and establishes principles of internal accountability.[20]

The SOS Collective engages in what George Lipsitz describes as "illogical oppositions" in his essay for this volume. These oppositions are "illogical" because they refuse to follow and abide by the normative logics of value under gendered racial capitalism and the US state apparatus. Rather than privileging individual gain at the expense of communal vitality, those who engage in illogical oppositions seek to model mutual sustenance and collective empowerment. As Stefano Harney and Fred Moten remind us, this work requires co-creating ways of being, seeing, and doing that are in a constant state of fugitive flight from processes that seek to co-opt, destroy, or neutralize their radical visions.[21] The perpetual threat of co-optation requires this radical fugitivity to stay ever-engaged with invention, improvisation, relationality, and creativity in order to exceed the epistemological and ontological reach of domination.

Like the SOS Collective's recognition that cultural work is vital to organizing, the Antiracism Inc. collective understands that poetry and activism are central to the project of developing new language, images, and ideas for gender and racial justice. The poetry and activist interviews in this collection provide blueprints for another world, a space to dream and activate alternative visions of social life — a collective refusal of the oppressive terms of experience meted out by heteropatriarchal

---

20 Tasha Amezcua, Long Ejeris Dixon, and Che J. Rene, "Ten Lessons for Creating Safety Without Police," *Truthout*, June 29, 2017, http://www.truth-out.org/opinion/item/36812-10-lessons-for-creating-safety-without-the-police-a-reflection-on-the-10-year-anniversary-of-the-sos-collective.

21 Harney and Moten, *The Undercommons*.

racial capitalism. Each section includes poetic and/or activist accounts of racial justice practices that continue to regenerate and re-conceptualize struggles towards justice. In short, each section seeks to model a dialogic interplay between Antiracism Inc. and the alternative epistemological and ontological frames that ground racial justice praxis.

Our Work Exists Within a Legacy

Antiracism Inc.: Why the Way We Talk about Racial Justice Matters grapples with the peculiar impasses produced when the empirical evidence of systemic racism's persistence fails to make a difference due to the assumption that liberal democracies *are already* antiracist. It contends with the very real problems people face in communities where their testimonies are refused, inverted, or incorporated toward agendas that further their oppression. The volume examines the ways intra-racial and intra-communal hurts and conflicts are negotiated given the dominant refusal to acknowledge systemic grievances.

Our collection clarifies antiracist incorporation and appropriation as one of the many technologies through which contemporary racism is deployed. This volume builds upon an important body of scholarship that catalogues the detrimental outcomes produced by colorblind, multiculturalist, and diversity discourses in political, legal, cultural, and educational contexts. Scholars have documented the repackaging and reproduction of racial power in the wake of mid-twentieth century freedom and decolonization movements. The "racial break" — the shift from segregationist, colonial, and apartheid practices and policies — challenged white domination in ways that connected antiracism with democracy. Liberalism appropriates antiracism in the service of reimagining US nationalism. As Melanie McAlister argues, those who were previously excluded, disenfranchised, and undeserving of citizenship are re-signified as proof of the nation's multicultural strength, particularly its military prowess.[22] Liberals incorporate antiracism in order to establish US exceptionalism and individual moral goodness, but radically fail to redistribute the socio-economic wealth and advantages obtained through systematic forms of racial discrimination in housing, education, employment, and governmental policy.

Eduardo Bonilla-Silva, George Lipsitz, Ruth Frankenberg, and others revealed the ways that white people evade their complicity with racism by invoking colorblind tropes.[23] In law, scholars of Critical Race Theory (CRT) such as Kimberlé Crenshaw, Patricia Williams, Neil Gotanda, Cheryl Harris, and Gary Peller interrogated the doctrinal basis of "racial non-recognition" that results in the legal impossibility of acknowledging a broad range of social, economic, and political race-based asymmetries.[24] Scholars like James Kyung-Jin Lee have shown how multiculturalism fails to create equitable structural transformation, opting instead to "imagine a new [national] fantasy than to dismantle the actual racial legacies that a previous fantasy permitted the United States to nurture."[25] As such, multicultur-

---

22 Melani McAlister, *Epic Encounters: Culture, Media, and US Interests in the Middle East Since 1945*, 2nd edn. (Berkeley: University of California Press, 2005).

23 Eduardo Bonilla-Silva, *Racism without Racists: Color-Blind Racism and the Persistence of Racial Inequality in the United States*, 2nd edn. (Lanham: Rowman & Littlefield, 2006); George Lipsitz, *The Possessive Investment in Whiteness: How White People Profit from Identity Politics*, rev. and exp. edn. (Philadelphia: Temple University Press, 2006); Ruth Frankenberg, *White Women, Race Matters: The Social Construction of Whiteness* (Minneapolis: University of Minnesota Press, 1993).

24 See Kimberlé Williams Crenshaw, "Race, Reform, and Retrenchment: Transformation and Legitimation in Anti-discrimination Law," in *Critical Race Theory: The Key Writings That Formed the Movement*, eds. Kimberlé Crenshaw, Neil Gotanda, Gary Peller, and Kendall Thomas, 103–26 (New York: The New Press, 1995). See also Patricia Williams, "*Metro Broadcasting Inc. v. FCC*: Regrouping in Singular Times," in *Critical Race Theory*, 191–204; Neil Gotanda, "A Critique of 'Our Constitution is Color-Blind,'" in *Critical Race Theory*, 257–75; Cheryl Harris, "Whiteness as Property," in *Critical Race Theory*, 276–91; Gary Peller, "Race-Consciousness," in *Critical Race Theory*, 127–58.

25 James Kyung-Jin Lee, *Urban Triage: Race and the Fictions of Multiculturalism* (Minneapolis: University of Minnesota Press, 2004), xiv.

alism becomes a way to manage racial antagonisms and evade structural racial inequalities. In *On Being Included,* Sara Ahmed demonstrates how institutional commitments to diversity are "non-performatives" that thwart the very thing those commitments name.[26] Chandan Reddy argues that official, state-based antiracist discourses reduce the demands made by race and gender-based social movements to the formal, legal remedies that the state provides.[27] Howard Winant claims that new racial politics simultaneously acknowledge the demands of egalitarian movements while extending the legacies of racial rule without ending white supremacy and the related expectations of racial and gender normativity.[28] Racial inequality therefore can thrive under colorblind and multiculturalist discourses, "still resorting to exclusionism and scapegoating when politically necessary, still invoking the supposed superiority of so-called mainstream (i.e., white) values, and still cheerfully maintaining that equality has been largely achieved."[29] Insisting that hegemonic emotional economies foreclose people's affective receptivity to the undisputed facts of systemic gendered racism, Paula Ioanide demonstrates how socially shared racial feelings contribute to sustaining the contradiction between colorblind claims and race and gender-specific attitudes that perpetuate racial violence and discrimination.[30] In *Represent and Destroy*, Jodi Melamed shows how liberal antiracist discourses seek to incorporate and neutralize the critiques made in literature authored by racially subordinated US populations.[31]

---

26 Sara Ahmed, *On Being Included: Racism and Diversity in Institutional Life* (Durham: Duke University Press, 2012).

27 Chandan Reddy, *Freedom with Violence: Race, Sexuality, and the US State* (Durham: Duke University Press, 2011).

28 Howard Winant, *The New Politics of Race: Globalism, Difference, Justice* (Minneapolis: University of Minnesota Press, 2004), 42.

29 Winant, *New Politics of Race*, xiii–xiv.

30 Paula Ioanide, *The Emotional Politics of Racism: How Feelings Trump Facts in an Era of Colorblindness* (Stanford: Stanford University Press, 2015).

31 Jodi Melamed, *Represent and Destroy: Rationalizing Violence in the New Racial Capitalism* (Minneapolis: University of Minnesota Press, 2011).

These important interventions allow us to develop a sophisticated analysis of the various ways racism can be deployed. Building on these critiques, this collection focuses on the relational dimensions of antiracism inc. and racial justice praxis. Like racism, this relationship is easy to see, but difficult to make sense of. As a technology of domination, antiracist appropriation and incorporation is not new. From Andrew Jackson's genocidal project of settler colonialism masqueraded as "benevolent paternalism," to placing the abolitionist Harriet Tubman on the $20 bill, symbolically incorporating the bodies, cultures, and social movements of aggrieved communities has long been a tactic for reifying national fantasies of US exceptionalism and concealing the workings of white domination. Hence, this collection examines the conditions of possibility that allow particular styles of racism (e.g., neo-fascist and antiracist appropriation) to become hegemonic.

We argue that antiracist appropriation creates distinct political paradoxes and discursive disorientations such that those on the right and those on the left appear to be making the same claims! For example, as Alison Reed argues in this collection, the framework for the free speech vs. political correctness debate remains tied to the idea that the basis of national social order demands a coherent politics.[32] Under this notion, free speech advocates purportedly seek to eliminate political correctness insofar as it seems to oppose a putatively constitutional national principle. Yet in practice, the opposition to political correctness in favor of free speech is a thinly veiled mechanism for protecting and reifying white racial hegemony. Hostility towards a politically correct term like "undocumented" for instance, is about preserving the right to discriminate against "illegal aliens" as a way to protect citizens and the nation. Resistance to the phrase "white privilege" and to critiques of traditional masculinity is about maintaining control over who represents the national collective. Debates over bathroom policies and Protestant religious

---

32 Cedric Robinson, *The Terms of Order: Political Science and the Myth of Leadership* (Chapel Hill: University of North Carolina Press, 1980).

freedom are about preserving the right to marginalize gender non-conforming bodies in order to define the proper citizen subject as heteronormative. These anxieties about race, gender, religion, and behavior echo the definitions of citizenship in the 1790s, but they also reveal mounting alarm over the redefinition of traditional social roles.

Political correctness, the production and use of speech that avoids representations, behaviors, and language that disparage historically marginalized populations, is regularly described as the basis for so-called liberal indoctrination, particularly in higher educational settings. As we discussed in relation to the struggle over Ethnic Studies in Arizona, education is a key site for developing both appropriations of antiracist discourses and expressions of racial justice praxis. Because the Alt-Right and conservative actors understand educational sites as central to knowledge production, they have increasingly intervened in those settings through appropriations of antiracist discourse. Inverting realities, conservatives claim that those who dare to speak about race and racism are themselves racist ideologues. As Secretary of Education Betsy DeVos argues, "the faculty, from adjunct professors to deans, tell you what to do, what to say and, more ominously, what to think. They say that if you voted for Donald Trump, you're a threat to the university community. But the real threat is silencing the First Amendment rights of people with whom you disagree."[33] The empirically confirmed realities of systemic racism are converted, under this logic, to something that is a matter of opinion and debate. By extension, white nationalist and racist ideologies are treated as equally legitimate claims.

Liberals often respond to these Alt-Right and conservative intrusions with staunch defenses of inclusion, diversity, multiculturalism and equality. Yet they also participate in wielding this

---

33 Valerie Strauss, "DeVos: Colleges Tell Students 'What to Do, What to Say And, More Ominously, What to Think,'" *Washington Post*, February 23, 2017, http://www.washingtonpost.com/news/answer-sheet/wp/2017/02/23/de-vos-colleges-tell-students-what-to-do-what-to-say-and-more-ominously-what-to-think/.

new nationalist protection of hate speech as free speech. Terms like "diversity," "inclusivity," "safe space," and "free speech" now circulate in a context governed by a supposedly gender-neutral and colorblind sense of fairness and equality. Because these terms have been divorced from critiques of systemic heteropatriarchal racism, such liberal concepts have been easily appropriated to include *any* notion of injury, especially those made by people in positions of power. Liberals have widened diversity to mean openness to any viewpoints, even if those views espouse misogyny, endorse police brutality, and contest the existence of transgender individuals. If diversity is code for counting underrepresented students but not the oppression marginalized students face, then creating space for diverse viewpoints can also mean openness to expressions against those who the champions of diversity once sought to protect.

Inclusion in this context means simply the opposite of exclusion writ large. Inviting campus speakers like Milos Yiannopoulous, Ann Coulter, and Ben Shapiro, who openly avow misogyny, transphobia, xenophobia, and racism, makes room for expressions of hate speech within the purportedly progressive discourses of "diversity," "inclusivity," "safe space," and "free speech". Within such discursive frameworks, white students are empowered to articulate themselves as "oppressed" by "political correctness," while students of color are asked to champion a type of patriotism that accepts hate speech — and the violence it emboldens — as another "diverse perspective." Women must tolerate misogynistic words and actions like US President Donald Trump's so-called locker room talk,[34] and LGBTQ people should convert themselves back into traditional binary gender roles or cease to exist. These contestations over national discourse are not simply matters of experiencing hurtful words. These discourses are always coupled with policy and implementation

---

34 Louis Nelson, "From 'Locker Room talk' On, Trump Fends Off Misconduct Claims," *Politico,* December 12, 2017, https://www.politico.com/story/2017/12/12/trump-timeline-sexual-misconduct-allegations-defense-292146.

technologies like executive orders, legislative bills, tanks, militarized policing, prisons, and vigilante violence meant to render aggrieved populations increasingly vulnerable to premature death.[35] Such frames require aggrieved groups to accept hateful representations of themselves in order to be accepted into this new national order.

These discursive moves indicate that the appropriative *rhetoric* of antiracism sometimes overshadows the *work* of antiracism and thus its desired outcome. Modeling transformative rather than assimilative approaches to justice, especially those that defy state recognition, moves us toward racial justice praxis.

Contributions

Each section of the collection includes scholarly essays on the multifaceted ways antiracist discourses are appropriated, incorporated, and neutralized as well as poetic and/or activist accounts of antiracist praxis that continue to regenerate and reconceptualize struggles towards justice. Thus, each section seeks to model a dialogic interplay between antiracism inc. and racial justice innovation, creativity, and regeneration across the color line and intra-racially.

In the first section, "Working Politics," we examine the ways we talk about race, racism, and antiracism in political domains. As Daniel HoSang argues in this collection, demands for racial inclusion and equality made in the context of Jim Crow exclusion have been appropriated by corporations and state institutions to advocate for the incorporation of people of color into the existing status quo, so long as they concede to the inherently unjust structures of corporate capitalism, the prison industrial complex, and the military. Such incorporative strategies seek to shrink racial disparities in corporate workforces, prisons, or the military, but leave the exploitative and violent operative logics of

---

35 Ruth Wilson Gilmore, *Golden Gulag: Prisons, Surplus, Crisis, and Opposition in Globalizing California* (Berkeley: University of California Press, 2007), 28.

those institutions intact. HoSang cautions that racial justice advocates must demand something more than forms of inclusion that seek to punish, incarcerate, and exclude in "racially equal" ways. Paula Ioanide examines the defensive appropriations of antiracist discourses and tactics made by white nationalist groups, police officers and the Alt-Right movement. She argues that these appropriative strategies fabricate affective economies of white victimhood, marginality, and rage irrespective of the empirical realities of white advantage. In re-asserting people of color as a shared object of hate/threat, whiteness reproduces the primary bases for constituting a sense of collective white identity: the power to exclude and violate with impunity. But these defensive appropriations also show the effectiveness of racial justice movements, and the need for persistent innovation. Diana Zuñiga, Statewide Coordinator for Californians United for a Responsible Budget (CURB) discusses her organization's tactics for negotiating and redefining policy decisions related to mass incarceration in an interview with Felice Blake. California, a so-called liberal "blue" state, is also the world's 6th largest economy, a center of technological innovation, and a leader in adult incarceration and correctional supervision. As Zuñiga discusses, the state simultaneously legitimizes prison expansion *and* reform by using a number of incorporative strategies that pervert or sanitize the critiques made by anti-prison activists. Daniel Silber-Baker and Jari Bradley's poems puncture the section by asking difficult questions about survival and resistance amidst the nation's antiracist appropriations and exacerbated racist violence.

The second section, "Educational Strategies" examines the ways educational institutions offer central sites for neutralizing radical propositions for racial justice while purporting to stand for diversity, multiculturalism, and inclusion. As Alison Reed shows, universities and colleges have established themselves as places where diverse viewpoints are welcome. Absent empirically-based critiques of systemic racism and power, such watered-down logics of diversity mean welcoming people who espouse hate speech against the very marginalized students diversity initiatives were meant to include. Similarly, the knowledge produced by people who are actively engaged with racial justice praxis is often misinterpreted and misused, and therefore in constant need of revitalization. Barbara Tomlinson shows how the radical concept of "intersectionality," as originally theorized by Crenshaw, has been appropriated and sanitized of its radical potential by feminist scholars across the globe. Poetic interventions by Dahlak Brathwaite and Sophia Terazawa grapple with the difficulty of finding language to express intergenerational traumas in a time of putative inclusion and recurring violence.

The "Cultural Productions" section provides analyses of antiracism inc. in the complex cultural terrain of contemporary popular film and music. Felice Blake asks us to consider the role of Black cultural criticism in an era fraught with antiracist appropriations. Black popular culture enjoys a dominant position in the US and Black cultural products circulate globally through markets eager for their unique forms of entertainment. Many audiences associate Black musical expression with the critique of injustice and the articulation of resistance. Blake examines how Black cultural incorporation attempts to perform an allegiance to antiracism without engaging the dynamic critiques of power this cultural work may offer. Instead, she meditates on how new artists trouble the terms of order that structure discourses about race, creativity, and representation. Kevin Fellezs considers how soft sounds that are normatively not associated with protest music have the ability to augment vibrant, antiracist legacies. Taking an in-depth look at *nahenahe,* the term native Hawaiians use to describe the aesthetic ideal for slack key guitar, Fellezs challenges the stereotyping of softness as acquiescence, cowardice or naivete. Rather, he shows how the epistemologies of native Hawaiians imbue *nahenahe* with meanings that are often illegible to masculinist protest aesthetics. The section includes interventions from poetic pedagogues Ebony Donnley, David Scott, and Daniel Silber-Baker, who craft language for naming both liberatory practices and the paradoxes created by the cultures of racism.

The final section, "Racial Justice Praxis," shows how antiracist discourses are being reclaimed, reimagined, and re-contextualized by activists in light of dominant appropriations, incorporations and neutralizations. George Lipsitz explores how antiracist co-optation encourages oppressed communities to buy into the profits and tokenized forms of recognition offered by racial capitalism at the expense of their community. By looking to various sites of resistance, Lipsitz offers examples of the ways people refuse such co-optation, privileging horizontal social relations and collective uplift instead. Phia Salter and Glenn Adams propose that the activity of intellectual decolonization is necessary to counteract the (often apparently progressive) forms of knowledge that promote ignorance about ongoing racial domination. They propose two provisional strategies for decolonizing consciousness, and they illustrate these strategies with examples from their research on the relationship between historical knowledge and perception of racism in US society. An interview of activist members of People Organizing for the Defense and Equal Rights of Santa Barbara Youth (PODER) and poems by Dubian Ade, Colin Masashi Ehara, Corinne Contreras, and Daniel Silber-Baker encourage us to consider the difficult work of healing trauma and the need for new language and visions for freedom.

This collection articulates how post-Civil Rights shifts revitalized strategies of antiracist appropriation, co-optation and incorporation in new ways. But it also shows that antiracist appropriations are not the only operative terms of order. The epistemologies and ontologies of the Black Radical Tradition are in a constant state of fugitive flight from the totalizing gestures of Eurocentrism. Although sanitized versions of Civil Rights or antiracism have been incorporated into normative nationalist discourses, the epistemologies, methodologies, and ontologies of the Black Radical Tradition are in a permanent excess to the frames and value systems of heteropatriarchal whiteness. Thus, they continue to guide those who struggle for justice.

Poetic Knowledge: On Why Art Matters to *Antiracism Inc.*

Alison Reed

> *We cannot exist without art.*
> — Angela Y. Davis[1]

On February 20, 2016, at a powerful public conversation Critical Resistance co-hosted titled "Profiles of Abolition: Abolition and the Radical Imagination," moderator Robin D.G. Kelley asked visionary Black freedom fighter and abolitionist Angela Y. Davis to reflect on the vital links between creativity and change. Davis, without hesitation, affirmed the role of art in social movements, elaborating: "Art is always embedded in our efforts to create a better world, to achieve justice. It gives leadership to us…it both allows us to see what is not yet possible but it also allows us to see those things that are right in front of our eyes and that we refuse to see."[2] *Antiracism Inc.: Why the Way We Talk About Racial Justice Matters* takes seriously this claim that art animates

---

1   Angela Y. Davis, public forum, "Profiles of Abolition: Abolition and the Radical Imagination," hosted by Critical Resistance and Los Angeles Poverty Department, Los Angeles, February 20, 2016.

2   Ibid.

DOI: 10.21983/P3.0250.1.03   41

possibilities for building livable futures in the present. In short, a world without art is not only unimaginable, but uninhabitable.

Key to this concept is an understanding of the gross limitations of the representational model of cultural production: the mistaken notion, especially attached to writers of color, that art merely reflects social realities. Instead, this book collection recognizes that acts of artistry are not only deeply imaginative, but transformative of the terms meant to dictate experience. Creative interventions critique power's brutal operation, while also engaging alternative forms of collective social life, amidst pain. All of the writers in this collection seek to model this poetic impetus, urged toward not only critiquing the present, but also reflecting on how community organizers and cultural producers prophesize and enact other ways to be.

Take, for instance, Kendrick Lamar's electrifying performance of "The Blacker The Berry" and "Alright" at the 2016 Grammys, which the audience at "Profiles of Abolition" joined Davis in praising robustly as indicating new horizons of possibility. It's no surprise why this is so, as Lamar at once evokes the unlivable (anti)social destinies of global racial capitalism and simultaneously imagines otherwise. Lamar's band enters the stage in a chain gang, while some are jailed, tracing the trajectory "from the prison of slavery to the slavery of prison."[3] Yet while Lamar spits rhymes between beats dropping like bullets, the saxophonist's blare behind bars affirms that cages cannot contain creative dissent. Amidst a deep historical pulse, the re-signification of racialized symbols, and a stunned audience that rose in standing ovation, lies the poetic knowledge that — to paraphrase Fred Moten's critique of Immanuel Kant — the creative wings of the Black Radical Imagination cannot be clipped.[4]

---

3 Angela Y. Davis, "From the Prison of Slavery to the Slavery of Prison: Frederick Douglass and the Convict Lease System," in *The Angela Y. Davis Reader*, ed. Joy James (Oxford: Blackwell, 1998), 74–96.

4 Fred Moten, "Knowledge of Freedom," *New Centennial Review* 4, no. 2 (Fall 2004): 269–310.

Poetic Knowledge in Outerspace

> *Poetic knowledge is born in the great*
> *silence of scientific knowledge.*
> — Aimé Césaire[5]

In discussing poetic knowledge, I evoke Robin D.G. Kelley's *Freedom Dreams: The Black Radical Imagination*. In this indispensable book, Kelley quotes Césaire's essay "Poetry and Knowledge" to elaborate Césaire's term, which explains how poetry is capable of generating creative solutions to social problems where science fails. In Kelley's words: "We must remember that the conditions and the very existence of social movements enable participants to imagine something different, to realize that things need not always be this way. It is *that* imagination, that effort to see the future in the present, that I shall call 'poetry' or 'poetic knowledge.'"[6] This statement about the necessity of poetry where science fails can be extended to social scientific methods of addressing systems of domination. As important as tracing the myriad untenable fates power engineers on purpose, equally critical is that which the social sciences often leave untouched: the way that grassroots organizers, community-based artists, and poets harness the "power to see the future in the present." In other words, research that exposes the brutal maneuvers of gendered racial capitalism, as significant as it remains, needs the antidote of artistry to chart new star maps to a livable social world.

I'll never forget sitting around uc Santa Barbara's American Cultures and Global Contexts Center director Felice Blake's table one afternoon, as we planned the next *Antiracism Inc.* event, when her daughter Malena dropped poetic knowledge, the wisdom of which far exceeded her years: she looked at us incredulously and explained, matter of factly, how any analysis

---

5   Aimé Césaire, cited in Robin D.G. Kelley, *Freedom Dreams: The Black Radical Imagination* (Boston: Beacon Press, 2002), 9.

6   Ibid., 9.

of anti-Black racism needed to account for outerspace. Her brilliance echoes the Afrofuturist funk of Sun Ra's *Space Is the Place*, Parliament Funkadelic's *Mothership Connection*, and Janelle Monáe's *The Electric Lady*. More specifically, it indicates the everyday awareness of Kelley's concept of a "more expansive, fluid, 'cosmos-politan' definition of blackness, to teach us that we are not merely inheritors of a culture but its makers."[7] It's easy to forget about the imagination as a necessary resource, amidst seas of statistics and the lived trauma — often fetishized in academic spaces — they point to.[8] Yet the poets gathered in this collection dream new worlds into existence, reminding us of the danger of forgetting the fundamental agency of, in Malena's words, not forgetting outerspace.

The Poetics of Activism, the Activism of Poetry

As Critical Resistance co-director Mohamed Shehk says, "abolition is both a beautiful vision but also a practical organizing strategy."[9] Poetic and abolitionist imaginaries continue to intervene in our current political and cultural landscape in ways that challenge the violent status quo. As our beautiful vision reminds us, we are not the passive observers of history; we are active agents in mobilizing to fight against the seemingly inevitable continuation of power across flexible regimes. Even more importantly, we build sustainable communities. To be *against* something suggests that someone else defines the terms of a dialectical relation. Yet the Black Radical Imagination moves to the *works*, which is to say, how we can model transformative approaches to justice, even and especially when they defy state recognition. Once the state assimilates our resistance, it no longer

---

7   Ibid., 2.

8   As Kelley warns against in *Freedom Dreams*, "There are very few contemporary political spaces where the energies of love and imagination are understood and respected as powerful social forces" (4).

9   Mohamed Shehk, emcee commentary, "Profiles of Abolition: Abolition and the Radical Imagination," hosted by Critical Resistance and Los Angeles Poverty Department, Los Angeles, February 20, 2016.

speaks to or for us. In an era of neoliberal multiculturalism that incorporates antiracist discourse through rhetorical traps of "inclusion" and "diversity," we refuse the possibility of reforming or "humanizing" fundamentally inhumane institutions.

This refusal of organizing as reactionary, and our insistence on deep creativity and world-building, also speaks to how and why "antiracism" as a term often interpellates those invested in the philosophy of white liberalism, not the Black Radical Tradition. The neoliberal progress narrative of reformist antiracism — or Civil Rights struggle as assimilation into rather than transformation of foundationally racist institutions — simultaneously occludes and reinforces ongoing brutality. Thus, it is largely the assimilative model of antiracism that has been incorporated, *not* modalities of the Black Radical Tradition. We came to *Antiracism Works* precisely on these terms, asking what flees incorporation through constant reinvention: not legal appeals to reform carceral power, but a transformative way of being in the world. Against an ethic of collective care, the antiracism that has been most fiercely co-opted is precisely the version that was about incorporation, and thus bedmates with the state.

Holding in tension both what confounds and what compels change — or how antiracism gets incorporated into oppressive regimes *and* how alternative social formations disrupt this co-optation — has been central to the *Antiracism Inc.* program. Rather than perceiving the persistence of domestic and border policing, the prison industrial complex and immigration control apparatus (with their invented wars on drugs and terror), labor exploitation, and other forms of state violence as signs of defeat, cultural producers continue to posit concrete visions of justice. While activist-oriented scholarship risks performatively enacting rather than dynamically investing in social change, our project has everywhere shaped and made us accountable to our coalitional work and vice versa. For example, the Coalition for Sustainable Communities formed in response to an *Antiracism Inc.* event series we hosted titled "Engaged Activism/Activist Encounters," which compelled our local engagements during the 2013–14 programming year. This second year of the program featured the subheading *Antiracism Works* and sought to extend the critical frames for addressing issues central to *Antiracism Inc.* by bridging intellectual work with coalitional possibility. From the Shawn Greenwood Working Group[10] in Ithaca, New York, to UC Santa Barbara Students for Justice in Palestine, "Activist Encounters" engaged grassroots responses to police murder, global security, drones, immigration, detention, occupation, and incarceration.

As the Coalition for Sustainable Communities learned in our fight against the proposed jail and ICE detention center projects in North Santa Barbara County, people will often be more receptive to critique if you propose alternative visions of safety and security without cops and cages. The creation of inventive solutions functions as a practical organizing strategy. Using creative tactics in public spaces, from community forums to an Isla Vista Earth Day Festival in 2014, we exposed how — amidst an economic crisis — the so-called public safety budget justified a proposal to spend over $153,000,000 to build the North Santa Barbara County Jail.[11] As the county increased investment in imprisonment, it decreased funding for health and public assistance — concretely demonstrating how unchecked expenditure on carceral power siphons resources away from a plethora of programs that actually sustain communities. Since the state is hemorrhaging money to uphold the inundated and ineffective punishment industry, the county also proposed to increase sales tax.[12] Instead of standing only in opposition to the expansion project, we fought for recognition of life-affirming alternatives to imprisonment — understanding that the proposed jail project

---

10 This grassroots working group convened to challenge clear injustices and discrepancies in the case of Shawn Greenwood, a 29-year-old Black man who was killed by Ithaca Police Department Officer Brian Bangs on February 23, 2010 in Ithaca, New York. The working group later focused on challenging police violence, militarization, and racism in the broader community.

11 Michael F. Brown, "New Jail Planning Study," County of Santa Barbara, 2005, http://www.countyofsb.org/ceo/asset.c/328.

12 Ibid.

would not alleviate overcrowding, but further bolster an inherently violent system that attacks the physical, mental, spiritual, and social health of our communities. In illustrating these realities, the Coalition for Sustainable Communities used our collective creativity as a resource to perform and embody the motto "Jails are Toxic." While we had some victories, what sustained us through the defeats is the knowledge of what we stand *for,* not only what we stand against.

Members of the *Antiracism Inc.* working group continually affirmed that a generative analysis produces hope, not just keen awareness of power's machinations. For example, in "Breaking the Chains and Steering the Ship," George Lipsitz insists that the ongoing struggle needs amplified dialogue between academics and activists to produce new sites of organizing in the academy that necessarily extend to larger collective networks.[13] Knowledge production, grassroots organizing, abolitionist frameworks, and arts practice remain generatively entangled and bound up together even and especially in their tensions and contradictions. As the co-founder of the Combahee River Collective, Barbara Smith, urged in "Toward a Black Feminist Criticism," the mutual exchange among artists, activists, and academics can create new epistemologies, cosmologies, and social formations capable of opening us to "not only know better how to live, but how to dream."[14] The poetry we find most compelling moves us toward our dreams of a just world.

Poetic Praxis

Since its inception in the fall of 2012, *Antiracism Inc.* centered the poetic work of imagining otherwise. In this section, I briefly outline how poetry intersected with three years of program-

---

13 George Lipsitz, "Breaking the Chains and Steering the Ship: How Activism Can Help Change Teaching and Scholarship," in *Engaging Contradictions: Theory, Politics, and Methods of Activist Scholarship,* ed. Charles R. Hale (Berkeley: University of California Press, 2008), 88–111.

14 Barbara Smith, "Toward a Black Feminist Criticism," *Conditions: Two* 1, no. 2 (October 1977): 25–44, at 42.

ming at UCSB's American Cultures and Global Contexts Center, housed in the English Department. While I served as graduate fellow of the program, Dr. Felice Blake's directorship constantly reminded us to not just create space for poetry, but to make poetic praxis the guiding logic of our organizing efforts.

In that spirit, we hosted a daylong workshop in the spring of 2013, "Poetic Interventions," which brought together community members, students, staff, and interested faculty, as well as New York and Bay Area-based hip hop and spoken word artists: Dubian Ade, Ebony P. Donnley, Daniel Hershel Silber-Baker, Gregory Mitchell, Colin Masashi Ehara, and David Scott. With these poetic pedagogues and radical visionaries we engaged our imaginations and collectivity. Through a series of writing prompts, community-building exercises, and captivating performances, we put our finger on the pulse of new language and strategies to intervene in the critical impasses our current racial landscape presents to possibilities for justice. "Poetic Interventions" did not remain in the space of critique but ultimately ushered us into the *works* — or, how we must constantly generate and manifest new propositions for antiracism, despite and especially because of its co-optation.

Elated and invigorated by our coming together for "Poetic Interventions," we invited these poets back to the *Antiracism Inc./Works Anticonference* in the spring of 2014. Our anticonference featured the voices of faculty, organizers, students, and poets from across the country, and focused on the reading and redefinition of antiracism in the Age of Obama. In lieu of a typical Q&A after a panel of speakers presented their work, invited poets led audience members through a series of exercises to address the questions, insights, and possibilities emerging from the conversation. Moreover, the Coalition for Sustainable Communities facilitated a teach-in, "How to Stop the North County Jail." Members from PODER (People Organizing for the Defense and Equal Rights of Santa Barbara Youth) also attended, offering their insight on the Santa Barbara gang injunction struggle, which they ultimately won. Our poetic praxis meant creating space for real engagement of pressing issues, rather than abstract analyses and academic performances divorced from the urgency that animates our organizing commitments.

As we leveraged institutional resources for community-based projects, we did not fetishize the space of the university as a privileged site of study. During the spring of 2014, we presented our work on fighting prison and jail expansion projects at community forums and local schools, such as San Marcos High School, where we collaborated with Ismael Huerta, an eminent youth educator and counselor. We also founded *Antiracism Writes*, an afterschool tutoring program for local junior high and high school students oriented toward critical and creative expression. Our work was guided by the motto "Writing is a Right and Form of Self-Empowerment."

Finally, our program featured a visiting poet in residence, Daniel Hershel Silber-Baker, who facilitated a course in the spring of 2014, "The Poetics of Struggle." It brought together students across campus interested in how words can reckon with and transform histories of struggle, how 36-letter alphabets can make room for marvelous analyses and channel ancestors whose spirits invigorate the work. From Nina Simone, Bootsy Collins, and Kendrick Lamar to Aimé Césaire, James Baldwin, and Audre Lorde, the class dove into the aesthetics of the Black Radical Tradition to emerge from the depths with new words and worlds between our open palms. The workshop-oriented class centered group activities, self-reflection, and self-revelation. In collectively studying Audre Lorde's "The Transformation of Silence into Language and Action,"[15] for example, we interrogated why we speak, of what we are afraid, what we have survived, how we resist, and how we heal. In the classroom, we held space for healing, and for the words we do not yet have. We then asked ourselves how our own healing is necessarily embedded in a larger project of developing holistic visions of collective

---

15 Audre Lorde, "The Transformation of Silence into Language and Action," in *Sister Outsider: Essays and Speeches by Audre Lorde* (Berkeley: Crossing Press, 2007), 40–44.

social life. Ultimately, the class was nothing short of a thesis on the work of poetry.

Star Map to What Follows

Acknowledging the limited authority of the dominant, this collection chooses to not only speak back to power but to radically reimagine the terms of how we connect meaningfully with each other. Exchanging a reactionary position for a creative one does not mean a naïve minimization of the material force of state violence on people's lives; it simply refuses to let that violence delimit the spiritual authority of our communities and commitments. The poems gathered here make powerful propositions for the future grounded in rich legacies of the past. These poems provide a through-line across each section of the book, from "Working Politics," "Educational Strategies," and "Cultural Productions" to "Racial Justice Praxis."

From the so-called "post-racial" era of Obama to antiracism in the time of Trump, or from the colorblind mechanism of disavowal to the current era of neo-fascist rule, *Antiracism Inc.* helps us interrogate the mechanisms through which we understand continuity rather than rupture across historical moments. For example, Dubian Ade's work addresses the tension between the Black freedom struggle and white liberal denial in a post-Civil Rights era. Dahlak Brathwaite's "The Good One" is also situated in a post-Civil Rights era where racism so often attempts to wear antiracist masks. His poem brilliantly indicts neoliberal multiculturalist incorporation: "I'm just playing the game with the tokens given / We already Willy Wonka's chocolate factory / Here's your golden ticket." He continues, mocking colorblindness ideology: "Your Barack Obama / You voted for him / You didn't even see he was black!" From Obama to Trump, Jari Bradley's "Trump 2016" gestures toward Black queer love as survival and resistance to the country's ongoing violences, which the neoliberal police state attempts to conceal: "This has always been America — a silent bloodlust / loud in the heart until it bursts."

Against this bloodlust that bursts, Colin Masashi Ehara's "Akira" affirms the presence and power of social movements led by young people of color. And David Scott's "Gangland Wonderama" theorizes how people negotiate the deep wounds born out of structural harm. Ebony P. Donnley explores the politics of desire amidst state-sanctioned death, and Black queer love as a revolutionary act: "black femmes / i didn't intend for this to be worship,/ but a deep longing for a call to arms,/ for us to lock ours." Corinne Contreras and Sophia Terazawa ground us in space to meditate on how knowledge of the traumatic rifts of hate speech and diasporic memory urge people toward one another through storytelling. Directly summoning his pedagogy and our collective philosophy, Daniel Hershel Silber-Baker's poems contest the state's attempted theft of the radical imagination and assert language's power to heal, create, and "hold spiritual space." As he testifies, the duplicitous face and brute force of state power has co-opted, sanitized, and incorporated antiracist discourse and strategies. Our volume as a whole intervenes in this oppressive "antiracism" by bearing witness to its brutality — and looking to poetry for an otherwise and otherwhere that hungers for another kind of collectivity.

Part I

WORKING POLITICS

graffiti hanging gently in an art museum

Daniel Hershel Silber-Baker

… the deployment of antiracist discourse as a strategy for advancing neoliberal and neoconservative agendas is a new phenomenon that requires careful interrogation and analysis.

Our swords which we wielded to break the chains
The very means by which we have forged
these languages of freedom
Are now hung and held as an artifice artifact
Of a long past struggle
wedged between the very chains
They were made to break
     A centerpiece for viewing

       Graffiti hanging gently in an art museum

DOI: 10.21983/P3.0250.1.04

2

A Wider Type of Freedom

Daniel Martinez HoSang

> *The African bruises and breaks himself against his bars*
> *in the interest of freedoms wider than his own.*
> — C.L.R. James, *A History of Pan-African Revolt*[1]

The formulation "Antiracism Inc." explored in this volume raises two interrelated questions. First, is there an articulation of "antiracism" that is not "incorporated" and thus remains in opposition to the dominant social, economic and political order? Second, in what ways has antiracism become incorporated, or rendered commensurate with rather than antagonistic towards these dominant structures?

This essay takes up both of those questions in turn. I first explore a tradition of racial justice that long imagined and required a fundamental reconstitution, rather than amelioration, of broad forms of governance and material relationships of power. I then discuss contemporary articulations of multiculturalism and racial inclusion that have proliferated in corporations, the military, and some conservative formations that speak in the putative language of antiracism. I conclude with a consid-

---

1 C.L.R. James, *A History of Pan-African Revolt* (Oakland: PM Press, 2012), 106.

DOI: 10.21983/P3.0250.1.05

eration of the hazards and challenges long-posed by these forms of antiracist incorporation.

In 1938, as the tremors of war began pulsating across Europe, the 37-year-old Trinidadian-born writer and political critic C.L.R. James penned a series of pamphlets from his London flat. Like many of his contemporaries on the Left, James sought to make sense of the broad political, economic, and social forces that shaped this moment of revolution and upheaval. What political traditions, popular struggles, and optics on life might have proved capable of liberating the world from perpetual violence, domination and crisis?[2]

James turned his attention to what he described as a "revolutionary history" that was "rich, inspiring, and unknown." A particular tradition of Black revolt and struggle, he argued, represented the repudiation of the West's most corrupting tendencies: slavery and labor exploitation; land appropriation and control; authoritarian governance and genocide. Published together as *A History of Negro Revolt* (and 31 years later, with a new epilogue under the title *A History of Pan-African Revolt*) the short essays took aim at a prevailing historical record that depicted Black people as passive objects of history, destined to realize a painful but inevitable fate of servitude. James subverted this narrative by describing a people in constant revolt: striking for better wages in the mines of West Africa; leading uprisings on the plantations of Haiti and Jamaica; acting decisively to win their liberation during the Civil War; building new churches, schools, and associations in the aftermath to secure their freedom. As he explained in another essay published a year later, "the only place where Negroes did not revolt is in the pages of capitalist historians."[3]

---

2   The pamphlets were published together as *A History of Negro Revolt* by the Independent Labor Party in Britain in 1938 and reissued by the Charles H. Kerr Publishing Company in 1939. See Robin Kelley, "Introduction," in James, *A History of Pan-African Revolt*, 106.

3   J.R. Johnson, "The Revolution and the Negro," *New International* 5 (December 1939): 339–43. As Robin D.G. Kelley explains in the Introduction to the 2012 edition, this essay was essentially a summary of the main arguments in *A History of Negro Revolt*.

James argued that these particular struggles for Black liberation had universal implications; they were responsible for nothing less than the "transformation of western civilization." This was not because of a predisposition within Black civilizations toward revolt, though James did note the cultural practices, memories and traditions that nourished these efforts. It was a quality of Black civilizations rather than particular forms of political consciousness, experience, and exchange produced in response to the domination they endured. In Haiti for example, James described the way in which slaves who lacked formal education and who suffered the degradations of bondage achieved "a liberality in social aspiration and an elevation of political thought equivalent to anything similar that took place in France." Similarly, after the Civil War, the forms of schooling, governance, and public development enacted by free women and men in the South reflected "the policy of a people poor and backward seeking to establish a community where all, black and white, could live in amity and freedom."[4] In the crucible of their despair, new understandings of freedom and human possibility emerged, ideas that could never be imagined by governments premised on the buying and selling of human flesh.

James urged others on the Left to pay attention to these traditions, stories, and histories, insisting that they held invaluable lessons for a world in permanent crisis. James concluded the last essay of *The History of Negro Revolt* in this way: "The African bruises and breaks himself against his bars in the interest of freedoms wider than his own."[5]

On first blush, James's assertion seems puzzling. Political struggles led by a particular group appear by definition to be parochial, meaning that they are applicable only to the specific conditions and experiences of those group members. Within market or interest-based interpretations of political conflict and power, one group's gain is often another group's loss. From this perspective, struggles authored in the interests of Black people

---

4 James, *A History of Pan-African Revolt*, 47.

5 Ibid., 106.

are at best relevant only to other Black people. At worst, they may threaten the interests and status of those who are not Black. If you win, I lose.

James thought and wrote from a much different perspective. He understood the modern concept of race to be premised upon the unequal ordering of humanity, a social and political ideology indispensable to the operation of capitalist economies and authoritarian governments. The specific and localized struggles he recounted — the abolition of slavery in the French colonies; the end of lynching in Alabama; the demand for fair wages in the Congo — produced wider interrogations of power.

In a 1948 essay, James noted that Black resistance in the United States had a "vitality and validity of its own" and "an organic political perspective" that was not simply derived from the broader labor movement or the dominant framework of rights-based liberalism. This "perspective" included a deep skepticism of "imperialist war[s]" that were never meant to secure the "freedom of the persecuted peoples by the American bourgeois." These insights consistently led to forms of self-organization and mass action because Black people in the South in particular understood that ordinary structures of representative government, including voting, the two-party system, and other routine forms of political participation (e.g., "telegrams to Congress") were incapable of addressing their grievances. As a result, Black movements have been able "to intervene with terrific force upon the general and social and political life of the nation…."[6]

At their best, this collective action achieved what the theorist Cedric J. Robinson described as "the force of a historical

---

6   C.L.R. James Meyer, "The Revolutionary Answer to the Negro Problem in the US (1948)," in *C.L.R. James on the "Negro Question,"* ed. Scott McLemee (Jackson: University Press of Mississippi, 1996), 138–47, at 139. For an important discussion of this essay, see Josh Myers, "A Validity of its Own: CLR James and Black Independence," *Black Scholar,* August 24, 2015, http://www.theblackscholar.org/a-validity-of-its-own-clr-james-and-black-independence/.

antilogic to racism, slavery, and capitalism."[7] In other words, in rebelling against the terms of their own subordination, these movements also confronted the broad foundations of violence, exploitation and despotism that defined so much of the development of the West. At particular moments in the development of the United States, James later contended, these rebellions "formed a force which *initiated* and *stimulated*" other sections of the population, acting "as a *ferment*" for much broader opposition.[8] They demanded structural changes including the redistribution of land and resources, and the reorganization of social and political life. Thus, James argued, Black people had long toiled "in the interest of freedoms wider than [their] own."[9]

The claim that particular struggles against racial domination can upend much broader structures of power is most closely associated with a tradition of Black radicalism. As scholars such as Cedric J. Robinson and Robin D.G. Kelley have demonstrated, a long history of Black organizers, leaders and intellectuals, including Ella Baker, Ida B. Wells, Fannie Lou Hammer, Ana Julia Cooper, W.E.B. Du Bois, and many others continually pressed the claim that the abolition of particular forms of racist domination and violence could yield universal horizons of freedom.[10] As the Black feminist organizers who penned the famed Combahee River Collective Statement in April 1977 explained, Black women could draw from their "position at the bottom" to initiate "revolutionary action." They argued that Black women's freedom would "mean that everyone else would have to be free since our freedom would necessitate the destruction of all the systems of oppression."[11] In fighting the particularities of their

7 Cedric J. Robinson, *Black Marxism: The Making of the Black Radical Tradition* (Chapel Hill: University of North Carolina Press, 1983), 248.

8 Meyer, "The Revolutionary Answer to the Negro Problem in US (1948)," 142.

9 James, *A History of Pan-African Revolt*, 106.

10 Robinson, *Black Marxism*; Robin D.G. Kelley, *Freedom Dreams: The Black Radical Imagination* (Boston: Beacon Press, 2003); Barbara Ransby, *Ella Baker and the Black Freedom Movement: A Radical Vision* (Chapel Hill: University of North Carolina Press, 2003).

11 Combahee River Collective, "Combahee River Collective Statement," in *Home Girls: A Black Feminist Anthology*, ed. Barbara Smith (New York:

subordination, they invoked, demanded, and pursued visions of freedom that exceeded the terms of their own oppression.

As George Lipsitz contends, "the intellectual, moral, aesthetic, political, and spiritual legacy of the radical Black tradition" serves as "a repository of ideas and actions important to all people. The freedom dreams of Black people have never been only about Blackness, but rather have sought always to create a world transcending citizenship that would eclipse sectarian identifications and allegiances."[12] Following Aimé Césaire, Lipsitz advocates for "a universalism that is rich with particulars, that entails the dialogue of all, the autonomy of each, and the supremacy of none."[13]

This understanding of antiracist struggle as a capacious interrogation of power also has traditions and origins beyond the Black Freedom Movement. For example, across time and place indigenous people have revolted against the appropriation, commodification, and desecration of their lands and against attempts to abolish their political, cultural, and spiritual practices and traditions. The specific demands and contours of such resistance is well-documented across a rich archive, foregrounding issues of sovereignty, genocide, land theft, and the destruction of tribal cultural, linguistic, social, and political practices. The particularized revolts over these issues often directly confront the same regimes of private property, environmental exploitation, and state violence that undergird and order the United States economy as a whole.

The Nishnaabeg (First Nation) poet and scholar-activist Leanne Betasamosake Simpson disputes the assumption that "Indigenous scholars and community organizers must therefore engage only in what is perceived to be Indigenous theory." She explains instead that "our intelligence includes all the thinking that has gone into making the realities we live in and that on

---

Kitchen Table: Women of Color Press, 1983).

12 George Lipsitz, "Introduction: A New Beginning," *Kalfou* 1, no. 1 (2014): 7–14, at 13.

13 Lipsitz, "A New Beginning," 8.

a more philosophical scale, internationalism has always been a part of our intellectual practices. With our complex ways of relating to the plant nations, animal nations, and the spiritual realm, our existence has always been inherently international regardless of how rooted in place we are."[14] Thus indigenous-led action against uranium mining on Diné (Navajo) lands in the Southwest and resistance against treaty violation and tribal sovereignty also have had universal bearing and implications. They too are bruising and breaking themselves across their bars in the interest of freedom wider than their own.[15]

Likewise, groups such as the New York-based DRUM-South Asian Organizing Center (formerly Desis Rising Up and Moving) that emerged in response to the profiling and detention of Muslim and South Asian Americans after 9/11, represent the latest chapter of a much longer history of Asian Pacific American resistance against militarism and racial profiling. The working-class Muslim, Arab, and South Asian communities DRUM organizes challenge both the particular surveillance and detention programs that wreak havoc on their lives as well as other interconnected forms of state violence, from the militarization of the US border with Mexico to drone strikes in Pakistan.[16]

Similarly, particular traditions of collective resistance emanating from Chicanx, Puerto Rican, and other Latinx communities have interrogated and resisted broad structures of power and domination. For example, in the 1970s in New York and Los Angeles, Latinas mobilized to end practices of coercive and involuntary sterilizations performed on thousands of women deemed unfit to make their own decisions about bearing children. Latina-led organizations such as the Committee to Stop

---

14 Leanne Betasamosake Simpson, *As We Have Always Done: Indigenous Freedom Through Radical Resistance* (Minneapolis: University of Minnesota Press, 2017), 56.

15 Roxanne Dunbar-Ortiz, *An Indigenous People's History of the United States* (Boston: Beacon, 2015), and *Say We Are Nations: Documents of Politics and Protest in Indigenous America since 1887*, ed. Daniel Cobb (Chapel Hill: University of North Carolina Press, 2015).

16 See DRUM — *Desis Rising Up and Moving*, http://www.drumnyc.org.

Forced Sterilizations centered their activism on the women most directly affected by abusive sterilization practices. But they explained that the stakes were much wider:

> The racism of the sterilizations goes further than who is actually sterilized. White workers are told that the reason taxes take so much out of their salaries is because they are supporting all those non-white people and their kids on welfare. Minority people are told that the reason they are poor is not because of job and education discrimination but because they have too many children. This helps direct the anger of these people towards poor people or towards themselves instead of against the corporations and the government of the rich.[17]

The Committee to Stop Forced Sterilizations linked their demand to eradicate compulsory sterilizations to a wider vision of economic justice and redistribution that would no longer view poor women of color as objects of social policy.

Broadly then, "the revolutionary history" described by C.L.R. James more than 80 years ago as "rich, inspiring, and unknown," extends across many communities and traditions of resistance. The events that constitute this history are linked by a shared understanding of the generative and complex connection that exists between the particular and the universal. Rejecting a market framework of politics rooted in a zero-sum understanding of interests and power, these episodes demonstrate the ways that particular antiracist struggles are capable of a broad interrogation and transformation of power.

Antiracism Inc.: The Depoliticization of Racial Justice

C.L.R. James argued that particular episodes of Black revolt against the conditions of their subordination produced far-

---

17 Committee to Stop Forced Sterilization, *Stop Forced Sterilization Now!* (Los Angeles: 1975), 5, http://www.freedomarchives.org/Documents/Finder/DOC46_scans/46.StopForcedSterilizationNow.pdf.

reaching conceptions of freedom and human possibility. There continues to be important examples today in which localized actions in the name of racial justice press wide-reaching claims for redistribution of economic, political and social power.

To many critics, however, the assumption that particular struggles against racial domination are central to the restructuring of political, social, and economic life in the United States is not tenable. A growing chorus of progressive scholars and writers insist that antiracist initiatives and campaigns no longer have transformative political potential. In an age of vast material inequalities, they reason, an emphasis on racial justice does little to interrupt the structures and cultural norms that continue to concentrate wealth and power in the hands of the few. At worst, such an emphasis could actually strengthen the hands of the same military, corporate, and elite interests that help to maintain and reproduce this inequality.

The literary theorist Walter Benn Michaels argues that liberal condemnations of racism, such as those centering on the lack of race and gender diversity in corporate boardrooms, seek only to diversify the class of economic elites who claim an ever-increasing share of global wealth. It is capitalism and the profit imperatives of an unrestrained market economy that produces inequality, not race-based discrimination. As Michaels contends,

> multiculturalism and diversity more generally are even more effective as a legitimizing tool, because they suggest that the ultimate goal of social justice in a neoliberal economy is not that there should be less difference between the rich and the poor — indeed the rule in neoliberal economies is that the difference between the rich and the poor gets wider rather than shrinks — but that no culture should be treated invidiously and that it's basically OK if economic differences widen as long as the increasingly successful elites come to look like the increasingly unsuccessful non-elites. [18]

---

18 Bhaskar Sunkara, "Let them Eat Diversity: An Interview with Walter Benn Michaels," *Jacobin*, January 1, 2011, http://www.jacobinmag.com/2011/01/

For Michaels this has produced "a contemporary anti-racism that functions as a legitimization of capital rather than as resistance or even critique."[19] Or as the influential political scientist and public commentator Adolph Reed Jr. bluntly put it, "antiracist politics is in fact the left wing of neoliberalism."[20]

Nikhil Singh explains that in this context, critics fear that an emphasis on race "risks a descent into parochialism and mystification, leaving foundational issues of capitalist domination and class inequality untouched."[21] To some extent, these assertions have rekindled long-standing debates about the relative importance of race versus class in explaining structural inequality in the United States. Thus we might understand figures such as Reed and Michaels, advocating a "class first" position, to be fundamentally opposed to the analysis and insights centered on race pressed by writers like C.L.R. James.

But on closer examination, this tension might be understood as productive rather than polarizing, helping to clarify the particular conditions under which resistance against racial domination might yield new possibilities of political transformation. That is, not every invocation of racial resistance, uplift, or progress produces wider visions of freedom. As critics like Reed and Michaels argue, some are fully commensurate with the status quo; others may even legitimate unequal distributions of power.

To this end, it is helpful to consider some contemporary examples in which particular invocations of antiracism serve to sustain rather than displace exploitation and inequality, or what we describe generatively in this volume as Anti-Racism, Inc. These cases demonstrate that many of the most familiar signifi-

---

let-them-eat-diversity.

19 Ibid.

20 Adolph Reed Jr., "How Racial Disparity Does Not Help Make Sense of Patterns of Police Violence," *Nonsite*, September 16, 2016, http://www.nonsite. org/editorial/how-racial-disparity-does-not-help-make-sense-of-patterns-of-police-violence.

21 Nikhil Singh, "A Note on Race and the Left," *Social Text Online*, July 31, 2015, http://www.socialtextjournal.org/a-note-on-race-and-the-left/.

ers of antiracism have become subject to far-ranging and sometimes reactionary political ends. The very institutions that drive
militarism, economic exploitation and inequality, and the appropriation of land and life in the United States and around the
world, also regularly incorporate people of color as spokespersons and representatives, emphasize themes of cultural diversity and pluralism, and uplift and empower non-white groups.
These gestures have become a mainstay of public discourse, devoid of any shared political meaning or intent.

Consider, for example, the various ways that units of the
United States military deploy and incorporate references to race
and cultural difference. In September 2011, the us Marine Corps
marked Hispanic Heritage Month by launching its "Values 2.0"
campaign. The initiative included a nationwide billboard campaign featuring a photo of a solemn, crisply dressed military
officer silhouetted by a faintly clouded sky. The adjacent text
read: "Celebrating Hispanic values and the Marines who act on
them." The campaign was partly aimed at helping the Marines
cast a wider demographic net in meeting its recruitment goals.
As Eric Lindsay, the Marine Corps Recruiting Command's diversity advertising officer explained, "the values of many Hispanic families are in line with our core Marine Corps values of
Honor, Courage and Commitment. We want to ensure that the
Marine Corps is representative of the different ethnic groups
across the country."[22] Representations of racial diversity in the
Marine's $100 million annual recruitment budget have another
intent too. A subsequent campaign titled "Fighting With Purpose" included web and broadcast-based videos and print ads
profiling an African-American infantry officer and a Latina
helicopter pilot, and a multi-media campaign that celebrated
the "Monford Point Marines," a segregated all-Black unit in the
1940s and 1950s, situating the Marines as an historic engine of

---

22 Lance Cpl. David Flynn, "MCRC Launches Campaign Celebrating Hispanic
    Heritage Month," Marine Corps Recruiting Command, September 20, 2011,
    http://www.mcrc.marines.mil/News/NewsArticleDisplay/tabid/5320/Arti-
    cle/519229/mcrc-launches-campaign-celebrating-hispanic-heritage-month.
    aspx.

Black progress. The campaign incorporated racially diverse figures and themes in part to stress the "humanitarian" reach of the Marines Corp, a theme that focus groups found to be appealing to potential recruits of all backgrounds. As a Black solider explains in one ad, "It's always been a part of me to fight for those who couldn't fight for themselves, whether on my block or around the world."[23] Marine recruiters suggest the campaigns "show the American people that their Marines are not just the world's finest war fighters; they are also some of the world's greatest humanitarians."[24]

At a time when the US military operates bases in some 150 countries, maintains an active force of more than one million personnel around the globe, and faces continued criticism for occupation, torture, and civilian and combatant deaths, the invocations of race here are crucial. Representations of racial diversity, narratives of racial uplift, and the incorporation of people of color to signify humanitarian and service-oriented commitments perform important political labor for the Marines and other units of the US military. In this context, racial colorblindness has little payoff. Racial incorporation, diversity, and uplift are articulated as fully commensurate with the military's global presence and mission. At the state and local level one can find hundreds of examples of law enforcement agencies pursuing similar strategies in order to both recruit people of color into their ranks and to "humanize" institutions that are continually accused of dehumanizing violence.

In several affirmative action cases heard by the Supreme Court since the early 2000s, both the US military and a coterie of Fortune 500 corporations have submitted amicus briefs

---

23 Tony Perry, "New Marine Ad Pitch: Think Diversity, Not White Male," *Los Angeles Times*, November 10, 2012, http://www.articles.latimes.com/print/2012/nov/10/nation/la-na-nn-new-marine-ad-campaign-20121110.

24 Lance Cpl. David Flynn, "'Toward the Sounds of Chaos' to Showcase Marines' Combat, Humanitarian Capabilities," Marine Corps Recruiting Command, March 8, 2012, http://www.mcrc.marines.mil/News/News-Article-Display/Article/519243/toward-the-sounds-of-chaos-to-showcase-marines-combat-humanitarian-capabilities/.

in support of race-conscious college admissions. As the military's amicus brief for the *Grutter v. Bollinger* case (2003) concerning the University of Michigan's affirmative action policies contended, "to lead our country's racially diverse enlisted men and women, our nation's fighting force requires a diverse office corps: affirmative action policies have helped our military build a top quality officer corps that reflects America's diversity."[25] Another brief in support of race-conscious university admissions was filed by sixty-five Fortune 500 corporations (whose collective revenues exceeded a trillion dollars) including Chevron-Texaco, Nike, Lockheed Martin, and Dow Chemical. The brief announces plainly that their support for affirmative action in higher education rests on the need to ensure their "continued success in the global market place."[26] The support of corporations and the military should not be taken as a sign that affirmative action is an inherently flawed or reactionary policy. To the contrary, it has played and continues to play an important role in challenging inequality and race-based subordination in higher education. Instead, corporate and military support for affirmative action demonstrates the ways in which some of the most dominant forces in the global political economy have become adept at incorporating the language and policy commitments of antiracism toward their own goals.

The brand managers and strategists of multinational corporations rely similarly on racially diverse images, spokespersons, and themes to win customers, raise profits, and build particular emotional and affective connections with their products.[27] Take, for example, a 2013 Coca-Cola commercial titled "It's Beauti-

---

25 Joe R. Reeder, "Military Amicus Brief Cited in Supreme Court's Decision In the University of Michigan Case, Grutter v. Bollinger," *Greenberg Traurig Law*, June 27, 2003, http://www.gtlaw.com/News-Events/Newsroom/Press-Releases/84047/Military-Amicus-Brief-Cited-in-Supreme-Courts-Decision-in-the-University-of-Michigan-Case-Grutter-v-Bollinger.

26 Grutter v. Bollinger et al., 539 US 306, February 18, 2003, diversity.umich.edu/admissions/legal/gru_amicus-ussc/um/Fortune500-both.pdf.

27 Sarah Banet-Weiser, *Authentic™: The Politics of Ambivalence in a Brand Culture* (New York: New York University Press, 2012).

ful" that incorporated a medley of diverse families describing why the nation's multicultural diversity was its greatest strength. Launched during the Super Bowl, the ad celebrated this diversity — from an interracial gay male couple holding the hands of their two children as they skate happily across an ice rink to a tearful teenager recounting the triumph of her immigrant experience — as emblematic of the nation's multicultural strength and identity, united by a shared passion for a sugar-laden soft drink.

During the 2016 presidential campaign, Celebrity Cruises launched its "Sail Beyond Borders" promotional campaign featuring a 30-second ad that debuted during the evening of the first presidential debate. The ad seemed to take direct aim at the sentiments witnessed at hundreds of Trump campaign rallies and events in which frenzied supporters chanted "Build the Wall!" Instead, over images of global cities, ports, and people, a somber-toned female narrator explained, "Far from the talk of building walls, far from the threats of keeping people out, far from the rhetoric of fear, is a world of differences — differences that expand and enrich us. Because, after all, our lives aren't made better when we close ourselves off to the world — they're made better when we open ourselves up to it." In an interview, company officials declared the ad to be an "unapologetic declaration of company ideology," and was not "a left or right issue" and because "millions reject this [anti-travel] rhetoric on the right."[28]

For Coca-Cola, Celebrity Cruises, and many other companies, neither racial colorblindness nor appeals to white fears of racial diversity seem profitable. Multicultural logics, incorporations, and representations are central to their core business strategy. These efforts demonstrate investments of corporations and economic elites in what some scholars have called "neoliberal multiculturalism," in which representations of pluralism, multi-

---

28 Many conservatives in fact took exception to the ad and voiced their displeasure online; the company pulled the campaign soon after the election. See Brittany Chrusciel, "Celebrity Cruises Debuting 'Sail Beyond Borders' Campaign During Presidential Debate," *Cruise Critic*, February 1, 2018, http://www.cruisecritic.com/news/news.cfm?ID=7253.

culturalism, and diversity are framed as fully aligned with a market-driven society, even one structured by vast racial disparities.

These connections are summed up succinctly in a 2013 report commissioned by the liberal W.K. Kellogg Foundation titled "The Business Case for Racial Equity," which contended that in addition to social justice considerations, "moving toward racial equity can generate significant economic returns as well."[29] Similarly, a 2017 report titled "The Competitive Advantage of Racial Equity" argues that "corporate America is missing out on one of the biggest opportunities of our time for driving innovation and growth: creating business value by advancing racial equity." Co-published by PolicyLink, an Oakland-based non-profit explicitly dedicated to advancing economic and racial equity, and FSG, a transnational consulting firm, the report profiles companies such as PayPal, the Gap, American Express, Prudential and other multinational firms to argue that "racial equity" represents a critical "source of corporate competitive advantage." And indeed, nearly every large corporation today boasts some version of a "diversity and inclusion" initiative. Lloyd Blankfein, the chairman and CEO of Goldman Sachs, proudly proclaims on the company's website that "diversity is at the very core of our ability to serve our clients and to maximize return for our shareholders."[30]

Consider also the reaction of many leading CEOs from multinational corporations in the aftermath of the August 2016 "Unite the Right" white nationalist rally in Charlottesville, Virginia that resulted in the death of an antiracist activist named Heather D. Heyer. After Trump refused to offer an unqualified condemnation of the white supremacist protesters, insisting that there was "hatred, bigotry, and violence on many sides," CEOs resigned en masse from Trump's two economic advisory councils, insisting the white supremacist commitments on display clashed with their values. As Inge Thulin, CEO of 3M explained, "Sustain-

29 Ani Turner et al., "The Business Case for Racial Equity," Altarum Institute, 2013, http://www.altarum.org/sites/default/files/uploaded-publication-files/WKKF%20Business%20Case%20for%20Racial%20Equity.pdf.

30 Lloyd C. Blankfein, "Diversity and Inclusion," Goldman Sachs, September 20, 2017, http://www.goldmansachs.com/who-we-are/diversity-and-inclusion/.

ability, diversity and inclusion are my personal values and also fundamental to the 3M Vision. The past few months have provided me with an opportunity to reflect upon my commitment to these values."[31]

The point here is that many of the most public and legible expressions of contemporary antiracism — celebrations of diversity, multiculturalism, and inclusion and condemnations of bigotry and extremism — are fully compatible with the dominant commitments of the neoliberal order. Jodi Melamed has argued that neoliberal policy itself "engenders new racial subjects, as it creates and distinguishes between newly privileged and stigmatized collectivities, yet multiculturalism codes the wealth, mobility, and political power of neoliberalism's beneficiaries to be the just desserts of 'multicultural world citizens,' while representing those neoliberalism dispossesses to be handicapped by their own 'monoculturalism' or other historico-cultural deficiencies."[32] Neoliberal multiculturalism performs historically specific work by "breaking with an older racism's reliance on phenotype to innovate new ways of fixing human capacities to naturalize inequality. The new racism deploys economic, ideological, cultural, and religious distinctions to produce lesser personhoods, laying these new categories of privilege and stigma across conventional racial categories, fracturing them into differential status groups."[33]

The contradictory uses of antiracism come into full view in a 2012 legal case titled *Vergara v. California* initiated by a group of conservative foundations and Silicon Valley investors seeking to weaken state laws concerning the job security, tenure, and employment rights of public school teachers in California. The suit

---

31 Kellie Ell, "Statements From CEOs Who Served On Trump's Now-disbanded Economic Councils," *USA Today*, August 18, 2017, http://www.usatoday.com/story/money/2017/08/18/statements-ceos-who-served-trumps-econ-dis-bands-two-councils-via-twitter-after-onslaught-resignation/572496001/.

32 Jodi Melamed, "The Spirit of Neoliberalism: From Racial Liberalism to Neoliberal Multiculturalism," *Social Text* 24, no. 4 (2006): 1–24, at 1, https://doi.org/10.1215/01642472-2006-009.

33 Ibid., 14.

claimed that these protections were unconstitutional because they violated the civil rights of African-American and Latinx students who disproportionately suffered the burden of being taught by bad teachers. If teachers lost these rights, the suit asserted, they could more easily be disciplined and fired, thus improving the learning conditions of Black and Latinx students. A Superior Court judge ruled in the group's favor, determining that statutes providing for the employment rights of teachers infringed upon the equal protection guarantees of the Fourteenth Amendment and the California constitution. And while it was conservative-leaning groups long hostile to the workplace protections of unionized teachers that initially pressed this claim, many people of color, including parents, students, elected officials, and judges, endorsed the idea that to promote racial equity, public school teaching must become a less secure profession. While the state court of appeals overturned the verdict in a 2016 decision, the underlying legal and political argument continues to find fertile ground in lawsuits filed in other states.[34]

Neoliberal multiculturalism has also come to shape political projects and mobilizations led by people of color. Take for example the Congressional Black Caucus (CBC), founded in 1971 by African-American members of Congress, that fashions itself today "as the voice for people of color and vulnerable communities in Congress."[35] Many early members of the CBC had deep connections to mass-based civil rights, feminist, and Black Power movements that helped make their election possible. Today, the CBC also has deep connections to corporate lobbyists and donors that covet the influence of many high-ranking CBC members. Lobbyists and executives from "Boeing, Wal-Mart, Dell, Citigroup, Coca-Cola, Verizon, Heineken, Anheuser-Busch and

---

34 Emma Brown, "California Appeals Court Upholds Teacher Tenure, A Major Victory for Unions," *Washington Post*, April 14, 2016, http://www.washingtonpost.com/local/education/california-appeals-court-upholds-teacher-tenure-a-major-victory-for-unions/2016/04/14/8dde2d94-0297-11e6-9d36-33d198ea26c5_story.html.

35 "About the CBC," *Congressional Black Caucus*, February 15, 2016, http://www.cbc-butterfield.house.gov/about.

the drug makers Amgen and GlaxoSmithKline" sit on the board of the CBC Foundation.[36] Between 2004 and 2008 alone, a time of growing Black poverty and rising corporate profits, these and dozens of other companies poured more than $55 million into the CBC's political and charitable arms, often at lavish fundraising galas hosted by corporate lobbyists for CBC members.

All of these examples demonstrate the political capaciousness of antiracism. Like race itself, antiracism "floats" as a signifier; it has no inherent political valence or meaning. As the US military, Fortune 500 companies, and anti-union elites have learned, invocations of diversity, multiculturalism, and racial inclusion and equality can be fully commensurate with their agendas and interests. In many ways, the current regime of neoliberal multiculturalism represents the rise of a *depoliticized antiracism* — efforts presumed to stand against racial inequality and hierarchy that simply invite incorporation into existing systems of domination and power.

To some commentators, antiracism has become so thoroughly depoliticized that it no longer holds any possibility of transforming social, economic, and political relations writ large. Thus, there is no wider type of freedom at stake in the particular and localized rebellions of racially subordinated groups. From this perspective, those rebellions cannot be universalistic or broadly emancipatory because they fail to address the structures of control that *really* matter: the organization of the capitalist economy and the forms of exploitation, abandonment, or regulation that capitalism always produces.

Yet what this analysis, and so many others like it, fails to recognize and engage is a political tradition of antiracism and racial justice that has forged, in the crucibles of racial domination and violence, demands for a world organized around new structures of power, possibility, and life — including possibilities of economic life beyond the demands of capitalism. Rather than

---

36 Eric Lipton and Eric Lichtblau, "In Black Caucus, a Fund-Raising Powerhouse," *The New York Times*, February 13, 2010, http://www.nytimes.com/2010/02/14/us/politics/14cbc.html.

seeking incorporation into dominant systems of power or a limited set of rights to participate in these systems, these traditions of political imagination, cultural production, and collective struggle seek not only to challenge racial domination but also to reconstitute the society that has produced such a diminished view of humanity.

Central to this tradition has been the recognition that antiracism has always had many articulations, including some that are devoid of any transformative or oppositional possibilities. While these politically attenuated projects have accelerated in the era of neoliberal multiculturalism, they are hardly new. Many thoughtful and engaged critics have long understood that many political demands and mobilizations led by people of color or executed in the name of ending racial domination are not premised on emancipatory ambitions. C.L.R. James himself noted in 1938 that the "colored middle classes are making great progress. They grumble at racial discrimination, but their outlook is the same as that of the rich whites, and indeed their sole grievances are that they do not get all the posts they want, and that whites do not often invite them to dinner."[37] At the end of World War II he noted the growth of organized elite efforts to "win the minds" of Black people through modest reform efforts aimed at reducing individual racial prejudice.[38] James offered these observations in order to clarify the relationship between particular struggles against racial domination and wider disruptions and transformations of power. But he does not presume that the parochial political vision of the "colored middle classes" necessarily poisons the emancipatory potential of all resistance against racial domination. To dismiss all such efforts as narrow or complicit misses their transformative and indeed universal potential.

Modes and experiences of racial domination are not singular or unitary, and resistance against racism does not always yield

---

37 James, *A History of Pan-African Revolt*, 97.
38 Meyer, "The Revolutionary Answer to the Negro Problem in US (1948)." In this speech, James presciently identified the recent publication of Gunnar Myrdal's *An American Dilemma* as expressive of a "powerful theoretical demonstration of the [bourgeois] position" on race.

new and transformative visions of justice. As many women-of-color feminists have long emphasized, there are significant and profound divisions and distinctions within communities of color. Their interests, identities, and experiences are not uniform, but are differentially shaped by the material forces of class, gender, sexuality, and place.[39] For example, as the scholar/activist Andrea Smith explains, because white supremacy, as a global framework of power and dispossession, operates through multiple "pillars" or modes of domination, it is often the case that the surest way to escape one mode of domination is to participate in another. In the early nineteenth century, a small number of indigenous groups in the us Southeast participated in the system of chattel slavery that dominated the Southern economy.[40]

These incentives have recruited even the most brilliant of antiracist thinkers and activists. At the end of the nineteenth century, the journalist Ida B. Wells penned devastating critiques of the lynching, extra-legal violence, and torture visited on hundreds of Black bodies each year. She explained that a nation that proclaimed itself to be at the vanguard of civilization and modernity was also one in which "butchery is made a pastime and national savagery condoned." One of the ways Wells challenged the hypocrisy of these claims was to liken lynching's brutal acts of dehumanization with the violence wrought by the "red Indian of the Western plains" who "tied his prisoner to the stake, tortured him, and danced in fiendish glee while his victim writhed in the flames." She argued that a society that tolerated the lynching of African Americans was debasing itself to the status of the Indian's "savage, untutored mind" which

---

39 Cathy Cohen, *The Boundaries of Blackness: AIDS and the Breakdown of Black Politics* (Chicago: University of Chicago Press, 1999); Kimberlé Williams Crenshaw, "Mapping the Margins: Intersectionality, Identity Politics, and Violence Against Women of Color," *Stanford Law Review* 43, no. 6 (1991): 1241–99; *This Bridge Called My Back*, eds. Gloria Anzaldua and Cherrie A. Moraga (New York: Kitchen Table: Women of Color Press, 1983).

40 See Brian Klopotek, *Recognition Odysseys: Indigeneity, Race, and Federal Tribal Recognition Policy in Three Louisiana Indian Communities* (Durham: Duke University Press, 2011).

knew of "no better way than that of wreaking vengeance upon those who had wronged him."[41] In a nation founded on both the dispossession of Black bodies and the theft of Native lands, Wells challenged the logic of the former by invoking the racist caricatures used to justify the latter. Andrea Smith argues that the structure of white supremacy rewards such forms of complicit resistance, as when Black and Brown soldiers from the US are summoned to participate in wars of imperialism abroad in order to secure basic rights and dignity at home. Similarly, one way for Asian Americans to struggle against the racist logic that renders Asians as permanently foreign and perpetual enemies of the state is to participate in forms of anti-Black subordination that demonstrate their belonging. In this perverse framework, one can escape some of the burden of racial subordination by partaking in the devaluation of others.[42]

Vincent Harding, the influential historian of the Black freedom struggle and an important confidant of Dr. King, suggests that the very struggle against segregation and racism produces the complicity to participate in such a system. As the crescendo of the civil rights movement began to recede, and Dr. King's appeal to struggle against the "triple threats" of capitalism, militarism, and racism faded from collective memory, Harding called for a critical self-examination that would "see how much over the past fifteen to twenty years we black folks have decided (consciously or not) to fight racism by seeking 'equal opportunity' or a 'fair share' in the nation's militarism and its materialism. In other words, we have chosen to struggle against one of the 'triple threats' by joining the other two, a destructive choice."[43] In pursuing such a course, Harding warned "we have imbibed much of the spirit...of greed, belligerency, fearful callouses, and

---

41 Ida B. Wells-Barnett, "Lynch Law in America," *The Arena* 23, no. 1 (January 1900): 15–24, http://www.digitalhistory.uh.edu/disp_textbook.cfm?smtID=3&psid=1113.

42 Lisa Marie Cacho, *Social Death: Racialized Rightlessness and the Criminalization of the Unprotected* (New York: New York University Press, 2012).

43 Vincent Harding, *Martin Luther King: The Inconvenient Hero* (Ossining: Orbis, 2008), 49.

individualism, a spirit that makes us anti-poor people, anti-immigrants, that creates injustice, that makes for war."[44]

Writing 40 years after Dr. King's death, Harding warned about the risks of such complicity, explaining that it would be "unfaithful to our own best history of struggle and to the hopes of the exploited peoples of the world, if black folk in the USA. were to settle for what is now called 'a piece of the pie' — some proportionate cut of the wealth amassed by this nation's military-industrial empire." Harding argued that Dr. King "understood how fundamentally the structures of military and economic domination are built on the exploitation and deprivation of our own poor people" and that "by definition, that the shares of *this* system could never be fair."[45]

For Harding and Dr. King, the possibilities for articulating what he called "a greater, richer vision of freedom"[46] lay precisely in those traditions of struggle and solidarity that refused such complicity. He asked: "How would history have judged us if our black fore parents had somehow managed to accompany the marauding American armies into Mexico in the 1840s and asked for our 'fair share' of the stolen, conquered land? And what would our children now be saying if in any large numbers we had followed the US troops on their genocidal sweep across the plains, stained with the blood of the Natives of this land, asking for our 'fair share' of their sacred places?"[47]

Harding explained that Dr. King "urged us to see ourselves moving forward always, urgently holding ourselves in the vanguard of humanity's best possibilities" and "asked us to see our freedom as empowering us to create new values, to envision a new society" that would "break beyond self-centered goals, to work for a new humanity."[48] Here, Harding follows not just King but a long tradition of Black women writers and organizers, including Lorraine Hansberry, Ella Baker, and Audre Lorde, in

---

44 Ibid., 51.
45 Ibid., 49.
46 Ibid., 53.
47 Ibid., 49.
48 Ibid., 909.

describing the wider forms of solidarity, consciousness, and empathy that can be produced through particular struggles.[49]

These stories do not cohere into a fully formed and coherent manifesto, platform or normative political vision. They are more productively understood as episodes of rebellion that have yielded an archive of political practices, perceptions, and enactments that offer important lessons for those hoping to reverse the widening gulf in power and freedom that marks contemporary life. They recount and excavate struggles that have always been particular in their form and aspiration, yet universal in their insights. As Audre Lorde explained, "there is no such thing as a single-issue struggle because we do not live single-issue lives… Our struggles are particular, but we are not alone."[50]

The wider type of freedom envisioned by C.L.R. James and so many others stands in bold contrast to the forms of "Anti-racism, Inc." through which contemporary neoliberalism operates. Lorde's understanding of ways that the particularities of specific struggles can contain the seeds of broad political transformation serves as one touchstone through which we might reverse the depoliticization of antiracism and realize an alternative future.

49 See for example Tricia Rose, "Hansberry's *A Raisin in the Sun* and the 'Illegible' Politics of Interpersonal Justice," *Kalfou* 1, no. 1 (2014): 27–60, https://doi.org/10.15367/kf.v1i1.9.

50 Audre Lorde, *Sister Outsider: Essays and Speeches* (Berkeley: Crossings, 2007), 138.

3

Trump 2016

Jari Bradley

We've both decided there is nowhere
to run — our bodies the first ones elected
for the push out & push over in this city.
We are closest to Land's End — salt licks
at the air as my love and I watch the line
that separates sea & sky disappear — the night's
shore becoming a thread of endless expanse.

Here, couples retreat to their backseats
& become a spontaneous splay of limbs —
an orchestra of moans syncopated to the blood
rush between legs & bitten lips. I see our future
between the intricate dance of sweat beaded
off fogged windows.

I am roused out of our slumber —
a loud smack of glass shattered against
concrete. The zigzag of white & blonde
greets my glazed over eyes — the liquor
poised to his lips; a flash of light scans
our car & I'm reminded of all the
feet on pavement tonight; of the police
that now hide their faces and badge numbers;
the tear gas tearing into crowds of unrest.

DOI: 10.21983/P3.0250.1.06

I search for something sharp, hard, blunt, heavy
& realize all I have are these fat fists, these teeth,
this hair that grows on my face — knowing
my presentation alone won't save us —
the man crosses the front of the car & I brace
for the smashing of the passenger window;
the scrawl of nigger hot off his drunken mouth;
I consider the spilling of blood from our bodies.

This has always been America — a silent bloodlust
loud in the heart until it bursts.

4

Defensive Appropriations

Paula Ioanide

To those who have not carefully examined or experienced white racist violence and domination in the United States, it may seem inconceivable that a phrase as uncontroversial as "Black Lives Matter" would quickly incite resentful and retaliatory responses among various factions in the United States. Even as the phrase and movement were still emerging in their popularity, the "All Lives Matter" counter-retort pierced the public sphere, particularly on twitter feeds like #TCOT (Top Conservatives on Twitter).[1] The appropriation of the Black Lives Matter (BLM) movement's discourse, which was originally created in 2013 by women of color organizers Alicia Garza, Patrisse Cullors, and Opal Tometi in response to the injustices of George Zimmerman's vigilante murder of Trayvon Martin, tries to accomplish two general things.[2] First, under the pretense of a universal concern for all human beings, the appropriation works to deny or minimize evidence that Black people (along with Latinx people, Native people, and LGBTQ+ people of color) are hyper-vulner-

---

1 Rashawn Ray, Melissa Brown, Neil Fraistat, and Edward Summers, "Ferguson and the Death of Michael Brown on Twitter: #BlackLivesMatter, #TCOT, and the Evolution of Collective Identities," *Ethnic and Racial Studies* 40, no. 11 (2017): 1797–813, https://doi.org/10.1080/01419870.2017.133542.

2 Black Lives Matter, "Herstory," *Black Lives Matter*, February 11, 2018, http://www.blacklivesmatter.com/about/herstory/.

able to premature death at the hands of police officers and that this violence is almost always deemed justifiable by state institutions.[3] By using a *universalizing* gesture about all human worth, this appropriative tactic attempts to erase the specific need to affirm the value of Black lives as a result of their *particular* subjection to racist state violence. Second, the "All Lives Matter" appropriation attempts to equate other groups' *perceived and/or fabricated* sense of victimization (e.g. white Americans, police officers) with Black people's empirically grounded, systematic vulnerability to racist violence and discrimination.[4]

Black sports celebrities like Floyd Mayweather and Richard Sherman have used the "All Lives Matter" phrase to maintain that the lives of police officers matter as much as Black people's.[5] Whether intended or not, the implication is that the two groups have equally legitimate grievances due to both groups' vulnerability to violence. Other Black celebrities like Fantasia have defended their use of the "All Lives Matter" phrase because they perceive any particular focus on Black people's grievances as socially divisive.[6]

---

3 "The Counted: Tracking People Killed by Police in the United States," *The Guardian,* February 11, 2018, http://www.theguardian.com/us-news/series/counted-us-police-killings.

4 See also Mark Orbe, "'#BlackLivesMatter Is Racist; It Should Be #AllLives-Matter!' #AllLivesMatter as Post-Racial Rhetoric," in *Getting Real about Race,* eds. Stephanie M. McClure and Cherise A. Harris, 2nd edn. (Los Angeles: SAGE, 2018), 305–17; George Yancy and Judith Butler, "What's Wrong With 'All Lives Matter'?" *New York Times Opinionator,* January 12, 2015, http://www.opinionator.blogs.nytimes.com/2015/01/12/whats-wrong-with-all-lives-matter/.

5 Brennan Williams, "Floyd Mayweather Wants You To Know Black, Blue And All Lives Matter," *Huffington Post,* October 11, 2016, http://www.huffingtonpost.com/entry/floyd-mayweather-black-blue-all-lives-matter_us_57fd1309e4b068ecb5e1e8d3; Domonique Foxworth, "Richard Sherman: As Human Beings, All Lives Matter," *The Undefeated,* July 26, 2016, https://theundefeated.com/features/richard-sherman-as-human-beings-all-lives-matter/.

6 Brennan Williams, "Fantasia and Her Huband Respond To 'All Lives Matter' Concert Critics," *Huffington Post,* September 27, 2016, http://www.huffingtonpost.com/entry/fantasia-all-lives-matter-concert-criticism_us_57eabe51e4b0c2407cd9faf2.

Most dominantly, however, "All Lives Matter" proliferates and intensifies white Americans' emotional attachments to the baseless and fabricated perception that anti-white discrimination is now higher than anti-Black discrimination.[7] Under this dominant logic, any discourse and movement that does not dominantly focus on, center, or include white people in its framing is taken as an attack on white Americans. In an astounding exercise of cognitive gymnastics, this constructed attack on white identity functions to invent a sense of white marginalization. That is to say, by interpreting "Black Lives Matter" as a discursive act of white exclusion, whiteness symbolically and affectively appropriates the historical positionality of the marginalized and assigns it to itself.

This emotional and ideological logic is similarly evident among white American students who sympathize with the need for "White Student Unions" on college campuses.[8] Even if many of the Facebook pages of White Student Unions on college campuses were later discovered to be fake, they capture sentiments and views that white American students often feel but are afraid to express for fear of social reprisal. Feeling attacked and/or excluded from diversity-related organizations and events that focus on Black, Latinx, Asian, indigenous, and other marginalized groups, White Student Union defenders argue that white students need a "safe space" to celebrate their identities, struggles, and sense of marginalization. This claim is usually made by conservative white students on liberal college campuses that institutionally endorse the value of diversity and inclusion, which is another way of saying, campuses that focus some attention on recruiting and retaining historically underrepresented students. Like Black Lives Matter, "diversity and in-

7   Michael I. Norton and Samuel R. Sommers, "Whites See Racism as a Zero-Sum Game That They Are Now Losing," *Perspectives on Psychological Science* 6, no. 3 (2011): 215–18, https://doi.org/10.1177/1745691611406922.

8   Yanan Wang, "More than 30 Purported 'White Student Unions' Pop up across the Country," *Washington Post*, November 24, 2015, http://www.washingtonpost.com/news/morning-mix/wp/2015/11/24/more-than-30-questionably-real-white-students-unions-pop-up-across-the-country/.

clusion" programming is understood to exclude whiteness and therefore produce white marginalization. In a remarkable shift away from whiteness as the sign of universality, the defenders of White Student Unions wish to attach *particularity* to white identity by inventing an affective economy of victimhood divorced from empirical realities.

In the post-Civil Rights era, normative discourses on whiteness have virulently avoided associations with group or collective identity, insisting that white Americans should be treated as atomized individuals. Anyone who violated this tacit rule of engagement by highlighting the ways white Americans benefited from patterns of racist discrimination and group advantages irrespective of individual intentions, were quickly accused of being "reverse racists." The charge of "reverse racism" functions to once again re-situate white identity as victim *par excellence*, this time through a denial of group identity.

In short, whiteness re-centers itself through universalizing appropriations (All Lives Matter) that deny the group disadvantages of nonwhite people; through particularizing appropriations (White Student Unions) that invent the marginalization of white identity; and through individuating appropriations (white people are only individuals, not a group) that deem anyone who highlights white group advantages as a "reverse racist." Yet all of these appropriative tactics share the common goal of fabricating an affective economy of white victimhood despite the material realities of white advantage.

It is critical to understand how and why many white Americans construct themselves as victims despite being the most advantaged racial group in the United States. Understanding these tactical moves is necessary for the health of racial justice movements whose discourses and tactics are always susceptible to theft, misuse, and neutralization. Moreover, it is critical to understand that the emotional and ideological structure of white victimization dismisses or distorts factual evidence that proves its baselessness. White victimization follows an affective logic where feelings trump facts.[9] That is, people rarely shift their emotional realities and beliefs because they are exposed to corrective facts and evidence. Understanding this affective logic is critical for anyone who wants to create effective racial justice strategies. Organizers must carefully study how socially shared emotions attached to the false belief in white victimhood operates in order to develop effective racial justice countermeasures.

To understand the specificity of white people's affective sense of victimhood invented through the appropriation of contemporary antiracist discourses and tactics — a process that helped propel Donald Trump to the presidency and fuel a massive resurgence of white nationalism and racist violence in the US — we must first understand the history of how the entitlements of whiteness became emotionally presumptive and embodied.

In her seminal essay, "Whiteness as Property," Cheryl Harris argues that white identity is inextricably linked to a set of presumed advantages and entitlements that have been codified and defended throughout US history:

> In ways so embedded that it is rarely apparent, the set of assumptions, privileges, and benefits that accompany the status of being white have become a valuable asset that whites sought to protect and that those who passed [as white] sought to attain — by fraud if necessary. Whites have come to expect and rely on these benefits, and over time these benefits have been affirmed, protected, and legitimated by the law. Even though the law is neither uniform nor explicit in all instances, in protecting settled expectations based on white privilege, American law has recognized a property interest in whiteness, that, although unacknowledged, now forms the background against which legal disputes are framed, argued and adjudicated.[10]

---

9 Paula Ioanide, *The Emotional Politics of Racism: How Feelings Trump Facts in an Era of Colorblindness* (Stanford: Stanford University Press, 2015).

10 Cheryl Harris, "Whiteness as Property," *Harvard Law Review* 106, no. 8 (1993): 1707–91, at 1713–14.

Using numerous legal and everyday examples, Harris establishes that the expectation to be socially, politically, and economically advantaged over and above other groups is historically constitutive of white identity. White entitlement, interpreted through Harris's careful argumentative frame, takes on a very specific meaning. White Americans expect not only to inherit an intergenerational birthright to the social, economic, and political advantages enjoyed by their ancestors; they also develop an affective corollary that manifests as an embodied performance of entitlement. Even in the absence of concrete knowledge or facts that these entitlements are under threat, the affective economies that structure white identity can construct a sense of loss, anxiety, fear and resentment anytime these advantages are projected to decrease in any way.

If we return to the example of white American students who feel the need to establish White Student Unions because they feel "excluded" from celebrations of diversity, the hauntings of whiteness as property become clear. Harris describes one specific attribute of white identity as the "right to use and enjoyment."[11] This is a form of property that gives whiteness the exclusive right to move about the world unrestrained — a right to leverage one's will and privileges, to enjoy life as one sees fit without being encumbered on the basis of race. In the embodied and affective realm, this property manifests as the entitlement to presume that all spaces are open and available to white people. It is an emotional economy that is radically inexperienced in the feelings and consequences of being excluded based on white racial identity.

Clearly, the unrestrained right to use and enjoy one's gifts was historically denied to people of color (in the US and other parts of the world) and continues to be severely circumscribed today. Because of the restrictions on people of color's "rights to use and enjoy," racial justice movements have always viewed the co-creation of sanctuary spaces for people of color to be essential tools for survival and organizing. That is, the experience of au-

---

11   Ibid., 1734.

tonomy, self-determination, and the development of collective antiracist identities often depends on cultivating physical and discursive spaces where whiteness is de-centered and subject to critique. At times, these spaces intentionally exclude white people in order to foster safety or to experience reprieve from overt, unintended, or ignorant forms of racism that often accompany white people.

Although Black, Latinx, Asian, and indigenous student unions on college campuses rarely exclude white students explicitly, they create the social expectation that whiteness cannot be "used and enjoyed" to access advantages and reproduce hierarchies in student of color spaces. If anything, white students' "right to use and enjoyment" is subject to open critique or implicitly circumscribed in student of color spaces. To be white in student of color spaces means confronting — in intellectual and embodied ways — what it might feel like to regularly face constraints and limits to one's right to use and enjoyment, since this is something that students of color deal with all the time. Yet for a white American who has experienced a limitless right to use and enjoyment for most of their lives, even a minor constraint on this white entitlement can be interpreted and affectively experienced as a loss or a threat. Rather than understand why student of color organizations elect to decenter whiteness and limit the use of white entitlement in their spaces, advocates for White Student Unions appropriate an antiracist strategy originally created to ensure people of color's safety, self-determination, and emotional reprieve from racism to restore whiteness's limitless right to use and enjoyment.

White college students' resentment over "being excluded" from celebrations of diversity is tied to another constitutive element of whiteness as property: the "absolute right to exclude." Harris argues that "mainly whiteness has been characterized, not by an inherent unifying characteristic, but by the exclusion of others deemed to be 'not white'... Whiteness became an exclusive club whose membership was closely and grudgingly guarded."[12] In other words, for centuries, to be white meant to reserve for oneself the exclusive right to tell others where they could go or not go, which houses, libraries, pools, universities they could occupy or not occupy. It meant presuming a managerial position of control. Viewed through this historical lens, organizations that center students of color are affectively experienced as an infringement on white people's *absolute* right to exclude and control people. As we have seen with the backlash to affirmative action, policies that specifically focus on the advancement of people of color are interpreted as a loss in white identity's presumed right to exclude under the erroneous presumption that affirmative action policies exclude white people. The realities that white women disproportionately benefited from affirmative action policies and that white Americans far outpace people of color in wealth, income, access to education, employment, health, and other life chances are irrelevant to the emotional politics of white entitlement.

Harris's discussion of the "absolute right to exclude" also helps us understand the affective rage experienced by neo-fascists and Alt-Right advocates when Barack Obama was elected president. To see the White House — the crowning symbol of national leadership and control — occupied by President Obama and his family from 2008 to 2016 symbolized a knock-out blow to white people's embodied entitlement to exclude. White nationalists presume that the government's responsibility is to defend and secure the permanence of white dominance, property advantages, and entitlements, including white citizens' right to exclude immigrants, Muslims, refugees, and unwanted nationals. Indeed, until mid-twentieth century freedom movements fundamentally ruptured the continuity of this presumption through mass protest, civil disobedience, and legal victories, the government consistently met this white nationalist expectation. In the post-Civil Rights era, the government's departure from overtly racist forms of exclusion to covert colorblind ones was emotionally experienced as a significant loss by white nationalists as well as

---

12   Ibid., 1736.

many white Americans. Even though *in practice* governmental policies largely continued to safeguard the property advantages and entitlements of whiteness, President Obama's rupture in the genealogy of white male leadership was equivalent to a symbolic declaration of war on the affective structure of white entitlment, particularly on the absolute right to exclude.

It is similarly important to understand that cultural shifts that center people of color in the social order necessarily perturb what W.E.B. Du Bois called the "psychological wages of whiteness,"[13] which are intimately embedded in the affective fabric of assumptive white entitlements. The mainstreaming of hip hop culture and music, the slow increase in leading roles for actors of color on primetime television and streaming services, and demographic shifts that project the gradual "browning" of America, converts even something as superficial as liberal multicultural inclusion into a threat to presumptive white entitlements.

Bonding Over the Power to Exclude and Control

Considered through an affective lens, Harris's analysis of the "absolute right to exclude" as a property of whiteness offers even more profound insights into the embodied processes that congeal white group identity. In arguing that whiteness does not have "an inherent unifying characteristic" and that its basis for group identity is "the exclusion of others deemed to be 'not white,'"[14] Harris suggests that white people have no shared cultural traits or communal practices that bind them into a community in any positive terms. Rather, white group identity is only held together through a negation, the exercise of excluding and controlling others.

This claim is echoed by historians like David Roediger and Noel Ignatiev, who show that in order to gain admission into the group-based benefits of whiteness, European immigrants had to

---

13 W.E.B. Du Bois, *Black Reconstruction in America: 1860–1880* (New York: Free Press, 1998), 700.

14 Harris, "Whiteness as Property," 1736.

publicly rescind their allegiance to their particular cultural, religious, and ethnic characteristics and identities.[15] These characteristics were deemed to be "impure" traits that would taint and degrade Anglo-Saxon biological, cultural, and racial superiority. The debasement of southern and eastern European immigrants' cultures in Anglo-Saxon discourse in late-nineteenth and early-twentieth century discourses cannot be understood outside of the fantasy constructions of blackness and indigeneity, which stand as foundational points of reference for fabricating notions of "impurity" and "inferiority." The process of broadening the definition of whiteness to include non-Anglo Saxon immigrants was therefore fundamentally linked to a social requirement to practice anti-blackness and anti-indigeneity.

The problem with white purity (aside from the fact that it's scientifically baseless, humanly impossible, and fictive), is not only that it required people to become culture-less in order to perform the scrubbed Anglo-Saxon, Victorian ideal devoid of sexual fun, funky smells, emotions, eclectic sounds, and all the other idiosyncrasies and "impurities" that give meaning to culture and community. Performing white purity also meant adopting an ontology of deadening oneself to one's own experience and the experience of others. In other words, the violence of white racism creates deeply detrimental consequences for white people's capacity to constitute community. Noting white settlers' shift toward this way of being and relating to indigenous people during the Jacksonian era, Michael Rogin argues:

Whites responded to Indian deaths by deadening their own experience. Indians were turned into things...and could be manipulated and rearranged at will. Money was the perfect representation of dead, interchangeable matter. It could not symbolize human suffering and human reproach. A money

---

15 David Roediger, *Working Toward Whiteness: How America's Immigrants Became White: The Strange Journey from Ellis Island to the Suburbs* (New York: Basic Books, 2005); Noel Ignatiev, *How the Irish Became White* (New York: Routledge, 1995).

equivalent could be found for Indian attachments; they had no intrinsic, unexchangeable matter. Indian love would give way to money; it could be bought. The "debt we owe to this unhappy race," converted into specie, could be paid.[16]

Central to the ontology of whiteness, Rogin argues, is the revocation of any ethos that privileges ecological sanctity, responsibility for others, and the wellbeing of the commons. To commit the violence of indigenous genocide and removal, white settlers normalized affective numbness and the inability to feel. These emotional states were transferred intergenerationally, since settler wars, land expropriation, and the racist and sexual violence of slavery required these affective corollaries to become normative to white identity. In fact, as Peter Linebaugh and Markus Rediker show in their discussion of multiracial coalitions like the one that staged the 1741 New York rebellion, white people who privileged the wellbeing of the multiracial commons over the property interests of the white elite were declared a traitor, and were consequently subject to punishment and death.[17] Thus, America's "racial contract,"[18] to use Charles W. Mills's conceptualization, necessarily requires white people's social alienation from people of color and among themselves. It constitutively depends on the exploitation, exclusion, and extermination of people of color but also requires white settlers' radical estrangement from themselves.

The process of cultural deracination and white purification in pursuit of the exclusive white club left only a few things for white Americans to affectively bond over: their property advan-

---

16 Michael Paul Rogin, *Fathers and Children: Andrew Jackson and the Subjugation of the American Indian* (New Brunswick: Transaction Publishers, 1991), 243.

17 Peter Linebaugh, *The Many-Headed Hydra: Sailors, Slaves, Commoners, and the Hidden History of the Revolutionary Atlantic* (Boston: Beacon Press, 2000).

18 Charles W. Mills, *The Racial Contract* (Ithaca: Cornell University Press, 1997).

tages; a shallow form of "competitive consumer citizenship"[19]; their shared hatred for nonwhite people's advancements;[20] or the sadistic pleasure derived from possessing the power to exclude and violate with impunity. These are not honorable reasons to constitute affective bonds and attachments. But they motivate the emotional politics of white victimhood and rage in the contemporary moment.

Without the right to exclude, white Americans would lose the *primary* basis for their group identity. Losing the right to exclude and control the movements and advancements of people of color entails losing the preferred psycho-emotional mechanism for constituting white group identity. All infringements on this entitlement facilitate the ontological death of white group identity. This is why Trump's actions to restore the right to exclude Latinx, African, Haitian, Puerto Rican and Muslim immigrants, to restore "law and order," and reestablish economies dominated by white workers resonate so deeply with more than half of white American voters. They not only affirm the affective sense of victimhood that fabricates white people as the most discriminated group in the nation, but re-establishes shared objects of hatred necessary for reproducing a sense of white group identity in a time of crisis.

When I ask my students "What is white American culture?," they struggle to define what it is beyond a set of commonly consumed foods, sports, and commodities. If I ask, "who is part of the white community?" and "where do we find it?" the closest thing people can point to is white nationalist organizations. Part of the reason they point to white nationalist organizations when thinking about white community is because white supremacists' bonding over nonwhite/immigrant exclusion generates a stronger sense of group identity than bonding over consumerism and a shared interest in individualist self-aggrandizement.

---

19 George Lipsitz, "Learning from New Orleans: The Social Warrant of Hostile Privatism and Competitive Consumer Citizenship," *Cultural Anthropology* 21, no. 3 (2006): 451–68, https://doi.org/10.1525/can.200621.3.451.

20 Carol Anderson, *White Rage: The Unspoken Truth of Our Racial Divide* (New York: Bloomsbury, 2016).

Put differently, the property interests of whiteness encourage white people to adhere to a way of relating that is necessarily instrumentalist, appropriative and competitive, and this relational modality is not limited to white people's interactions with people of color. People who are primarily vested in "thingifying" others exhibit this manner of relating among white people as well.[21] This is why white people rarely have the ability to create affective bonds in the absence of a shared object of hatred.

Allow me to briefly illustrate this point concretely. After spending a year with a white nationalist organization that advocated for racial separatism, sociologist Matthew Hughey found that the organization's members regularly looked to people of color's antiracist movements for tactical and strategic inspiration. In essence, they appropriated antiracist tactics and discourses to advance overtly racist goals, all while denying that they were racist. The following quote by a speaker at the white nationalist organization observed by Hughey perfectly illustrates such cognitive gymnastics:

> White civilization has fallen off and been led astray, often by black and Latino people... At the same time, the passion and commitment of blacks is something we presently lack... We can reclaim our former glory and rightful place by building relationships and friendships with people of color. Become their friends; explain to them our agenda and how it helps both of us. Let them know we do not hate them; we only wish to separate. Take with you their passion for racial identity... and use your friendships with them as a valuable commodity... That will build a new white nationalism, a new white identity.[22]

21 Aimé Césaire, *Discourse on Colonialism*, trans. Joan Pinkham (New York: New York University Press, 2001)."

22 Matthew W. Hughey, *White Bound: Nationalists, Antiracists, and the Shared Meanings of Race* (Stanford: Stanford University Press, 2012), 156.

Here, the white nationalist speaker encourages his audience to mimic Black people's passion and commitment for racial justice to reinvigorate white supremacy. He asks white nationalists to befriend people of color not only to discredit the popular perception that white supremacists are hateful and bigoted but also to adopt the "passion" involved in forging a common "racial identity." For the white nationalist, connections with people of color are instrumentalist, consumptive, appropriative, yet necessary. As Hughey argues, whites display "a paradoxical desire for contact with, and imitation of, nonwhites over whom they exercise power."[23]

As they sought to appropriate tactics and strategies born out of racial justice movements, white nationalists showed a deep fascination with and desire for nonwhite cultures, styles, and communities. It is as if whiteness had entangled them into an impossible web; even as they sought to re-assert their dominance and advocate for their absolute right to exclude nonwhite people from the nation, white nationalists were desperately dependent on people of color. Paul, a five-year member of the white nationalist organization Hughey observed, reveals precisely these paradoxical symptoms of white identity as he considers which antiracist tactics to appropriate from Black people:

> PAUL: I admire black people. I do. It's not like we're hate-mongers. They have a style and substance to them that is admirable…We can learn from black power, black pride, whatever. When they say that "black is beautiful," well, "white is beautiful" too. We have to take this strategy…Well, that's not it…It's not like this is a strategy, it's their natural style and flair.

> MWH: What do you mean exactly? Can you give me some examples?

> PAUL: Yeah, okay, look at the, uh, okay, the black power movement and how that was transferred over to actual items like

---

23 Ibid., 149.

black leather jackets, afro combs, berets and other things that became romantic icons for their agenda. We don't have that. People think whites are boring. [laughing] I mean sometimes we're pretty plain. But when blacks talk and organize, they do it with a charismatic flair that is natural to them…Anyway, we have to take this kind of natural style or flair or whatever and fill the gaps in how we organize and speak about white nationalism. Don't get me wrong, I don't mean like, you know, pollute things, but…take what works and fill in the holes.[24]

Though he seeks to steal antiracist strategies to advance white supremacy, Paul admits that he longs to embody the vivacity he sees in Black organizers. Paul imagines that the suffering and passion that motivates racial justice movements can be replicated by white nationalists. In other words, white nationalists hope to compensate for the alienated and fragmented bonds in white group identity through their appropriation of people of color's cultural and communal capital.

Paul's convoluted logic is symptomatic of something James Baldwin astutely theorized long ago. Baldwin argued that white racist hatred and self-victimization are actually over-compensations for white ontology's essential problem: the inability to connect. Baldwin identified white Americans' private failure to connect to and be responsible for others as the root cause of public racist projections and violence:

"Only connect," Henry James has said. Perhaps only an American writer would have been driven to say it, his very existence threatened by the failure, in most American lives, of the most elementary and crucial connections. This failure of the private life has always had the most devastating effect on American public conduct, and on black–white relations. If Americans were not so terrified of their private selves, they would never have needed to invent and could never have be-

24 Ibid., 162–63.

come so dependent on what they still call "the Negro problem." This problem, which they invented in order to safeguard
their purity, has made of them criminals and monsters, and
it is destroying them; and this not from anything blacks may
or may not be doing but because of the role a guilty and constricted white imagination has assigned to the blacks. That
the scapegoat pays for the sins of others is well known, but
this is only legend, and a revealing one at that. In fact, however the scapegoat may be made to suffer, his suffering cannot
purify the sinner; it merely incriminates him the more, and it
seals his damnation….People pay for what they do, and, still
more, for what they have allowed themselves to become. And
they pay for it very simply: by the lives they lead.[25]

In this passage from *No Name in the Street*, Baldwin is claiming
that in order to avoid confronting individual and group trans-
gressions, white Americans project their sins and repressed
desires onto people of color, or more accurately, on white
people's fantasy-constructions of people of color. But Baldwin
warns that these externalized projections do not spare white
Americans from ultimately reaping the degradation and alienation that they sow. As postcolonial theorists Paulo Freire,
Aimé Césaire, and Aishis Nandy have similarly argued, those
who degrade others necessarily degrade themselves.[26] Baldwin
argues that the self-degradation resulting from the practice of
oppressing others manifests most visibly in white Americans'
intra-racial alienation. He shows how white familial and intimate relationships are plagued by symptoms rooted in the loss
of connection, community, culture.[27] He traces certain intra-
racial sexual and commercial abuses to white people's intergenerational legacy of violating, exploiting, and excluding people

25 James Baldwin, *No Name in the Street* (New York: Vintage, 2007), 55.
26 Paulo Freire, *Pedagogy of the Oppressed*, 30th anniversary edn. (New York:
    Continuum, 2000); Aimé Césaire, *Discourse on Colonialism*; Ashis Nandy,
    The Intimate Enemy: Loss and Recovery of Self Under Colonialism (Oxford:
    Oxford University Press, 2009).
27 Baldwin, *No Name in the Street*.

of color with unfettered license. In essence, Baldwin warns that this loss of connection leads to revoking the ethos of communal wellbeing and interdependence, and therefore to the moral and social disintegration of US society.[28] While white Americans attempt to fill these voids through the appropriation of nonwhite cultures, wealth aggrandizement, or consumerist distractions, until the alienated structure of white ontology is confronted and reversed, fulfillment and healing is not forthcoming.

Indeed, the symptoms of white self-degradation become increasingly conspicuous when white property advantages are in decline. For example, Anne Case and Angus Deaton have documented that, between 1993 and 2013, a marked increase in the mortality rate of middle-aged white people in the US took place. The increasing death rates were particularly acute for less educated white people, with white women in rural locations outpacing other whites. The increase was unique to the US and did not affect Black non-Hispanic and Hispanic people (who continued to experience declining mortality rates). Case and Deaton attribute the cause for this increase in death rates to drug and alcohol poisonings, suicide, and chronic liver disease and cirrhosis. They also note increases in morbidity rates, whose causes include opioid abuse, obesity, mental health problems, and chronic pain.[29]

Scholars have interpreted these rising rates in white mortality and morbidity to be linked to the economic losses experienced by white working-class Americans in the post-Civil Rights era. Yet it is noteworthy that Black and Latinx people, who have been facing much worse conditions of poverty and joblessness for decades, have not shown similar increases. Sociologist Andrew Cherlin suspects that the contemporary rise in white self-destruction may be linked to the "dashed expectations" theory. This theory "says that whites who used to benefit from discrimi-

---

28 James Baldwin, *Going to Meet the Man* (New York: Dell, 1988).

29 Anne Case and Angus Deaton, "Rising Morbidity and Mortality in Midlife Among White Non-Hispanic Americans in the 21st Century," *Proceedings of the National Academy of Sciences of the United States of America* 112, no. 49 (2015): 15078–83.

natory hiring policies for blue-collar jobs and unions, but now find themselves out of work or struggling to keep their jobs are having trouble adapting to conditions that have plagued black and Hispanic Americans for decades."[30]

This is not surprising. The fusion between white identity and property is so tightly bound that when white property advantages and entitlements suffer from the effects of deindustrialization, globalization, climate chaos, the corporate elite's greed, as well as demographic, cultural and political shifts that de-center whiteness, white identity loses the primary basis on which it has historically constructed its self-worth and hope. Moreover, because white identity revoked any substantive commitment to the wellbeing of the commons, there is rarely a "white community" bound by an ethos of mutual aid and interdependence to support white people in times of crisis.

To be clear, the overall death rates for all groups of white Americans (e.g. women, less educated, etc.) are still much lower than the overall death rates of Black communities.[31] The recent increases in the mortality rates for white working-class Americans, particularly white women, do not make up for persistent racial disparities in life expectancy. Black people continue to experience the lowest life expectancy among racial groups.[32] But the increasing morbidity and mortality rates of white America does help us foreshadow how white Americans will respond to the socio-economic conditions purveyed by neoliberalism. White Americans will either continue to fight to restore real, prospective, or imagined losses in entitlements and advantages through nativist, neo-fascist, white nationalist movements and

---

30 James Wilkinson, "Rural America's White Women Are Now Dying up to 48 Percent Faster than 25 Years Ago," *Daily Mail*, April 11, 2016, http://www.dailymail.co.uk/news/article-3534768/Drugs-drink-obesity-smoking-suicide-rural-America-s-white-women-dying-48-percent-faster-25-years-ago.html.

31 "Number of Deaths per 100,000 Population by Race/Ethnicity," Henry J. Kaiser Family Foundation, http://www.kff.org/other/state-indicator/death-rate-by-raceethnicity/.

32 Ibid.

climate change denials, or they will awaken to the fact that a system that privileges property over people, individualist self-aggrandizement over mutual benefit, and environmental exploitation over ecological sanctity will eventually sink us all. The Black Radical Tradition has attempted to reveal the reality of the latter for centuries. As Felice Blake and I argue in the introduction to this collection, it is why the Black Radical Tradition has always organized for the *transformation* of social relations and economic structures toward mutual sustenance rather than simply demanding an inclusive seat at the table of racial capitalism.

Why Racial Justice Movements Are Working

A contemporary manifestation of this Black Radical Tradition ethos can be found in the remarkable agenda outlined by the Movement for Black Lives (MBL). In a document titled "A Vision for Black Lives: Policy Demands for Black Power, Freedom and Justice," over 50 organizations representing thousands of Black people across the US outlined a common vision. Yet, as has been the case in earlier articulations for Black freedom, the Movement for Black Lives fundamentally understands the liberation of Black people to be linked to all people's liberation. "We are a collective that centers and is rooted in Black communities, but we recognized we have a shared struggle with all oppressed people; collective liberation will be a product of all our work."[33] In essence, the MBL collective seeks a transformation in the dominant hegemony of white heteropatriarchal ontology — its appropriative, consumptive, exclusionary, authoritarian, dominating, and exploitative way of relating to others. This way of relating is not specific to white Americans, though it is most acutely evident in white ontology; it is hegemonic precisely because it recruits and incentivizes all people, including immigrants and people of color, to conform to it.

---

33 "A Vision for Black Lives: Policy Demands for Black Power, Freedom, and Justice," Movement for Black Lives, https://policy.m4bl.org/wp-content/uploads/2016/07/20160726-m4bl-Vision-Booklet-V3.pdf.

At the top of the demands outlined by the Movement for Black Lives is the immediate end to the criminalization, incarceration, and killing of Black people. The section outlines very specific and logical strategies to bring about this end. Central to this demand is the "reallocation of funds from police and punitive school discipline practices to restorative services."[34] This demand invites us to imagine a future without prisons, surveillance, militarization and police institutions. And as is clear in the responses of police departments to Black Lives Matter organizers across the US, it is a vision that is interpreted by many Americans as a direct threat to police officers and the state.

How have police officers and their supporters responded to the critiques and mobilizations staged by Black Lives Matter organizers? To be sure, the most obvious response has been to declare war on Black protestors and anyone who supports them using degrading and dehumanizing tactics. As Keeanga-Yamahtta Taylor documents in her seminal work on the Black Lives Matter movement, Ferguson police officers left Mike Brown's body "to fester in the hot summer sun for four and a half hours after killing him, keeping his parents away at gunpoint, and with dogs."[35] When Black residents returned day after day to protest Brown's murder, Ferguson police officers used tanks, machine guns, tear gas, rubber bullets, and swinging batons to suppress and demoralize them.[36]

Yet, despite all their militarized violence against protestors and unending exonerations of police officers who have killed unarmed Black and Brown people, police departments across the US are currently in a defensive stance. Since Black Lives Matter mobilizations began illuminating racist patterns in policing and the criminal justice system, police departments have attempted to re-invent themselves as victims. This affective strat-

---

34 Ibid.

35 Keeanga-Yamahtta Taylor, "What's the Point of 'Black Lives Matter' Protests? Black Lives Matter as a Movement, Not a Moment," in *Getting Real about Race,* eds. Stephanie M. McClure and Cherise A. Harris, 2nd edn. (Los Angeles: SAGE, 2018), 232.

36 Ibid., 232.

egy tries to restore police legitimacy by highlighting police officers' vulnerability to violence from everyday encounters as well
as protests.

This defensive, self-victimization tactic was evident when the
Ferguson Police Department grossly appropriated an antiracist
strategy to garner sympathy for Darren Wilson, the police officer that killed Mike Brown. As they were warring against unarmed, civilian people engaged in legal demonstrations, Ferguson police officers were seen wearing wristbands that declared
"I AM DARREN WILSON."[37] This was an overt reference to and
appropriation of BLM protesters' repetitive use of the phrase "I
AM TRAYVON MARTIN" in 2012. Black and Brown youth across
the country sported hoodies stating "I am Trayvon," chanted
the phrase in protests, and made social media posts to discur-
sively reveal the systematic and arbitrary nature of anti-Black
and anti-Brown police killings.[38] After the Department of Justice prohibited the Ferguson Police Department from wearing
the bracelets,[39] pro-police supporters across the country began
appropriating the very mantra of the Black Lives Matter movement, coining the phrase "Blue Lives Matter."

Were police officers so lacking in creativity that they couldn't
figure out any other phrases to express pro-Wilson/pro-police
solidarity? Was their appropriation of BLM's antiracist discourses an intentional, sadistic, degrading, in-your-face "fuck you"
to the racial justice movement? Or was it an attempt to shift
public focus away from the systematic police killings of Black
and Brown people by inventing the hyperbolic victimization of
police officers?

I don't have evidence-based answers to these questions. But
I do know that the effects of these antiracist appropriations are

---

37 Ibid.

38 Paul Lewis et al., "'I Am Trayvon Martin' Rallies across US Voice Anger at
    'Humiliating' Verdict," *The Guardian,* July 21, 2013, http://www.theguard-
    ian.com/world/2013/jul/21/trayvon-martin-protests.

39 Brittany Levine, "Ferguson Police Banned From Wearing 'I Am Darren
    Wilson' Bracelets," *Mashable,* September 26, 2014, http://www.mashable.
    com/2014/09/26/i-am-darren-wilson-bracelets-banned/.

twofold. On the one hand, for those who already identify with policing, law and order, and anti-Black racism, "I AM DARREN WILSON" and "Blue Lives Matter" attempts to re-signify police officers as the "true" victims. At the very least, this appropriative tactic has the effect of equating Black and Brown people's hyper-vulnerability to police killings with police officers' vulnerability to dying in the line of duty. Such false equivalences create ideological conditions that make police officers' and Alt-Right Movement's claims to victimhood appear to be as valid as the empirically-based claims of the Movement for Black Lives. Indeed, by the time Pres. Donald Trump defended neo-fascist protesters' killing of a white antiracist protestor in Charlottesville, Virginia by stating that there was "hatred, bigotry, and violence on many sides,"[40] American factions increasingly believed in these false equivalences.

On the other hand, for those who are emotionally receptive to the empirical evidence of Black and Brown people's hyper-vulnerability to police violence and therefore identify with the BLM movement, "I AM DARREN WILSON" and "Blue Lives Matter" should be interpreted as signs that the police are losing legitimacy and power. Put differently, BLM mobilizations and struggles have created a crisis for one of the most powerful state apparatuses, and therefore a moment of opportunity to shift power relations.

This may seem like a radical claim. After all, police officers still have the right to kill with impunity. They still have an entire governmental and military apparatus that protects their right to kill generally. Still, the police's defensive appropriations of BLM discourses and tactics reveals the police's moral degradation, guilt, culpability, and institutional lack of integrity. Institutions that operate with integrity and transparency rarely feel the need to defend themselves. Indeed, if such integrity and transparency

---

40 Ben Jacobs and Warren Murray, "Donald Trump under Fire after Failing to Denounce Virginia White Supremacists," *The Guardian,* August 13, 2017, http://www.theguardian.com/us-news/2017/aug/12/charlottesville-protest-trump-condemns-violence-many-sides.

were integral to policing, the proof would be evident in their institutional outcomes and there would be no need for appropriative tactics to restore their legitimacy.

I highlight the current crisis in policing because I want to emphasize the significance of the Black Lives Matter movement and everyday people's agency. A politics of hope is at stake here, and the question of whether BLM-identified people can sustain the emotional energy to fight institutional structures of policing that they have already successfully ruptured. Organizers can interpret attempts to dilute and delegitimize the Black Lives Matter movement through appropriative tactics like "Blue Lives Matter" as signs that they are losing. The hopelessness produced by appropriative tactics can diminish and stunt the long-term energy organizers need to create institutional shifts in power. Indeed, many young organizers expend a tremendous amount of emotional and intellectual energy critiquing the Alt-Right Movement's and pro-police people's appropriations of BLM tactics, particularly on social media like Twitter. I would argue that instead of dispelling this energy toward people who are emotionally and ideologically unreceptive to the injustices of Black and Brown people's hyper-vulnerability to premature death, BLM organizers should smile with self-assurance each time they witness defensive appropriations of their tactics, whether by white nationalists, White Student Unions, or Blue Lives Matter. These defensive appropriations not only indicate that racial justice movements have (once again) produced a national crisis in the legitimacy of white domination and institutionalized racism; they should also signal organizers to turn their energy toward the critical work of intracommunal movement building with people who are already identified and ready to work.

Intracommunal movement building is where transformations in ways of seeing, being, and relating have the potential to take place. It is where everyday people who are enraged by the injustices they witness come to figure out the difficult work of transforming local institutions, consider tactical ways to hold police departments accountable, and create educational settings for people to deepen their analysis. It is where people determine whether they are capable of trusting and loving each other in ways that are fundamentally anathema to the ontology of whiteness, which privileges forms of relating that breed division, hierarchy, and individualist self-aggrandizement. It is where people co-create and practice the ethos of mutual benefit and interdependence. It is where people gather the intellectual, emotional, and financial resources of the commons and begin building the worlds they would rather occupy.

When we do this work, it is important to remember George Lipsitz's caution at the *Antiracism Inc./Works Anticonference* that today's victories may be tomorrow's losses.[41] Who could have foreseen, for example, that the demand for women prisoners' rights would be co-opted by the state to legitimate the expansion of "gender-responsive" prisons? Who could have imagined that Martin Luther King Jr.'s radical critiques of militarism, capitalism, and racism in *Where Do We Go From Here? Chaos or Community* would be watered down to legitimate colorblind ideology and the abolishment of Tucson Unified School District's La Raza Studies Program? Who could digest the collective joy experienced by water protectors when, after months of indigenous-led resistance, construction of the Dakota Access Pipeline was halted, and who could process the devastation the same resistors felt when Trump overturned the decision by executive order only a month and a half later?[42]

My point is that if we understand racial justice organizing solely as "winning" or "losing," we are bound to lose the energy and hope we need to sustain our struggle in the long-term. By

---

41 George Lipsitz, "Idea Exchange 1: Antiracism Inc./Works on Activism," conference presentation, "Antiracism Inc./Works: The Anticonference," University of California, Santa Barbara, May 16, 2014.

42 Nathan Rott and Eyder Peralta, "In Victory For Protesters, Army Halts Construction Of Dakota Pipeline," *NPR*, December 4, 2016, http://www.npr.org/sections/thetwo-way/2016/12/04/504354503/army-corps-denies-easement-for-dakota-access-pipeline-says-tribal-organization; David Smith and Ashifa Kassam, "Trump Orders Revival of Keystone XL and Dakota Access Pipelines," *The Guardian*, January 24, 2017, http://www.theguardian.com/us-news/2017/jan/24/keystone-xl-dakota-access-pipelines-revived-trump-administration.

contrast, if we understand racial justice movement building and defensive appropriations as ebbs and flows that are inherent to organizing, we can focus our precious energy on transforming our ways of relating intracommunally and co-creating new racial justice discourses. So long as movements themselves mirror the ontology of whiteness — ways of relating that privilege selfish property interests over people, hierarchies and ego-boosting over co-created mutual benefit, exploitative environmental practices over ecological sustenance — we can win temporary victories, but we won't transform ourselves and our institutions. Movement victories are never guaranteed and always subject to appropriation, incorporation, and neutralization. By contrast, the transformations people experience when they attempt to establish interdependent relationships rooted in love, trust, dignity, and the desire to heal from the internalized and external oppressions can never be stolen.

the white supremacy waiting game

Daniel Hershel Silber-Baker

… consider how arguments about racism and power are to be made in a context that refuses to see or hear the grievances of oppressed people.

<u>IT</u> = *Appropriation, Incorporation, and Neutralization of Antiracist Discourses*

<u>IT</u> is the white supremacy waiting game
a still portrait
painted over the rearview window
    hidden in the backseat a mural of the 'peculiar' institutions
        which it said were

Immutable
PRISON-SLAVERY
Perpetual
PRISON-SLAVERY
Invariable
PRISON-SLAVERY

DOI: 10.21983/P3.0250.1.08

Unmodifiable
PRISON-SLAVERY

A history deferred is
Benjamin's Angel of History,   a-cannon-ball-on-a------chain
a single catastrophe hurled at our feet

IT is a maniacal game of red light green light of inclusion and
exclusion
IT Simon says
      Disavow history and let it grow smaller
      Sanitize the streets so we can't see the graffiti scrawled
        across the block to remind us

Histories in mirror may be closer than they appear
      Tied to us by the fact of
        its-and-our-inseparable-existence
                  a-cannon-ball-on-a------chain

      For how long will we let IT tear through the streets of our
      present
                &----white----supremacist---wrecking---ball

        IT calls history a melancholy mausoleum
but really it is a house party on the axis of space and time

6

Antiracism Works:
Interview with Diana Zuñiga

Felice Blake

Californians United for a Responsible Budget (CURB) began in 2003 with the goal of closing down prisons. The organization is a statewide coalition of grassroots organizations that has helped defeat over 140,000 proposed new prison and jail beds since 2004. Working with elected representatives, media actors, activists, and artists, CURB continues to divert public spending from the death economies associated with corrections and policing toward life-affirming services.

Diana Zuñiga is CURB's statewide coordinator in Los Angeles, California. In 2014 the *Antiracism Inc./Works* program invited Diana to speak with scholars, staff, students, and community members at the University of California, Santa Barbara about the proposed construction of a new jail and detention center in Northern Santa Barbara County. The *Antiracism Inc./Works* program sought to raise awareness and a discussion about carceral expansion in our community. The event generated the Coalition for Sustainable Communities, a group of UCSB scholars, students, activists, and local community members dedicated to opposing the proposed jail and to informing the public about

DOI: 10.21983/P3.0250.1.09

mass incarceration. Felice Blake was director of the *Antiracism Inc./Works* program series at UCSB.[1]

Blake: How do you understand prison abolition?

Zuñiga: My understanding of prison abolition is that it is the dreaming of the total elimination of prisons and jails in our world, and I think additionally it is also the reimagining of what we would want instead — so, how community members would want to address harm and violence in communities because in the world we are going to experience those things. How we would want to create systems to be able support people with mental health needs, just like we support people with health needs at the same rate. I think it's not only the total elimination of oppressive systems and institutions that continue to incarcerate our communities, but also the reimagining of what we as folks that have experienced oppression and violence and what we could imagine could be created in our world instead.

Blake: What are the obstacles in the way of that imagination?

Zuñiga: I think sometimes people feel that they don't have the tools to not just imagine but practice. And I think that's the other thing about abolition in that it is about imagining, but it's also about practically utilizing what we think could be created. And that piece of practicing takes a lot of work, takes sometimes… Sometimes we're not successful: sometimes it takes years and with those pieces I think folks find it hard how to practically see their visions come to fruition. So I think that that's a big piece of it. I feel like one of the things that comes to mind for me is just the ideas of transformative justice as a means to address harm and violence and sexual violence in our community. That type of transformative justice practice that a lot of people are engaging in right now take trust in community, takes trusting relationships, takes time. I think sometimes a lot of folks don't think

---

1   This phone interview occurred on January 18, 2017.

that we have that time, or are so in the crux of trying to figure out how to support their loved one with a mental health need or their loved one with a substance abuse need that sometimes it may feel easier to look at what resources the *state* has instead of thinking about what resources *we* actually have.

I can say myself that even doing the work that I'm doing, transformative justice and the idea of envisioning different things is a hard thing to do. But I do think we have a lot. We have to lean on our networks, lean on our own resources and knowledge and our instincts and intuition to be able to really think about how we're going to care for our communities and our loved ones.

Blake: Do you spend equal amounts of time dealing with communities impacted by policing and the prison or dealing with communities that represent the state?

Zuñiga: What we spend most of our time doing is trying to move elected officials and staff members at the local and state level. So it is a lot of trying to have those conversations with people who are the decision-makers. that may not have the same experiences and realities that we have. So our work is spending a lot of time figuring out how to present messages to decision-makers that will actually move them to make different decisions that will benefit us and benefit them in the long run as well.

The other piece of our work is really the community organizing piece, which is really thinking about how we can connect our member organizations, organize new member organizations into the coalition to shift the minds of our decision-makers. Most of the organizations we work with are led by formerly incarcerated people, people of color, family members of folks who are on the inside. So we really utilize our network as a coalition to really pull up and lift up basically the voices of those folks who are most impacted and also to support their leadership development in being able to engage in a budget and legislative process at the state and local level that can be really hard and really difficult to navigate as you're navigating all of these personal things that you're experiencing at the same time.

So it's a little bit of both. Those are the two sectors that we focus on the most.

Blake: We spend a lot of time talking about what is "going wrong" in terms of organizing against mass incarceration, but what are some of the things that you see "going right"? For example, what alliances have been built? What campaigns have been successful?

Zuñiga: I think some of the things that have been successful are for example:

Our grassroots power in the span from 2004–16. We've been able to stop almost 9 billion of prison and jail funding and construction funding, which is crazy! There has been jail and prison construction in the budget, but there would be so much more if the CURB network did not exist and if our member organizations weren't activated to stop that money from moving forward. So that has been very successful, a huge success for us.

I think, some other pieces are that we have been able to pass several different policies through the budget and legislative propositions in California. Propositions 36,[2] 47,[3] and 57[4] have

---

2   California Proposition 36 (2000), the Substance Abuse and Crime Prevention Act. Qualifying defendants convicted of non-violent drug possession offenses to receive a probationary sentence in lieu of incarceration. See https://ballotpedia.org/California_Proposition_36,_Changes_in_the_%22Three_Strikes%22_Law_(2012).

3   California Proposition 47 (2014), the Reduced Penalties for Some Crimes Initiative. Nonviolent, non-serious crimes were reduced to misdemeanors, unless the defendant has prior convictions for murder, rape, certain sex offenses or certain gun crimes. The measure included the personal use of most illegal drugs. See https://ballotpedia.org/California_Proposition_47,_Reduced_Penalties_for_Some_Crimes_Initiative_(2014).

4   California Proposition 57 (2016), the California Parole for Non-Violent Criminals and Juvenile Court Trial Requirements Initiative. Increased parole and good behavior opportunities for felons convicted of nonviolent crimes and allowed judges, not prosecutors, to decide whether to try certain juveniles as adults in court. See https://ballotpedia.org/California_Proposi-

been huge, have been ways that we've been able to decrease prison populations. And we have also been able to pass an elder parole program, which California didn't have three years ago. That was years after years of advocacy far beyond the time I've been with CURB. So those are really amazing policies that have been able to bring people back to their communities.

I think some other pieces that I think are really great are these community reinvestment pieces that are happening. For example, in Alameda County the Ella Baker Center for Human Rights (EBC) and several other organizations that were part of a coalition up there were able to get 50% of realignment dollars away from basically law enforcement and into community-based services. They also created (two organizers with EBC Darris Young is one of them) a fund that was specifically for formerly incarcerated people to be able to access so that they can create and expand their own programs in their community. So that is beautiful and wonderful, and I think a real success and is something were trying to implement in Los Angeles now given Alameda County's success.

I think the redirection, reinvestment piece is an amazing part and is really the third demand of CURB — to really redirect resources. I also think that the kind of coalition building that we've been successful at has been really amazing to witness. When I first started with CURB, our focus was always on state budgets, state institutions. We never really took a stance on any sort of issues around private facilities, private prisons, or jails. About three years ago we started bringing in new organizations that were really focused on immigrant justice work. And you can't talk about immigrant justice (and now the connection to criminalization) without talking about private issues as well. There are a few members in particular who have been in a three-year conversation as to how do we think about the organizing against private and public facilities. What are the contradictions that existed? What are the barriers that have limited us from working

tion_57,_Parole_for_Non-Violent_Criminals_and_Juvenile_Court_Trial_ Requirements_(2016).

together? And what are the actual examples of where we've been able to work together and been successful? To me, that is a huge, amazing success because it was something I was interested in for a long time with CURB and now we're actually engaged in this conversation and creating a resource that other people can actually use as they're trying to generate these alliances and stronger coalitions with each other.

Blake: As you can see, there is growing interest on college campuses in Prison Studies as well as faculty, students, and/or staff getting involved in or creating educational programs in correctional facilities. What is it you think that academics are contributing to the overall goal of closing down prisons? What things do they see or fail to see? What contributions would you want from them?

Zuñiga: Three things come to mind.

The first thing is, I think it's wonderful that professors and academics invite community voices and folks that are doing this kind of grassroots work to the classes that they're teaching these theories and these historical issues in. I think it really helps to put a face and a name and share what the movement is actually doing on the ground for students to be able to understand and access and know that this isn't just theory or this isn't just in the past. It's happening right now and *this* is how it's happening. This is how you can plug in. I really appreciate that and think that has been an amazing experience for me to be able to participate in. And I know [it has been] for others as well. And to be quite honest, it's also leveraged students to want to intern with organizations like CURB, which has been super helpful in us being able to sustain a small organization. So I think that that's great.

I really appreciate the partnership in Los Angeles that we're having with Dr. Kelly Lytle Hernandez [at UCLA]. She has been part of our LA No More Jails group for a while and basically started sensing some things that we were needing, specifically arrest data that advocates and organizers actually needed.

Through a collaborative effort with UCLA, LA No More Jails, Critical Resistance, CURB, Dignity and Power Now, and Youth Justice Coalition we've been able to generate the Million Dollar Hoods project (milliondollarhoods.org/), which is thriving and basically shows by neighborhood how many people have been incarcerated, how much money that's cost per neighborhood, and what people are being incarcerated for. Largely we see again that people are getting arrested for low-level offenses, drug offenses, DUIs, things that are very low-level issues. The issue that we are seeing though, is that there are a lot of domestic violence cases, which is again why we have to figure out how to address interpersonal violence in our communities in a different way, because people are just getting arrested for them. These are people that are part of families that are again being torn apart. So those are some of the things that we're seeing in the Million Dollar Hoods project and that's a perfect example of the kind of convergence between academia, technology, and grassroots organizations to really create something that is helpful and beneficial for our advocacy efforts — to really think about where the money's going and to think about how this is impacting our folks.

The last thing that I was thinking about was [education]. My uncle, for example, has been able to participate in a lot of academic programs on the inside. He's been inside now for 22 years, but he has two AA degrees and is an amazing person who does a lot to support folks on the inside as well as himself. One of the things that happens, as a result of academics going into the prisons, is that I hear his experience. For him it has been really impactful and helpful to be able to access these classes because for a long time my grandmother had to pay for him to be able to access those classes, and that's expensive! So this is a huge thing for a lot of people on the inside, that now these academic partnerships are being generated to actually provide access to classes.

One of the barriers that I'm seeing is that in the past, people who have completed any sort of academic achievement program have not been able to utilize good time credit. So they haven't been able to get a decrease in their sentence although they're participating in a positive program like academic advancement. In this year's budget [for 2017], we see the state saying that they will have a one-time credit for these academic or vocational courses, which is great, *and* we could do so much more. I think that that's where I wish academia would push a little bit more. Like, you all are providing these amazing services and these classes. You're creating these connections with people on the inside, [but] we want to see them out [of prison or jail] sooner. We don't want them to have to be in there. And I think that academia could advocate for good time credit to be expanded for the people that they're supporting and teaching on the inside. And I would like to see that.

Blake: We know that when people receive degrees, the recidivism rates start to plummet.

Zuñiga: My uncle had a graduation inside of the prison, and he invited me. And to see this entire visiting room of men, *many* men of color, in their gowns getting their diplomas and getting their certificates! It was just really amazing to see that. For me it was also sad to see that in a prison setting. But I also heard so much laughter and saw smiles from them that I was like, "something positive is happening on the inside of *them* as individuals."

Blake: How has working with CURB changed you?

Zuñiga: I started working with CURB when I was twenty-five years old. And I just turned thirty! Just to think about these past few years of how much CURB and its members have taught me and guided me and held me in these moments when this work is hard and we're continuously being attacked on so many different levels! Even our positive reform efforts are being attacked in a way where they're trying to create new facilities or CDC is generating different procedures for itself to *change* the positive things that we're passing…those things are really hard to manage. I have definitely built up a lot more strength and understanding and connection to a community that is experiencing the same thing, that is down to continue fighting, and that will continue to be resilient. I think that's how CURB has changed me in my trajectory of getting "here." At first I thought it was just my family, then I realized how many more families there were. And now I am lucky to have a community that understands exactly what we're experiencing and is dedicated to fighting against these systems of oppression. So I feel really grateful for that community.

When I first started with CURB, it was hard to manage all of the different opinions and perspectives in a coalition and come to an agreement. [laughter] It definitely took me awhile to build up that skill. But now it excites me that we have all these different opinions, that we have these questions, that we're being analytical, that we're thinking about the unintended consequences of policies that we're supporting. I think that that's definitely built up my own awareness of the need for the critical analysis in order to get to very intentional changes, whether it's within policy or within different organizing strategies. I really appreciate that about CURB and have really learned and changed a lot from those different perspectives.

Blake: We've been talking about how you've grown. What is it that sustains CURB, the organization and the people inside? What is the funding structure? What sustains CURB as a coalition?

Zuñiga: CURB as a coalition has a lot of different components. We have several different work groups, and that's really how people are able to plug into our work in very intentional ways based on their particular skills or a skill they want to build up. We have a media team, we have an advocacy team, fundraising, coordinating that really deals with human resources for us and bigger picture conversations and guiding membership to really think about political issues that are popping up.

Every month we have a CURB "member call" that happens at the beginning of the month so that we can share what's happening with our work. But we also use that space as a way to create trainings that will support leadership development for our members or to have a member talk about a new campaign or a new strategy that they're using. So we also use those member calls as building moments and sharing opportunities between the coalitional members to discuss what the coalition is up to.

Every year we have an annual "face-to-face," which is a two-day event when we bring together our members to really think about what we're experiencing on the ground — how state and local policy is impacting our work. This year we're going to talk about how the Trump administration may impact our work as well. This gives us time to see each other (because we're all in different parts of California), to connect with each other in person, and to imagine what we want to break down or create the next year. Also, it's a time to just laugh and eat and share personal stories with each other. Sometimes I think that everybody really loves the "face-to-face" for that purpose.

I think that those are the ways that we're able to function. The way that we're able to sustain financially: we have our fundraising committee that helps us figure out what foundations to reach out to. That is growing and we're hoping that it will grow more. But because of the work we do, CURB can't always get as much support from particular foundations, or any support from them at all. We also have built up a grassroots donor base where a large number of individuals are now donating to CURB, which is totally sustaining our work. And this past year we replicated an art auction that Critical Resistance had in 2015. For our auction, we had high profile artists and folks that are incarcerated in San Quentin donate their pieces and we auctioned them off as a way to generate revenue to sustain the coalition. It was amazing. A certain percentage of the proceeds went to the artists that requested that so we also shared resources. We always have to be creative. I think the art auction gave us the opportunity to also network with a new group of people — artists who may not normally be able to contribute to a small coalition like ours, but through their gift are able to give a piece of their work.

How are we able to sustain this personally? You know, I don't think we have a formula for that, but we do try to laugh a lot. We do try to be very patient with each other. If people need to take some time away from CURB or away from the organization they've been working for, that is encouraged and supported in order for people to be able to really take care of themselves. So I think that we're very patient, open, and flexible with folks, and that really helps people engage in the coalition in the capacities and in the ways that they can. I do think there is a large number of CURB members who have been around CURB or around our member organizations for a long time. Their historical knowledge, but also their personal support for folks like me who came into the CURB alliance at twenty-five years old, those mentorship opportunities also support how we sustain ourselves in this coalition.

Blake: You already started talking about this a little bit, and I'd be remiss if I didn't bring it up: the aftermath of the 2016 US presidential election! What do you think about the new president-elect and yet the simultaneous mainstreaming of the discussion about mass incarceration? The new president claims to be a law-and-order president. Are these contradictions producing new ideas and energies or do we keep doing what we've always known to do?

Zuñiga: It is a little bit of "we know that this existed and we're going to continue to fight and continue to do what we've been doing." But I do think that there are a lot of interesting connections that are also being made. Some of the things that I see are a continued connection to the work around immigrant justice and how that connects to criminalization, mass incarceration and mass deportations. For us right now, it's really about thinking locally. In a moment when we're also seeing cities and counties saying that they're sanctuary cities, how do we really hold people to what a sanctuary city is actually supposed to look like, and not just lean on the continued ways that undocumented folks with criminal convictions have been targeted for deportations? How do we generate these services and resources that we're talking about for *all* community members in this moment when these cities and counties are saying that they will be a sanctuary place? That is definitely a conversation that is popping up for us, and it's also bringing together a lot of organizations working on both issues to really think about what type of reinvestment campaigns we have to think about, and making sure those reinvestment campaigns don't leave people out and allow for access of services for everybody.

I do also see these new groupings of organizations coming together to create legal service clinics for undocumented folks who have criminal convictions because we know, Prop 47[5] for example, would impact them. That's also really exciting in our space — Drug Policy Alliance, Immigrant Youth Coalition, and ACLU just had a [legal service clinic]. These things are really a convergence of organizations that are practicing what we want to see in our communities.

Statewide, we're excited about the "face-to-face" that will allow us to be in a room together. It's a little bit hard to talk about our reactions and what's happening over the phone. We're thinking about that [meeting] as a way to recommit to our mission and think about how this federal administration could impact that. I do think that, and we've been talking about this already, it leaves us with the opportunity to really continue to strengthen efforts with people working on healthcare, housing, for example, because we know that those programs will likely be cut. It gives us an opportunity to push on our state to cut corrections and move that money into the sorts of services that we know are going to be negatively impacted by federal changes.

---

5   California Proposition 47 (2014), the Reduced Penalties for Some Crimes Initiative. Nonviolent, non-serious crimes were reduced to misdemeanors, unless the defendant has prior convictions for murder, rape, certain sex offenses or certain gun crimes. The measure included the personal use of most illegal drugs. See https://ballotpedia.org/California_Proposition_47,_Reduced_Penalties_for_Some_Crimes_Initiative_(2014).

Part II

EDUCATIONAL
STRATEGIES

7

The Good One

Dahlak Brathwaite

I'm a good nigga.

If we're gonna use labels

I am

I'm a good nigga.

Like…
I recycle and shit

I'm a good nigga.

At least that's what
I've managed to gather
From the random white people
Who might have
Thought of it
A compliment
To say
"I like black people like you"
Or "you're one of the good ones"

DOI: 10.21983/P3.0250.1.10

Which my Rosetta stone
For RACISM
Translated into
You're a good nigga.

I didn't mind it
Actually I kinda liked it
I wouldn't call myself that
But it kinda made me proud

For me,
Being a good one
WAS like being a nigga
Black folks could say it to me
Endearingly
White folks probably shouldn't say it
Out loud

I always got the feeling
Like I was born with a strike already
That through goodness
I could prove myself worthy of
Penitence
Forgiveness
For a sin not my own

And yeah
I am good
And bright
And qualified
And polite
I'm nonviolent
I got a pretty good outlook on life

I smile a lot
My teeth are bright
They think I'm cute

My nose just right
Lips just big enough
Dick just big enough
Wasup
You like?
What it do?
Is you in the mood
For a little bit of taboo
I like to read
I like Chekov
And I know you like to check off your to do

I'm the desire without the fear
I'm trustworthy
I'm safe
You need diversity
In the workplace?
Great!
I need a career

I'm just playing the game with the tokens given
We already Willy Wonka's chocolate factory
Here's your golden ticket
A fix for your fixation
Your methadone prescription
Starbucks equivalent to your fantasy addiction

Your guiltless pleasure
Your diet soda
Your fat free loaf
Your coke free crack
Your Barack Obama
You voted for him
You didn't even see he was black!

We the element of surprise
The black white elephant in the room

The beauty in the pain
Of Ella Fitzgerald's tunes
I naturally channel
The channel your television assumes
It suits me fine
Fuck what you tailored it to
I'm the talented tenth
And a tenth of
11 percent is
So few
So few
So few

So cool.

8

Gentrifying Disciplines: The Institutional Management of Trauma and Creative Dissent

Alison Reed

On Friday May 23, 2014, a tragedy interrupted heated debate over the recently publicized words of one University of California, Santa Barbara undergraduate, Bailey Loverin, and her student government-sponsored call for the institutionalization of trigger warnings.[1] Requisite trigger warnings, argued Loverin and her contingent, would serve as a preventative measure against classroom content that could potentially negatively impact students, particularly those experiencing post-traumatic

---

[1]   Bailey Loverin's call for campus policies on trigger warnings garnered national media attention after she published opinion pieces on mainstream platforms such as USA *Today*, where she writes: "Rarely does one not know the subject of a business meeting or the themes of a movie playing in theaters. In a classroom, however, professors screen independent films or self-made documentaries with no public information available. Like movie ratings, trigger warnings can make a world of difference." The problem lies not so much with Loverin's point as with its framing, which cannot be untied from the commodification of higher education, and the embedded expectations that attend the student-as-consumer model. See Bailey Loverin, "Trigger Warnings Avert Trauma: Opposing View," USA *Today*, April 21, 2014, http://www.usatoday.com/story/opinion/2014/04/21/trigger-warnings-ptsd-bailey-loverin-editorials-debates/7985479/.

DOI: 10.21983/P3.0250.1.11

stress disorder (PTSD).[2] While, as the Black Youth Project and others argue,[3] trigger warnings have long served as activist tools for recognizing people's lived experiences in social space, the move toward institutional codification here represents a co-optation of those tools of recognition to invisibilize the structures of power that make situated identities salient. Locating higher education in a managerial and entertainment context, the move to censor potentially triggering (i.e., "political") content disproportionately impacts the humanities and social sciences in general, and the justice-oriented classroom in particular.

Bailey Loverin's trigger warning editorials rehashed nationwide conversations about the institutional management of pain and eerily anticipated heightened discourses of trauma that would circulate on campus in the coming weeks. On May 21, 2014, academic blogger Valéria M. Souza prophesized: "It is as though Loverin is suggesting that one kind of 'trigger warning' will help prevent another, more gruesome 'trigger warning' — that of the school shooting."[4] Certainly unbeknownst to

---

2   Like much of the contemporary debate around trauma, tragedy, and trigger warnings, Loverin reverts to a popular discourse of trauma that occludes the idiosyncrasy of what triggers traumatic flashbacks and professional recommendations from research indicating that trigger avoidance may in fact prolong the healing process.

3   Two recent articles published on the Black Youth Project's blog address the complexity of trigger warnings, understanding their imprecision in navigating psychic trauma and yet the necessity of their activist roots in acknowledging situated identities and lived experiences, which provide the vital fabric of classroom conversation. See Jenn M. Jackson, "On Living with Triggers for Which There Are No Warnings," *Black Youth Project*, January 22, 2016, http://blackyouthproject.com/on-living-with-triggers-for-which-there-are-no-warnings/, and Jordie Davies, "U Chicago: 'We Do Not Condone Intellectual Safe Spaces,'" *Black Youth Project*, August 25, 2016, http://blackyouthproject.com/u-chicago-we-do-not-condone-intellectual-safe-spaces/. On the important distinction between intellectual discomfort and student of color unsafety, see Brittney Cooper, "Stop Mocking 'Safe Spaces': What the Mizzou & Yale Backlash is Really About," *Salon*, November 18, 2015, http://libertyunyielding.com/2015/11/18/stop-mocking-safe-spaces-what-the-mizzou-and-yale-backlash-is-really-about/.

4   Valéria M. Souza, "Triggernometry," *It's Complicated: Writings on Disability, Academia, Architecture, and Everything in Between,* May 21, 2014, https://

Souza, two days later 22-year-old Elliot Rodger went on a killing spree, stabbing and opening fire on residents of Isla Vista, California. Before taking his own life, he murdered six UC Santa Barbara students. Of those six, two of the three Chinese Americans killed were his roommates.[5] Rodger left behind a manifesto in which he self-identified as "half White, half Asian," exalting the former and reviling the latter — more specifically, Chinese descent on his mother's side.[6] Documented in his manifesto as well as chauvinist "Men's Rights" Internet forums and YouTube videos,[7] Rodger's deep hatred of people of color, interracial relationships, and his misogynistic idealization of white women as sexually available symbols of white supremacy and British aristocracy, fueled his rage against the world. However, few on campus wanted to acknowledge his deep investments in whiteness and misogyny, much less link them to the culture of Isla Vista.[8]

---

mariaxlopes.wordpress.com/2014/06/11/triggernometry-redux-the-trigger-warning-as-speech-act/.

5   Tami Abdollah, "Man in Isla Vista Rampage Rehearsed Stabbing Roommates," *Press Democrat,* February 20, 2015, http://www.pressdemocrat.com/news/3556059-181/man-in-isla-vista-rampage.

6   Josh Glasstetter, "Elliot Rodger, Isla Vista Shooting Suspect, Posted Racist Messages on Misogynistic Website," *Southern Poverty Law Center Hatewatch,* May 23, 2014, http://www.splcenter.org/hatewatch/2014/05/23/elliot-rodger-isla-vista-shooting-suspect-posted-racist-messages-misogynistic-website.

7   Megan Garvey, "Transcript of the Disturbing Video 'Elliot Rodger's Retribution'," *Los Angeles Times,* May 24, 2014, http://www.latimes.com/local/lanow/la-me-ln-transcript-ucsb-shootings-video-20140524-story.html.

8   I here define whiteness not as an essentialist or biological racial identification, but, in the vein of critical race scholars Cheryl Harris and George Lipsitz, as a kind of property invested with legal, material, and cultural privileges. Whiteness accumulates value in the exploitation and subordination of the lives and labor of people of color but can be accessed to varying degrees (and in complicated ways) by whites from all socioeconomic backgrounds and migration histories as well as people of color. See Cheryl Harris, "Whiteness as Property," *Harvard Law Review* 106, no. 8 (1993): 1707–91, and George Lipsitz, *The Possessive Investment in Whiteness: How White People Profit from Identity Politics* (Philadelphia: Temple University Press, 1998).

As the unruly academic blogosphere continued to irrupt over trigger warnings, and what came to be known as "the Isla Vista massacre" gained international visibility and media attention, the link between the two events emanating from UC Santa Barbara remained only implied. However, explicitly connecting the discourse surrounding trigger warnings and the Isla Vista tragedy shapes the politics and perils of how trauma gains institutional legibility.[9] More specifically, I argue, the co-optation of real political contestations for the neoliberal management of harm appropriates racialized suffering for its own sanitized version of multicultural "antiracist" praxis in which whiteness emerges, miraculously, as both victim of proximal pain and tonic to the toxicity of race talk. Rather than indicating a real investment in navigating trauma within the context of institutional white supremacy, the co-optation of the language of trauma points to the disciplining of diversity central to what Chandan Reddy calls "post-racial multiculturalism."[10]

In the immediate aftermath of the Isla Vista massacre, students, faculty, staff, and administrators at UC Santa Barbara mourned Elliot Rodger's brutal acts in competing and contra-

---

9 I am less interested, for the purposes of this essay, in how educators engage with trigger warnings in their classrooms, and more in the institutional effect of their evocation.

10 Post-racial multiculturalism accounts for how multiculturalism can exist alongside "colorblindness" ideology without being perceived as contradictory — an apparent paradox insofar as multiculturalism seemingly embraces ethnic if not racial difference while colorblind logics pretend not to notice difference at all. In a society that disavows the existence of systemic forms of racism and celebrates "post-identity" politics in which all identity is constructed and thus supposedly equal, multiculturalism's safe containment of certain kinds of societally sanctioned difference allows it to coexist alongside colorblindness. See Jodi Melamed's *Represent and Destroy: Rationalizing Violence in the New Racial Capitalism* (Minneapolis: University of Minnesota Press, 2011) on "neoliberal multiculturalism" and Barbara Tomlinson and George Lipsitz on neoliberal racial deployment and disavowal, or the racialization of the collective good in order to make the public more hospitable to privatization, in "Insubordinate Spaces for Intemperate Times: Countering the Pedagogies of Neoliberalism," *Review of Education, Pedagogy, and Cultural Studies* 35, no. 1 (2013): 3–26, at 9, https://doi.org/10.1080/10714413.2013.753758.

dictory ways. Rodger's manifesto articulated his alignment, as a biracial man of white British and Malaysian Chinese descent, with heteropatriarchal white supremacy. Yet his "Day of Retribution" quickly got folded into the dominant discourse of senselessness apportioned only to racially unmarked (that is to say, white) forms of violence. As scholars and journalists have shown, US legal and cultural frameworks uniquely treat white crime as a problem of the individual rather than proof of pre-existing racialized pathology.[11]

Artistic interventions, however, name the violence of what George Lipsitz describes as "a possessive investment in whiteness"[12] and, more importantly, call forth new forms of collective social life. During a memorial event at which the English department chair asked me to say some words, I read a poem by Nayyirah Waheed that questions when a white man is "born with such a rabid / starvation … why he is in so much pain / he needs to rip the roots of happiness / from the earth / and / burn them into / his smile."[13] Despite having received approval from the chair, the selection was met with shock and dismay by other faculty and students gathered in the space — for my apparently distasteful appropriation of a tragedy to further my own political agenda.[14] When my choice was critiqued through the lan-

---

11 See Felice Blake, "Global Mass Violence: Examining Racial and Gendered Violence in the Twilight of Multiculturalism," *Ethnic and Racial Studies* 40, no. 14 (2017): 2615–33, https://doi.org/10.1080/01419870.2016.1237669. As Blake argues, the popular reversion to discussion of the perpetrator's psychological state avoids the clear evidence — Rodger and other mass shooters left behind manifestoes explicitly detailing their motivations. This is not to discount a more complex study of the relationship between racism, misogyny, and mental illness. See also Shaun King, "Another Mass Shooting. Another Case in Which Signs of White Violence Didn't Raise Alarms.," *The Intercept,* February 16, 2018, https://theintercept.com/2018/02/16/florida-shooting-nikolas-cruz/.

12 Lipsitz, *The Possessive Investment in Whiteness.*

13 Nayyirah Waheed, "Psyche" (via nayyirahwaheed-deactivated20180), July 14, 2013, http://flymetothemoon13.tumblr.com/post/55441425521/i-have-never-understood-will-probably-never#notes.

14 The fact that I was asked to speak in my capacity as an educator and organizer actively committed to justice work added to the perhaps all too predict-

guage of needing to protect the traumatized from further harm, I began thinking more about how current trigger warning and free speech rhetoric has been wielded to not only silence dissent, but also to dictate the boundaries of recognizing, grieving, and redressing trauma.

Given accusations leveled against my reading of this poem for being unsuitable to the demands of "senseless" violence and the necessity of "safe" (read: power-evasive) spaces in its wake, conversations about trigger warnings and free speech — both of which acknowledge that language *matters* — seemed ominously timely. Carefully, but perhaps naïvely, I stood by the appropriateness of what seemed like an exceedingly relevant poem to an event that shook me and about which I was deeply engaged in mourning and processing with my colleagues, friends, and students. For us, Rodger could not simply provide a convenient scapegoat for social ills around gun control and mental health reform, but indicated a larger structural issue around the psychic *and* material harm of toxic identity investments. Rodger was deeply wedded to the logics of heteropatriarchal white supremacy, which in my classrooms and social spaces felt inseparable from discussions of how his violence traumatized already vulnerable communities. Moreover, the administrative response to dramatically increase the police presence on campus in the tragedy's wake further compounded the limits of whose communities warrant protection.

It was clear from the endless repetition of a discourse of unspeakability — we have no words, no analysis of such senseless violence — that institutional authorities and social actors have a vested interest in actively refusing to engage with the structural forces that make such violence systematic and bound to happen again. Trauma does not exist as an aberration for people who experience routinized violence in their daily lives, yet the dominant public's discourse of "senselessness" publicly mourns tragedy while disavowing its underlying causes. When we come

---

able irony of the poem's reception.

together "as a community," are we mourning our own inability to truly mourn?

Popular responses to trigger warnings, and the Isla Vista tragedy writ large, miss a key point about the discursive limits of *trauma* and *safety*: for many students who experience the daily impact of racism, sexism, homophobia, transphobia, and endemic sexual violence on college campuses, the university never was a trauma-free space. Because of its leveraging power to privilege the presumed safety of certain lives over and against others, I situate trauma as a cultural discourse and a technology of silencing. This is not to minimize the very real need to treat ongoing experiences of trauma, and the wounds of heteropatriarchal white supremacy, with care in pedagogical and communal spaces. But understanding trauma as exceptional — rather than woven into the social fabric of oppressive regimes — perpetuates a discourse of suffering as detached from daily lived experiences.

In this essay, I contend that the co-opted language of trigger warnings and free speech indicates a broader post-Civil Rights cultural investment in protecting entrenched white interests while divesting from the demands of radical social movements on university campuses, as well as the students who originally championed them. This dynamic of co-optation and exclusion I identify as a process of gentrification. Gentrification must be understood in the historical contexts of President Lyndon Johnson's War on Poverty and President Richard Nixon's War on Drugs through Reaganomics and the explosion of the prison industrial complex. But as Eric A. Stanley reminds us, it has a long and bloody history — from 1492 to our present era of multicultural incorporation and ongoing racial capitalist exploitation.[15] In *Urban Triage*, James Kyung-Jin Lee describes how the carceral state indeed provides the enabling mechanism of multiculturalism's empty promise, the "tragic bridge" between the

---

15 Eric A. Stanley, "Safe Space: Gay Neighborhood History and the Politics of Violence by Christina B. Hanhardt (review)," QED: A Journal in GLBTQ Worldmaking 2, no. 2 (Summer 2015): 218–23.

post-Civil Rights embrace of multiculturalism and its undoing.[16] Multiculturalism thus exists not alongside, but *through*, the death economies of policing, surveillance, and imprisonment.

While radical students, inspired by broader social movements during the 1960s and 1970s, fought for the presence and recognition of their voices in college classrooms, the crackdown on dissent happened on campus as well as in the streets. In the neoliberal university, what I call "gentrifying disciplines" emerges out of the struggle first for the curricular presence of coursework attentive to social identities and power and now against the evacuation of its vital political referent. Thus the gentrification of disciplines, specifically fields of study born out of struggle, tokenizes trauma while absenting the people of color for whom its experience is ongoing and systematic. In the social justice-oriented classroom, educators must contend with the contradictions of a neoliberal university that at once vilifies radical thought and cashes in on the market value of a sanitized antiracism divorced from praxis — precisely by attempting to replace discussions of institutional racism with respect for so-called "difference."

The co-opted language of trauma and safety protects the vested interests of white anxiety and their centrality in the universe and university. Moreover, such rhetoric provides administrative rationale for heightened surveillance and policing of students of color on college campuses following the historical rise of multiculturalism and the prison industrial complex. Ultimately, the *incorporation* of the antiracist language of trauma (e.g. "safe spaces") protects white interests and polices the bodies, activism, and intellectual labor of people of color — those most likely to be actually harmed by the university. In what follows, I extend my case study of UC Santa Barbara (UCSB) to elaborate on the institutional management of trauma in three sites — the gentrification of disciplines, trigger warnings, and free speech,

---

16 James Kyung-Jin Lee, *Urban Triage: Race and the Fictions of Multiculturalism* (Minneapolis: University of Minnesota Press, 2004), xv. Lee theorizes a key tension of "multicultural privilege and racial misery" (xxiv).

all of which simultaneously co-opt and exclude radical voices through liberal pleas for dialogue.[17] Then, moving to how anti-racism *works*, I end by gesturing toward how modalities of the Black Radical Tradition and creative dissent reclaim trauma, not as spectacle, but as the basis for new sites of struggle.

Trauma Inc. as a New Canon War Formation

Despite its refusal of radical racial justice visions mobilized in the 1960s and 1970s, multiculturalism as a tool and trap of state power nonetheless poses a threat to white students who have operationalized the language of safe space to claim bereaved whiteness. Multicultural discourse reduces race and racism to bureaucratic diversity management that fetishizes the surface of "difference" but disavows the systematic traumas of racialized groups. Within this rubric of multicultural incorporation and disavowal, whiteness conjures fantasies of its own demise as more people ascend its symbolic structure by assimilating into exploitative capitalism. In a neoliberal order, white anxieties find appeasement through asserting their right to "safe space" and "free speech" from the very peoples whose activist labor made their claims possible.

In other words, civil rights and racial justice movements in the 1960s and 1970s made way for programmatic changes, curricular addition of historically absented voices, and the emergence of justice-oriented and socially-located disciplines — such as Ethnic Studies and Women's Studies — over and against "neutral" (read: white) departments. It is clear that these gains prompted the Canon War backlash of the 1980s and 1990s. Despite the fact that these changes did not fundamentally trans-

---

17 I began writing this piece at UC Santa Barbara (UCSB), and my analysis of its unfolding remains grounded in West Coast politics, rather than in the South, where I currently work and live amidst what Clyde Woods, in *Development Arrested: The Blues and Plantation Power in the Mississippi Delta* (New York: Verso, 1998), calls a blues epistemology. The fact that UCSB is a purportedly liberal university system in a liberal state makes it an ideal place to consider the neoliberal university in a "crisis" of its own design.

form the university but merely conceded to some activist demands, white students, faculty, and administrators nonetheless perceived these shifts as a very real threat to the perpetuity of "neutral" universalism. The presence and politics of people of color in the academy, particularly those who offer a radical rather than establishment critique, threaten white students and white supremacy.

For example, UCSB Feminist Studies associate professor Mireille Miller-Young's encounter with abortion protestors, and subsequent highly publicized legal battle,[18] was fueled by much more than a skirmish between pro- and anti-choice positions; the well-documented backlash provides ample evidence that this media event was a tremendous assault on Black women as intellectual authorities and interlocutors in the university.[19] Meanwhile, the innocent and redeemable whiteness of anti-

---

18 For a detailed account of the event and its fallout, see Christopher New-field, "Abortion in the Culture Wars: Some Effects of Academia's Weakness (Updated)," *Remaking the University*, March 17, 2014, http://utotherescue.blogspot.com/2014/03/abortion-in-culture-wars-some-effects.html.

19 A cursory Internet search yields descriptors of Dr. Miller-Young ranging from "mammy" to "jezebel" to "thug," effectively capturing the gamut of racism's dependence on mythological stereotypes of Black hypersexuality and criminality. For research on how Internet search tools are not neutral, see Safiya Noble's *The Algorithms of Oppression: How Search Engines Reinforce Racism* (New York: New York University Press, 2018). For just one example of the racist and sexist attack on Miller-Young's professionalism and intellectual rigor, see "When Enlightened Professors Attack!" *Clearly Caneda*, March 23, 2014, clearlycaneda.wordpress.com/2014/03/23/when-enlightened-professors-attack/. This random blogger's response, which turns up near the top of Internet searches on the topic, remains moderate compared to *Fox News* and *Breitbart*. See, for example, Joel B. Pollack, "Video: Pornography Professor Assaults Pro-Life Activist at UCSB," *Breitbart News*, March 21, 2014, http://www.breitbart.com/big-government/2014/03/21/video-pornography-professor-assaults-pro-life-activist/. Such responses are documented and critiqued in *The Feminist Wire*, which released two statements of solidarity with Miller-Young: David J. Leonard, "Challenging the 'Hard Right' Playbook: In Solidarity with Dr. Mireille Miller-Young," *The Feminist Wire*, March 20, 2014, http://www.thefeministwire.com/2014/03/mireille-miller-young/, and Stephanie Gilmore, "Why I Am In Solidarity with Mireille Miller-Young," *The Feminist Wire*, March 20, 2014, http://www.thefeministwire.com/2014/03/mireille-miller-young-standing-with/.

choice members of "Survivors of the Abortion Holocaust" can be protected in the name of free speech in a supposedly free country, once again proving white injury as the only legible form of wounding warranting administrative and state redress. What's more, the hate group's rhetoric of *survivor* and *Holocaust* co-opts the language of sexual and racial trauma. Anti-choice advocates often descend on college campuses with their shock tactics, visually aligning abortion with graphic images of the Shoah and lynching. Yet no one asked Dr. Miller-Young if she could have been triggered by the sign of a bloody fetus, since the free speech of two white girls took precedence. Professors such as Dr. Miller-Young, who impede on the white nationhood of neoliberal higher education, can be fought through claims to trauma, safety, and inclusivity that protect the comfortability of white people. Ultimately, this theft of real political contestations — safe space, trigger warnings, and free speech — can be understood as a *new canon war formation*.

Within this formation, coalition, confrontation, contestation, and change became siphoned out of the academic vernacular of race. The neoliberal university has wielded the moral panics Stuart Hall and his colleagues famously describe in *Policing the Crisis* to co-opt and exclude people imagined as a threat to its perpetuity.[20] Radical professors teaching critical race and ethnic studies (or, as often formulated, "doing race") across the humanities and social sciences serve as tokens of progress, providing they do not evoke the specter of racism.[21] Thus the sanitized inclusion of multicultural curricula serves racism by

---

20 Stuart Hall, Chas Critcher, Tony Jefferson, John Clarke, and Brian Roberts, *Policing the Crisis: Mugging, the State, and Law and Order* (London: Palgrave Macmillan, 1978).

21 For a discussion of how "symbolic inclusion" paralleled racial re-entrenchment and the subsequent absenting and depoliticizing of Black feminist thought from university life, see Patricia Hill Collins, *Black Feminist Thought* (New York: Routledge, 1990), 6. See also Grace Kyungwon Hong, "'The Future of Our Worlds': Black Feminism and the Politics of Knowledge in the University under Globalization," *Meridians: Feminism, Race, Transnationalism* 8, no. 2 (2008): 95–115.

offering false evidence of its demise, articulated as an *absence of talking about racism.*

This silencing of dissent enacts disciplinary gentrification, which describes the affective scripts of racial danger and decay that prompt the so-called revitalization of fields of inquiry into the artisanal statecraft of multiculturalism. In the process, the disruptive bodies and ideas of professors invested in the ongoing struggle out of which justice-oriented disciplines emerged bear the brunt of negotiating the white rage of multiculturalism's perceived threat to white supremacy. This echoes the ethos of gentrification wherein storefronts of so-called local color provide the gritty urban backdrop of privileged hipster artists eager for a grunge aesthetic that reeks of the exploitation and evacuation of actual people of color from their newly fashionable neighborhoods — and parallels the fact that Black and Latinx college admissions were in fact on the decline during the rise of a bereaved whiteness that claims victimhood.[22] What's more, as Leslie T. Fenwick and H. Patrick Swygert have shown, institutional racism persists in tenure-track faculty appointments, as commitments to diversity are not reflected in recruitment, hiring, promotion, and retention.[23] White folks find themselves caught in and complicit with the drama of bulldozing culture to make room for its commoditized presence in cafés and classrooms alike. Gentrifying disciplines, then, fetishize trauma while evacuating its historical referent.

Institutionally, places of higher education claim victimhood by hearing the appellation of racism as injury. As Sara Ahmed explains, "racism is heard as an injury to an institution and as

---

22 Lee, *Urban Triage*, 74. See also Roderick Ferguson's analysis of the Lumumba-Zapata experiment at UC San Diego in *The Reorder of Things: The University and Its Pedagogies of Minority Difference* (Minneapolis: University of Minnesota Press, 2012), 50–54.

23 Valerie Strauss, "It's 2015. Where Are All the Black College Faculty?" *Washington Post*, November 12, 2015, http://www.washingtonpost.com/news/answer-sheet/wp/2015/11/12/its-2015-where-are-all-the-black-college-faculty/?utm_term=.44b83bec38f0.

damaging to an institutional reputation for 'being diverse.'"[24] Ahmed thus describes how diversity work transforms its goal into "*changing perceptions of whiteness rather than changing the whiteness of organizations.*"[25] Building on Ahmed's intervention, I argue that the gentrifying of disciplines seeks to transform whiteness by fashioning difference into a hip new space to take up residence. Thus, the ultimate expression of gentrified disciplines manifests as white professors teaching "multicultural" classes without adequately addressing histories of racism, much less being actively committed to those struggles off campus.

In other words, gentrifying disciplines as an analytic identifies the process whereby multiculturalist logics replace radicalized people of color actively committed to abolitionist imaginaries with neoliberal subjects divorced from antiracist practice. Within this framework, faculty of color must be figured as unthreatening *representations* of race unaccountable to racial justice movements, while white professors get positioned as moral authorities on experiences and identities absented from university life. The privatization of public institutions, rising tuition costs, the normalized realities of staggering student debt, and the dismantling of affirmative action policies meant to redress systematic inequity, all the while shrinking tenure lines and subsisting on exploited adjunct labor, have made institutions of higher education less desirable or accessible for students historically excluded from their walls — such as the working class and people of color.

Nonetheless, those who materially and socially benefit from gendered racism now position themselves as victims of a "hostile" feminist and antiracist praxis that (in its *radical*, as opposed to liberal, forms) is targeted for vigilante violence and administrative crackdown. Despite material realities of entrenched power, white men now see themselves as oppressed by the presumed liberal bent of institutions of higher education. Online

---

24 Sara Ahmed, *On Being Included: Racism and Diversity in Institutional Life* (Durham: Duke University Press, 2012), 17.

25 Ibid., 34 (emphasis in original).

platforms such as *Campus Reform* and *Professor Watchlist* exist to endanger the careers and lives of so-called dangerous leftist professors while protecting the perceived victimhood of white people and their right-wing allies, traumatized by trauma-talk. The very existence of conservative media rancor, and abysmal institutional responses to professors whose unpopular opinions or provocative courses get thrusted into the national spotlight,[26] can make social justice-minded educators paranoid and maybe even less likely to broach controversial topics, such as the BDS (Boycott, Divestment, and Sanctions) movement, in their class-rooms. Right-wing professor watchlists are doing the vigilante work of the neoliberal university's attempts to silence radical voices and maintain law and order.

Winter is Coming: Trigger Warnings in the Time of Trump

On May 23, 2016, to memorialize the two-year anniversary of the Isla Vista tragedy, UC Santa Barbara hosted an iteration of the Table of Silence Project formed by choreographer Jacqulyn Buglisi following 9/11. The project was created, according to UCSB Chancellor Henry T. Yang, as "a tribute to the lives lost. It is also a call for peaceful dialogue in times of conflict."[27] This 9/11-infused language typifies multicultural victimhood, where specifically American lives — coded as white, patriotic, and thus deserving of mourning — can find refuge from the racialized threat of the "terrorist," couched in tacit anti-blackness and Is-

---

26 To name just a few professors targeted by white supremacist harassment and death threats: Lee Bebout (an associate professor of English at Arizona State University, for a course on "United States Race Theory & the Problem of Whiteness"); Keeanga-Yamahtta Taylor (an assistant professor of African American studies at Princeton University, for noting Trump's racism and sexism during a commencement speech); and George Ciccariello-Maher (a former associate professor of politics and global studies who resigned after a tweet poking fun at the alt-right's popular hashtag, #WhiteGenocide, made his teaching career at Drexel University unsustainable).

27 Henry T. Yang, "Table of Silence Project UCSB: We Remember on May 23." Email message to "Members of our Campus Community," Office of the Chancellor, May 19, 2016.

lamophobia. The call for peaceful dialogue, then, can only be enacted through the disavowal of accountability to the US Empire's ongoing production of war and violence. When Debbie Fleming, assistant vice chancellor for student affairs, noted in a UCSB periodical that "high levels of compassion and caring in our community helped us all to heal and begin to recover after the tragedy, and that compassion and caring are still strong now, stronger even, two years later,"[28] I assume she was not referring to the specter of Elliot Rodger — the proliferation of Internet fan clubs, even — and the consolidation of his murderous ideas and fascist ideals in a group logic that has spewed hate speech across campus before, during, and after Trump's terrifying, though unsurprising, presidential election.[29]

As one obvious example of white backlash to racial justice gains, on December 1, 2015, the UCSB White Student Union (a Facebook group, if not actual community organization, as their page claims, and certainly not the first of its kind) issued a press release parodying the nationally resonant demands of student activists of color across the country — following University of Missouri President Tim Wolfe's resignation in November 2015. White Student Union members made fallacious claims to systematic marginalization, oppression, and the need for more resources, cultural spaces, "non-self-hating" white faculty and administrative support, as well as heightened campus policing to protect white students from hate speech. As student activists of color were protesting in solidarity with Mizzou and making their own demands, the White Student Union announced a solidarity walk-out for people of European descent and their

---

28 Shelly Leachman, "Table of Silence Project UCSB: We Remember," UC Santa Barbara Current, May 17, 2016, http://www.news.ucsb.edu/2016/016804/table-silence-project-ucsb-we-remember.

29 In the weeks following Trump's election, Democracy Now! reported over 400 documented incidents of racist, sexist, homophobic, transphobic, and xenophobic harassment and attack. See "400+ Reports of Attacks & Harassment in Wake of Trump's Election," Democracy Now!, November 18, 2016, https://www.democracynow.org/2016/11/18/headlines/400_reports_of_attacks_harassment_in_wake_of_trumps_election.

allies. They write, mocking the at sign often used in Chicanx and Latinx Studies: "We, students of Europe@n descent at UCSB, refuse to accept the negative social climate created towards our peers of Europe@n descent and other marginalized groups. We have begun this movement, UCSB White Student Union, in an effort to change the status quo for a more just and inclusive environment within our campus."[30] Their claims use the language championed by social movements to cash in on white injury while violently denying, through satirical strategy, the realities of people of color. Claims to injury so often authorize violence, from white feminist platforms for reform that reinforce the carceral state, to the fallacy of "reverse racism" that rolled back affirmative action policies, to institutional demands for "safe space" that exclude the very people for whom safety does not function as an entitlement of racial privilege.[31]

Lest we think this move stops at a pathological kind of satire that exploits lived social realities, another group with ties to Facebook pages UCSB White Student Union and UCSB Unsafe Space demanded recognition by UCSB Associated Students and garnered the anxious support of administrators. Funded by a right-wing libertarian organization, the Young Americans for Liberty (YAL) UCSB is a local iteration of a group with over 900 chapters and growing nationwide. UCSB faculty members were told by John Majewski, the dean of humanities, to be "inclusive" of their events in the name of "free speech" after YAL threatened to sue the university. Margaret Klawunn, the vice chancellor for student affairs, adopted a similar tone in an email

---

30 UCSB White Student Union, *Facebook,* December 1, 2015. While their online profile is now defunct, the press release of their demands was widely shared by right-wing websites. See, for example, Jennifer Kabbany, "UCSB's 'White Student Union' Releases Hilarious 'List of Demands,'" *The College Fix,* December 3, 2015, https://www.thecollegefix.com/post/25374/.

31 See Dean Spade, "Intersectional Resistance and Law Reform," in *Intersectionality: Theorizing Power, Empowering Theory* (special journal issue), eds. Sumi Cho, Kimberlé Williams Crenshaw, and Leslie McCall, *Signs* 38, no. 4 (Summer 2013): 1031–55, https://doi.org/ 10.1086/669608. See also Christina B. Hanhardt, *Safe Space: Gay Neighborhood History and the Politics of Violence* (Durham: Duke University Press, 2013).

she wrote to faculty "who teach about issues related to social justice, free speech, community values and ethics" asking for a meeting on April 12, 2016 to discuss YAL events with members of the Bias Response Team about "some events scheduled for our campus this spring that are intended to challenge our principles of community," such as "Safe Space for White Students," "Transgenderism is Absurd," and "Feminism is Cancer." Rather than prohibiting such deliberate provocations to actual student safety, Klawunn invited a conversation about how best to manage these events in "a campus environment that values diversity and free speech." In contrast to the administrative response, students waged powerful counter-protests against YAL events, and the department of Feminist Studies released an official statement, noting rightly that the proclamation "Feminism is Cancer" constitutes hate speech. As the department writes in a public announcement archived online, "calling feminism 'cancer' is not dialogue. It is backlash against the gains we have made. Along with the words of hate inscribed on our campus in the first week of April, this event attacks a long tradition of scholarship and activism committed to intellectual rigor, social justice, and critical citizenship."[32] The "words of hate" to which this response refers summon a concurrent wave of pro-Trump graffiti that has littered college campuses from coast to coast, with UCSB as no exception.[33]

YAL members distanced themselves from these racist, xenophobic, Islamophobic, homophobic, transphobic, and misogynistic chalk drawings that spread like wildfire across the country and social media, referred to as the "chalkening" by neoconservative student groups and archived under the Twitter hashtag #TheChalkening. Yet, they insisted on the right to express them-

---

32 "A Statement on the Message that 'Feminism is Cancer,'" *UC Santa Barbara Department of Feminist Studies,* May 24, 2016, http://www.femst.ucsb.edu/news/announcement/536.

33 Willa Frej, "These Are The College Campuses Dotted With Hateful Pro-Trump Graffiti," *Huffington Post,* April 15, 2016, http://www.huffingtonpost.com/entry/college-campuses-trump-graffiti_us_5710fd91e4b06f35cb6f503b.

selves freely and assemble in a "safe space" on campus — safe from the university's injurious liberal agenda, of course. Similar events have occurred throughout the University of California, from UCLA to UC Riverside, where on April 6, 2016, an anti-Muslim hate crime targeted women of color professors in the Department of Ethnic Studies.[34]

While many activist writers have noted the proliferation of Trump-fueled ignorance on college campuses nationwide, racist hate crime in the university is not historically new. Yet the dense network of events during March and April 2016 at UCSB provides an opportunity to reflect on for whom the university offers protection, and what strategies are deployed at its behest. The dialectic of white backlash and administrative response is an old and tired one — from the founding of the White Citizens' Council in the wake of *Brown v. Board of Education* to Ronald Reagan, in the words of poet David Scott, as one "villain to a very long bedtime story."[35] The fascistic rise of Trump makes all the more urgent the critique and collapse of an ongoing crisis of whiteness.

Freedom of Expression, Hate Speech, and Civil Discourse?

Since Loverin's widely publicized call emanating from UC Santa Barbara, and in the wake of massive student protests against campus racism across the nation, from the University of Missouri to Yale to Oberlin, the debate over the contested terms of trigger warning and safe space discourse has resurfaced many times over to protect institutional investments in maintaining

---

34 See, for example, Jillian Frankel, "Offensive Posters Targeting SJP Resurface on Campus for Third Time," *Daily Bruin,* November 12, 2015, http://www.dailybruin.com/2015/11/12/offensive-posters-targeting-sjp-resurface-on-campus-for-third-time/. See also "Police Investigating Vandalism at UC Riverside as Hate Crime," *CBS Los Angeles,* April 5, 2016, losangeles.cbslocal.com/2016/04/05/police-investigating-vandalism-at-uc-riverside-as-hate-crime/.

35 David Scott, *Years Like Fevers* (Seattle: CreateSpace, 2013), 38.

an oppressive status quo.[36] In August 2016, for example, the University of Chicago's Dean of Students, John Ellison, defended the right to freedom of expression, much like other institutions across the country, to implicitly protect white interests and silence dissent, demonizing protests with law-and-order rhetoric. (To understand how the rhetoric of freedom of expression protects white interests, we need look no further than prisons, where you can study Hitler's *Mein Kampf* and other white supremacist classics, but not the Black Radical Tradition.[37]) It should come as no surprise, then, that Dean Ellison's letter to the Class of 2020 was met with approval by far-right blogs and media organizations such as *Fox News*.[38] In said letter, Ellison states that the University of Chicago does not provide "so-called 'trigger warnings'" or "condone the creation of intellectual 'safe spaces.'"[39] He almost mocks students by dismissing their awareness of power in educational institutions with a patronizing tone: "You will find that we expect members of our community to be engaged in rigorous debate, discussion and even disagreement. At times

36 *New Yorker* staff writer Nathan Heller grapples with how the "new activism of liberal arts colleges" navigates the contradictions of post-racial multiculturalism. Pointing to a trigger warning plea for *Antigone,* he initially seems dismissive of student demands as privileged millennial stabs at educational comfort, but ultimately concedes their power to understand a political landscape Heller himself is at pains to address. See Nathan Heller, "Letter from Oberlin: The Big Uneasy," *The New Yorker,* May 30, 2016, http://www.newyorker.com/magazine/2016/05/30/the-new-activism-of-liberal-arts-colleges.

37 Dan Slater, "Texas Prisons Banned My Book About Texas Prisoners: The Texas Department of Criminal Justice's Literary Censorship Policy is a National Disgrace," *Slate,* September 27, 2016, http://www.slate.com/articles/news_and_politics/jurisprudence/2016/09/texas_prisons_banned_book_policy_is_a_national_disgrace.html.

38 See, for example, the comments appended to "University 'Warns' Incoming Freshmen: No Safe Spaces or Trigger Warnings Here," *Fox News,* August 25, 2016, http://insider.foxnews.com/2016/08/25/university-warns-incoming-freshmen-no-safe-spaces-or-trigger-warnings-here.

39 Jordie Davies, "Uchiletter," *Black Youth Project,* August 25, 2016, http://www.blackyouthproject.com/u-chicago-we-do-not-condone-intellectual-safe-spaces/uchiletter/.

this may challenge you and even cause discomfort."[40] Ellison's rhetorical moves indicate a broader investment in re-centering "post-racial" methods in the classroom by at once fashioning and dismissing student protests as a privileged retreat into identity politics minus the politics.

This move silences two facts: 1) student protesters respond to real concerns and thus threaten to expose and undo institutional inequities, yet these dissenters get caricatured as privileged millennials — the smoke and mirrors to occlude institutional injustice such as recent allegations of mishandling reports of sexual assault, and 2) as Anna Merlan writing for *Jezebel* reports, this letter cannot be divorced from how University of Chicago Student Body President Tyler Kissinger was almost expelled just before graduation for his participation in last May's occupation of the president's office demanding a livable wage for campus workers and fossil fuel divestment.[41] The Dean's letter thus makes visible the co-opted language of activist efforts, now wielded against activists. The University of Chicago also recently shamed as attacks on freedom of expression "protests that threaten safety, silence speakers with different points of view, prevent members of our community from listening to speakers, or prevent campus events from proceeding," even though acts of hate speech, not protests, actually threaten student safety. It is those defenses of hate speech under the banner of free speech to which I now turn, as the co-opted language of safety and inclusivity quell white rage against the gains of mid-century civil rights and racial justice movements.

In the 1960s, dissenting and rebellious voices of social movements fought for the right of free speech on college campuses such as UC Berkeley, where Stokely Carmichael lectured on the necessity of speaking truth to power. The crackdown was immediate, as Ronald Reagan used conservative backlash to "mal-

---

40 Ibid.

41 See Anna Merlan, "UChicago Tells Incoming Students It Doesn't Believe in Safe Spaces or Trigger Warnings," *Jezebel*, August 25, 2016, http://jezebel.com/uchicago-tells-incoming-students-it-doesnt-believe-in-s-1785737747.

contents" to fuel his 1966 gubernatorial election.[42] While the free speech debate has a long and storied past, here I focus on its racialized intersection with criminalization. As Jelani Cobb argues, bringing to the surface what free speech deliberately occludes:

> Two weeks ago, we saw a school security officer in South Carolina violently subdue a teen-age girl for simple noncompliance, and we actually countenanced discussion of the student's culpability for "being disruptive in class." The default for avoiding discussion of racism is to invoke a separate principle, one with which few would disagree in the abstract — free speech, respectful participation in class — as the counterpoint to the violation of principles relating to civil rights.[43]

What Cobb rightly describes as "victim-blaming with a software update" evades conversations about very real material harm enacted against people of color with recourse to free speech. Thus, liberals and conservatives alike attack activists unwilling to play nice. Such invocations of free speech co-opt activist efforts in an effort to silence and threaten people of color. As Robert Jones, Jr. (aka Son of Baldwin) writes, "We can disagree and still love each other, unless your disagreement is rooted in my oppression and denial of my humanity and right to exist."[44]

The institutional management of trauma and crisis is linked to the criminalization of blackness and the dismissal of a critique of gendered racism. It is no coincidence that current debates over sexual harassment and assault policy on college campuses wield blame-the-victim rhetoric to minimize the ubiquity

42 Jill Lepore, "Flip-Flopping on Free Speech," *The New Yorker,* October 9, 2017, http://www.newyorker.com/magazine/2017/10/09/flip-flopping-on-free-speech.

43 Jelani Cobb, "Race and the Free-Speech Diversion," *The New Yorker,* November 10, 2015, http://www.newyorker.com/news/news-desk/race-and-the-free-speech-diversion.

44 Robert Jones, Jr., *Twitter,* August 18, 2015, 7:19am, https://twitter.com/sonofbaldwin/status/633644373423562753.

of rape culture,[45] rhetoric that flies in the face of the #MeToo movement, started by longtime Black feminist activist Tarana Burke.[46] Moreover, racialized patterns of sexual harassment and assault charges disproportionately expel Black men, while granting leniency to white perpetrators such as Brock Turner.[47] The myth of a liberal campus oppressing innocent white men is reinforced by Donald Trump, Betsy DeVos, and their supporters, hellbent on undoing President Barack Obama's policies on sexual assault. For example, the deeply offensive notion that survivors of sexual assault are partially to blame, while scapegoating men of color for an endemic problem, indicates how steadfast the linked operation of racism and misogyny remains in this country.

Bitingly, the co-opted language of safe spaces and trigger warnings emerged in part out of student activist mobilizations around heteropatriarchal rape culture on college campuses. The self-professed "alt-right" has deployed the rhetoric of trigger warnings to gaslight people's very real grievances, as evidenced in its depiction of the Left as overly sensitive, easily triggered "snowflakes."[48] Yet this accusation points to a deeper hypocrisy — it is white people, after all, who perceive the very presence of people of color in traditionally white spaces as a threat

---

45 Madison Pauly, "Betsey DeVos Is Being Sued for Rolling Back Campus Protections for Sexual Assault Victims," *Mother Jones,* January 26, 2018, http://www.motherjones.com/politics/2018/01/betsy-devos-is-being-sued-for-rolling-back-campus-protections-for-sexual-assault-victims/.

46 "Meet Tarana Burke, Activist Who Started 'Me Too' Campaign to Ignite Conversation on Sexual Assault," *Democracy Now!,* October 17, 2017, https://www.democracynow.org/2017/10/17/meet_tarana_burke_the_activist_who.

47 Peter Yang, "The Question of Race in Campus Sexual-Assault Cases: Is the System Biased against Men of Color?" *The Atlantic,* September 11, 2017, https://www.theatlantic.com/education/archive/2017/09/the-question-of-race-in-campus-sexual-assault-cases/539361/.

48 For a brief history of the term "alt-right" (coined by white nationalist Richard Spencer and which, at its core, sees white people as victims of racial justice agendas), see the Southern Poverty Law Center, "Alt-Right," *Southern Policy Law Center,* http://www.splcenter.org/fighting-hate/extremist-files/ideology/alt-right.

to their very existence, as suggested by the alt-right's popular hashtag #WhiteGenocide.

Alt-right political cartoonist Ben Garrison's work thrives in this climate. A viral 2017 Garrison cartoon, published on his widely followed Twitter account and blog, captures his demands for an end to "the tyranny of 'political correctness.'"[49] He, like his following, sees "Social Justice Warriors" as abusive and illogical emotional wrecks, whose activism centers solely on calling out people's innocent slips of tongue. One particularly popular cartoon, "Attack of the Cry Bullies," features three racialized and gendered caricatures running amok in diapers. One holds a protest sign reading "#HoldYourBreathforJustice," viciously echoing the last words of Eric Garner taken up by Black Lives Matter activists — "I can't breathe." A pearl-clutching feminist with an edgy aesthetic, and a stomach emblazoned with the words "Special Snowflake," follows another bawling social justice warrior with a racism rattle. Meanwhile, an adult baby coded as queer pouts in a "Safe Space" pen. These four figures are presented as ironic assaults on the US Constitution, curriculum, and reason, all up in flames, as they threaten to crush well-intentioned and apologetic liberals who fail to meet their demands. The very real grievances of people of color are here mocked in spectacular absurdity, making room for the real victims of multiculturalism — white men like Ben Garrison.

In the Trump era, the term special snowflake with its accompanying refrain of "you triggered, snowflake?" has been a favorite of alt-right spokespersons and viral memes that circulate widely on the Internet.[50] Here, the alt-right manipulates a popular strategy across the political spectrum: by reducing institutional racism to individualized feelings, white people make claims to "anti-white racism" and neglect social facts of housing

---

49 Ben Garrison, "Attack of the Cry Bullies" (cartoon), *GrrrGraphics*, November 13, 2015, https://grrrgraphics.files.wordpress.com/2015/11/crybullies_ben_garrison.jpg.

50 Dana Schwartz, "Why Trump Supporters Love Calling People 'Snowflakes,'" *GQ*, February 1, 2017, http://www.gq.com/story/why-trump-supporters-love-calling-people-snowflakes.

discrimination, the shrinking welfare state, asymmetric educational and professional opportunities along racial lines, the prison industrial complex, etc. Ironically, ring-wing ideologues use an argument rooted in the feelings, or "feewings," they loathe to dismiss material realities of systematic oppression while claiming that the Left has abandoned all logic in favor of emotional overreactions to imagined trespasses of political correctness.

Ultimately, the tactics of the alt-right and the liberals they revile converge in silencing radical movements for social justice through racially-coded appeals to civil discourse. Popular calls for so-called peaceful dialogue with speakers such as Richard Spencer, Ann Coulter, and Milo Yiannopoulos — in the name of free speech — unsurprisingly vilify activists who protest such displays of overt bigotry and hatred. Because of hard-fought gains of student activists of color in the 1960s and 1970s, universities in the 1980s and 1990s convened committees and wrote statements in service of multicultural and inclusive curricula and programming. Diversity on college campuses, though, has mostly meant shallow gestures rather than a fundamental rethinking of the role of the university. Thus, student activists continue to mobilize for deeper, more transformative institutional change. Yet, their experiences with systematic trauma have been minimized as the whining of privileged millennials.

The shallowness of institutional proclamations of diversity and inclusivity is nowhere more evident than in the failure to recognize an obvious fact: hate speech is not free; its price is paid in human lives. One need not be reminded of the white nationalist "Unite the Right" rally in Charlottesville, Virginia, organized by Richard Spencer and others, where counter-protesters were viciously attacked, resulting in the death of Heather Heyer and injuries to nineteen others. The injured included DeAndre Harris, who was brutally beaten by white nationalists yet subsequently arrested and charged with a felony.[51] This gross

---

51 Creede Newton, "Black Man Attacked at Charlottesville Rally Charged," *Al Jazeera,* October 13, 2017, http://www.aljazeera.com/news/2017/10/black-man-attacked-charlottesville-rally-charged-171013065312451.html.

injustice speaks to how policing works in tandem with vigilante white supremacists: with the criminalization of Black resistance forefronted, cops protect white free speech against dissent. Universities are complicit with this drama as they continue to use institutional monies to invest in openly hateful speakers in the name of diversity of thought and open dialogue, such as the University of Chicago's defense of a professor's recent invitation to Steve Bannon, already widely protested by faculty and students.[52] Yet, the rhetoric of free speech and triggered snowflakes paints those standing against white supremacy as the close-minded ones who actually oppose diversity. While free speech and trigger warnings were originally championed by radical social justice actors, their language has been thoroughly co-opted to silence the movements backing their refrains of #BlackLivesMatter and #MeToo. Yet, those movements persist, offering a powerful counter-narrative to the sanitized insistence on diversity and dialogue that aligns liberals with the right.

In this climate of intense Zionism, Islamophobia, misogyny, and racism, we must develop new tools for articulating visions of justice that wrest the co-opted terms of inclusion and safety back from institutions (including, but not limited to, the university) that sanction such violence. Particularly in the wake of Trump's election, cultural workers, community members, and student activists organized grassroots networks of care to overpower the wave of hate. The dense fabric of identifications and identities most impacted by post-election Trump terror — Black, Latinx, Indigenous, Muslim, undocumented, disabled, queer, trans, femme, anarchist, and otherwise dangerous to the reign of straight, white, racist, "Christian," able-bodied, toxic masculinity — has been mobilizing with fury and fortitude, using collective grief as a galvanizing force to fight fascism.

---

52 Dawn Rhodes et al., "U. of C. Professor Invites Steve Bannon to Campus Debate, Prompting Protest," *Chicago Tribune,* January 25, 2018, http://www.chicagotribune.com/news/ct-met-steve-bannon-university-of-chicago-20180125-story.html.

Trauma Works

The maelstrom surrounding trigger warnings provides an opportunity to reflect on the complex relationship between trauma and identity. As the administrative and popular response to the Isla Vista massacre on campus testifies, asking students to understand the violence apart from the social and political investments to which it spoke maintains an illusion of whiteness and toxic masculinity as unaccountable and innocent. Trauma, now an infinitely malleable term, has been wielded more often to silence conversations than to open them up, to claim injury rather than an *identity formed through trauma* that acknowledges its constitutive force. In "Black Study, Black Struggle," Robin D.G. Kelley writes, "Resistance is our heritage. And resistance is our healing. Through collective struggle, we alter our circumstances; contain, escape, or possibly eviscerate the *source* of trauma; recover our bodies; reclaim and redeem our dead; and make ourselves whole. It is difficult to see this in a world where words such as *trauma*, PTSD, *micro-aggression*, and *triggers* have virtually replaced *oppression*, *repression*, and *subjugation*."[53] To recognize the traumatic nature of identity production through differentially felt systematic suffering can motivate political investment and participation in a broader social world. This is certainly not to diminish identities to the individual and collective sites of trauma in which they live and love.

Following critiques by Robin Kelley, Jack Halberstam, and others of how the rhetoric of injury functions under neoliberalism,[54] we must then ask how experiences with and ethical witnessing of trauma can be used in service of trans-

---

53 Robin D.G. Kelley, "Black Study, Black Struggle," *Boston Review,* March 7, 2016, http://bostonreview.net/forum/robin-d-g-kelley-black-study-black-struggle.

54 See, for example, Jack Halberstam's provocative and widely debated "You Are Triggering Me! The Neo-Liberal Rhetoric of Harm, Danger and Trauma," *Bully Bloggers,* July 5, 2014, https://bullybloggers.wordpress.com/2014/07/05/you-are-triggering-me-the-neo-liberal-rhetoric-of-harm-danger-and-trauma/.

formative justice work — rather than commodified as a voyeuristic display of pain legible to the state only in its exceptionality. Co-opting the language of trigger warnings and trauma works precisely by decontextualizing harm from larger social forces — often in turn redoubling violence as an ahistorical fetish. Such spectacles of violence may attempt to elicit humanistic gestures of empathy at best or pity and pleasure at worst, but this spectrum of feeling privileges individualized interiority over collective commitments to justice. When "issues" of race, including the appellation of race *as issue*, get institutionally managed through human resources instead of human rights, racism gets relegated to the discursive sphere of public relations trainings on how to learn and so *to master* difference. This mastery can only happen when the specter of racism remains a long shadow in a myopically short cultural memory.

While I started writing this piece directly following the 2014 Isla Vista massacre, I want to end by addressing Kelley's question: "Can we acknowledge students' pain in a culture that reduces oppression to misunderstanding and psychology?" In "Black Study, Black Struggle" as well as his response to the *Boston Review*-curated thread opened by his provocation cited above,[55] Kelley powerfully addresses how instead of dismantling institutional racism, social actors theft the language of trauma to emphasize self-help solutions to structural problems. While holding close Kelley's critique of curtailing the Black Radical Imagination with claims to the same trauma wielded to protect white interests, I insist on examining how trauma, despite its incorporation, might actually *work* to disrupt the neoliberal production of antiracist subjects divorced from praxis. I define trauma not in the individualized medical or juridical sense, but as a collective negotiation of everyday confrontations with state power. Instead of ignoring or instrumentalizing the pain of others, the recognition of one's own situated relation to personal

---

55 Robin Kelley, "Black Study, Black Struggle: Robin D. G. Kelley's Final Forum Response," *Boston Review,* March 7, 2016, bostonreview.net/forum/black-study-black-struggle/robin-d-g-kelley-robin-d-g-kelleys-final-response.

and social traumas can motivate political consciousness, accountability, and action.

Community organizers and cultural producers, through creative dissent, work to expose the violence of structural oppression and protest the terms meant to dictate experience. Racism, heterosexism, and other intersecting structures of power/knowledge exist as socially sanctioned and actively produced psychic sicknesses predicated on violence against targeted groups and in need of institutional acknowledgment and redress. To point to the psychic sickness of whiteness is not to alleviate it from culpability, as the mental health defense has been leveraged to protect whiteness from racialized charges of predisposed criminality. Rather, part of this making visible of material and discursive violence has been to demand that a critique of institutional power ask individuals who benefit within those institutions to take collective responsibility for their unearned advantage and interpersonal interactions.

Resisting the white appropriative urge to possessively claim another person's trauma as one's own, social actors must recognize their situated relation to a culture of systematic trauma. For white people, this means reckoning with a racial identity predicated on the "privilege" to subject others to suffering while maintaining a murderous innocence. It means facing the ugliness and horror of history and making an active commitment to doing something about it: not because of some misguided notion of benevolent help for others, but as the basis for a new identity rooted in an active commitment to *love, study,* and *struggle* (to use Robin Kelley's beautiful post-it note reminder mentioned in "Black Study, Black Struggle"). Instead of pathologizing aggrieved groups for structural injustices, it is time for a traumatized dominant culture to wake up from the fantasy of its injury to the reality of the devastating impact ideologies of inferiority and power-evasiveness have on its collective mental health.

Against the gentrification of disciplines, the study of the Black Radical Tradition, particularly Black feminist thought, offers active commitments to interrogating transnational manifestations of gendered racial capitalism. Humanities-based approaches to social justice, then, must not buy into the *Eat, Pray, Love* model of existential angst resolved through the New Age romance of traveling to spiritually consume "otherness." This multiculturalist move finds its way into institutional objectives of broadening student horizons through literary encounter of and empathy for the so-called other's experience. While under fire for their lack of "relevance" to an increasingly technologized world of warfare, the humanities can honor the power of social movements without thefting racialized moral compasses. Rather than appropriate the text of the body, students and teachers must study the massive body of texts, largely written by people of color, that address global capital in a moment of antiracist incorporation — and create activist and artistic blueprints for its undoing. Humanities-based analyses of social identities and power can dream into being provisions for justice actionable in coalitional spaces, from classrooms to protests to block parties.

Spaces of serious reflection, critical cultivation, and creative imagination provide the raw material for transformative action in and beyond the crumbling façade of neoliberal education. While both the language and strategies of justice movements will continue to be co-opted by the dominant order, it cannot replicate the strength of social relations. So, *in* the university but not quite of or beyond it,[56] we study, we decolonize dominant knowledge formations, we act, and we manifest new visions of collectivity born out of struggle.

I close by returning to Nayyirah Waheed's poetry, in many ways the impetus for this essay, to emphasize the cultural work of creative dissent in addressing and redressing collective traumas. While never simply reducible to the glue that binds communities, trauma remains intimately tied to subject formation, holding in tension self-division and pain alongside resilience and survival. For example, Waheed's *Salt* locates possibilities

---

56 Many radical scholar-activists and organizers, such as members of Undercommoning (undercommoning.org), have taken up the formulation of being in but not of the university that Fred Moten and Stefano Harney describe in their influential *The Undercommons: Fugitive Planning and Black Study* (New York: Autonomedia, 2013).

for poetic justice in wresting trauma from its institutional incorporation, providing the often-unseen evidence in which new practices of collective healing and being-together take root. I'll end with her words, which follow Audre Lorde and Hortense Spillers in saying yes to the *mother within*, mapping an erotics of non-hierarchical relationality in the face of trauma: "i want more 'men' / with flowers falling from their skin ... flowers pouring from [their] chest."[57]

---

57 Nayyirah Waheed, *Salt* (Seattle: CreateSpace, 2013), 47, 41.

9

After My Uncle Elbowed a Soldier in the Face on the Beach of Pulau Bidong

Sophia Terazawa

When the boy was dragged away,
they used my mother's tears. She
won't say why or who told her
to plug her mouth with sand.

She says I know not hate or
war. I know not hunger, real
hunger, the smell of protest
shed from flesh and bone. I

know not Third World. Woman. Home.
I know not bellies gutted,
not how to beg in someone
else's language, not how

to be named Cockroach. Monkey.
Dog. I know not how to take
comfort in knowing I can
let go of this body.

DOI: 10.21983/P3.0250.1.12

I know not how to bleed for
loss of words, to pass down what
I choose to tell and nothing
more, to tell my daughter

that raising one's voice without
fear of death is the highest
form of privilege in the
United States of Hope.

I know not how to lose this, too.
I know not taste of Rope. Stone.
Of daily executions.
I know not genocide.

I know not how to make one
memory into twenty
years of silence after they
drag my brother away

except in knowing you will
remember only what I choose to tell.

10

Wicked Problems and Intersectionality Telephone

Barbara Tomlinson

Antiracism Inc.: Why the Way We Talk about Racial Justice Matters reveals how arguments that frame themselves as antiracist may perpetuate racial injustice by appropriating, incorporating, misusing, and neutralizing antiracist discourses.[1] This chapter demonstrates how academic discourses can work to misrepresent and neutralize the concept of intersectionality. Intersectional thinking emerged from the theorizing of women of color as a tool against structural subordination, an analytic to challenge structural inequality and call for institutional transformation.[2] It is a political and analytic concept, a sensibility or disposition, a heuristic for thinking in supple and strategic ways about so-

---

1   Parts of "Wicked Problems and Intersectionality Telephone" are adapted from *Undermining Intersectionality: The Perils of Powerblind Feminism* (Philadelphia: Temple University Press, 2018), re-published here by permission of Temple University Press.

2   Anna Carastathis, *Intersectionality: Origins, Contestations, Horizons* (Lincoln: University of Nebraska Press, 2016); Patricia Hill Collins and Sirma Bilge, *Intersectionality* (Malden: Polity, 2016); Ange-Marie Hancock, *Intersectionality: An Intellectual History* (New York: Oxford University Press, 2016); Vivian M. May, *Pursuing Intersectionality: Unsettling Dominant Imaginaries* (New York, Routledge, 2015).

cial categories, relations of power, and the complexities of same-ness and difference in terms of conceptions of *both/and* rather than *either/or*.[3] Intersectional analysis reveals how single-axis theories of subordination inscribed in law and social life, but also utilized in self-defense by aggrieved groups, can obscure shifting and multiple axes of power. As a conceptual framework that focuses attention on the degree to which all identities are multi-dimensional, intersectionality is a nexus of complex arguments about race, gender, ethnicity, sexuality, religion, nation, hierarchy, power, control, and value. Intersectionality has demonstrated enormous value as a political and analytic tool.

Intersectionality has become a central frame in speaking about power and social categories for both activists and academics. Activists have used the concept of intersectionality to argue the need for recognizing the intersectional, multidimensional nature of subordination rather than approaching different axes of subordination separately. Academic discourses have in many ways embraced intersectionality: using it widely, citing it as a generative tool, framing it as central to feminist inquiry, for example, to the point that it appears to be hegemonic. Yet the very discourses appearing to incorporate intersectionality effectively undermine it by failing to interrogate the conventions of academic argument. These conventions are not by themselves racist but when wielded uncritically promote racist analyses and interpretations. For example, white feminists find useful intersectionality's critical analysis of gendered power but tend to jet-

---

3 Patricia Hill Collins, "It's All in the Family: Intersections of Gender, Race, and Nation," in *Decentering the Center: Philosophy for a Multicultural, Postcolonial, and Feminist World,* eds. Uma Narayan and Sandra Harding (Bloomington: Indiana University Press, 2000), 156–76; Kimberlé Crenshaw, "Demarginalizing the Intersection of Race and Sex: A Black Feminist Critique of Antidiscrimination Doctrine," *University of Chicago Legal Forum*, no. 1, art. 8 (1989): 139–67; Kimberlé Crenshaw, "Mapping the Margins: Intersectionality, Identity Politics, and Violence against Women of Colour," *Stanford Law Review* 43, no. 6 (1991): 1241–99; Kimberlé W. Crenshaw, "From Private Violence to Mass Incarceration: Thinking Intersectionally about Women, Race, and Social Control," *UCLA Law Review* 59 (2012): 1418–72.

tison its antiracist implications and obligations. The academic disciplines are not innately racist, but a disciplinary conservatism causes many scholars to see social problems as raw materials for disciplinary critique rather than moral and political challenges that might require tools beyond their discipline. A case in point is the reflexive embrace of social science methodologies when confronted with complex problems that require more capacious tools. As a result, the argumentative strategies and rhetorics of many white feminist critiques neutralize the radical antiracist potential of intersectionality by deprecating the intellectual production of its originating women of color.[4]

These critiques, I argue, are replete with what I term "powerblind" discursive practices that reinforce racial hierarchies.[5] The use of powerblind strategies — strategies that purport to be antiracist but in fact reinforce racial hierarchy — is generally obscured by taken-for-granted attitudes toward academic

---

4   The dominant subject position of the white (middle-class heterosexual) woman that characterizes what I call "white feminist critiques of intersectionality" is not an embodied identity but a privileged standpoint and structural advantage, a matter of foregrounding dominant interests and deprecating the interests of anti-subordination scholars and activists. Hence, when I talk about white critique, I am not necessarily talking about white people, but about a conditioned acceptance of certain ideas rather than about an embodied identity grounded in color or phenotype.

5   For other critical analyses of such critiques of intersectionality, see Nikol Alexander-Floyd, "Disappearing Acts: Reclaiming Intersectionality in the Social Sciences in a Post-Black Feminist Era," *Feminist Formations* 24, no. 1 (2012): 1–25, https://doi.org/10.1353/ff.2012.0003; Sirma Bilge, "Intersectionality Undone: Saving Intersectionality from Feminist Intersectionality Studies," *Du Bois Review* 10, no. 2 (2013): 405–24, https://doi.org/10.1017/S1742058X13000283; Sirma Bilge, "Whitening Intersectionality: Evanescence of Race in Current Intersectionality Scholarship," in *Racism and Sociology: Racism Analysis Yearbook* 5-2014, eds. Wulf D. Hund and Alana Lentin (Berlin: Lit Verlag, 2014), 175–205; Devon Carbado, "Colorblind Intersectionality," *Signs: A Journal of Women in Culture and Society* 38, no. 4 (2013): 811–45, https://doi.org/10.1086/669666; Kimberlé Williams Crenshaw, "Postscript," in *Framing Intersectionality: Debates on a Multifaceted Concept in Gender Studies,* eds. Helma Lutz, Maria Teresa Herrera Vivar, and Linda Supik (Burlington: Ashgate, 2011), 221–33; Vivian M. May, "'Speaking into the Void'? Intersectionality Critiques and Epistemic Backlash," *Hypatia* 29, no. 1 (2014): 94–112, https://doi.org/10.1111/hypa.12060.

discourse. The routine conventions of academic argument are generally treated as neutral technologies for conveying information, ideas, and explanations. In theory, scholars at the scene of argument identify the sites and the stakes of new research by reviewing relevant prior literatures, quoting and citing source materials, and highlighting their new original and generative contributions to the conversation. In practice, however, the scene of argument is suffused with interests and ideologies, shot through with hierarchical social power. The matter that makes up scholarly debates cannot be separated from the manner in which it is delivered. Academic arguments framing themselves as antiracist can be especially susceptible to subtle and surreptitious distortions. Scholarly research is, like activist struggles for social justice, innately dialogic, collective and collaborative. The structures of reward and recognition that prevail in scholarly research, however, are structured in dominance, allowing unacknowledged and unwitting deployment of powerblind hierarchical arguments. They encourage authors to view the scene of argument as a competitive enterprise, to elevate themselves by disparaging others, to claim as one's personal property ideas and arguments that emerge from polysemic and rhizomatic conversations inside and outside the academy. These practices do not reflect so much the personal flaws of individuals as the fact that in a hierarchical society, all discursive practices will be structured in dominance, unless they are challenged and refuted by conscious efforts to interrogate the routine conventions of argument and revise the terms of reading and writing.

Addressing Wicked Problems

The widespread and intersectional nature of structures of racial and gender subordination make them difficult to counter. Dispossession and violence against women and racialized people are often treated with impunity. These are "wicked problems" in the common meanings of the term "wicked." They are entrenched, reprehensible, iniquitous, heinous, vicious acts of domination and degradation that are nonetheless overlooked, treated as local anomalies, defined out of serious consideration. They are systematically evaded and ignored by local and national governments as well as the United Nations and other world organizations whose charge includes the improvement of living conditions and human rights for all.

The term "wicked problems" has also been developed by design theorists and been utilized across other academic disciplines to describe a specific kind of problem, one that is difficult to address. In this sense, "wicked problems" are problems in social life that "are ill-formulated, where the information is confusing, where there are many clients and decision makers with conflicting values, and where the ramifications in the whole system are thoroughly confusing."[6] Wicked problems are complex problems characterized by indeterminacy. They are fundamentally political and rhetorical, rather than scientific.[7] Academic discourses framed as antiracist or antisexist may fail to come to grips with problems of subordination if they use powerblind conventions instead of considering the full scope of subordination as a wicked problem.

6   C. West Churchman, "Wicked Problems," Editorial "Free for All," *Management Science* 14, no. 4 (1967): B141–42, at B-141, https://doi.org/10.1287/mnsc.14.4.B141.

7   I am grateful to Jodi Rios for alerting me to the importance of "wicked problems" and the differences between social sciences and design revealed by their differing approaches to wicked problems. While the term "wicked problem" was used by Karl Popper (1972), design theorists have developed a widespread and robust theory of wicked problems. See also Horst W.J. Rittel and Melvin M. Webber, "Dilemmas in a General Theory of Planning," *Policy Sciences* 4 (1973): 155–69, http://www.jstor.org/stable/4531523; Richard Buchanan, "Wicked Problems in Design Thinking," *Design Issues* 8, no. 2 (1992): 5–21, http://www.jstor.org/stable/1511637; Anna Rylander, "Design Thinking as Knowledge Work: Epistemological Foundations and Practical Implications," *Journal of Design Management* 4, no. 1 (2009): 7–19, https://doi.org/10.1111/j.1942-5074.2009.00003.x. I base much of my discussion here on Raymond McCall and Janet Burge, "Untangling Wicked Problems," Paper presentation, 6th International Conference on Design, Computing and Cognition, University College, London, June 23–25, 2014, and "Untangling Wicked Problems," *Artificial Intelligence for Engineering, Analysis and Manufacturing* 30, no. 2 (2016): 200–210, https://doi.org/10.1017/S089006041600007X.

To demonstrate this predicament, I contrast here two kinds of discourses: first, collaborative activist discourses developing the concept of intersectionality to address widespread practices of racial and gender subordination; then, academic discourses that frame themselves as promoting antisubordination while at the same time deploying powerblind strategies that support structures of racial dominance. The discourses I contrast concern the use of several "traffic" or "intersections" metaphors originally developed by legal theorist Kimberlé Crenshaw to illustrate some of the complexities of thinking intersectionality. Crenshaw has developed several metaphors to make the abstraction of multiple categorical discriminations more concrete by describing the movement of traffic through intersections. For example, Crenshaw argues: "Consider an analogy to traffic in an intersection, coming and going in all four directions. Discrimination, like traffic through an intersection, may flow in one direction, and it may flow in another. If an accident happens in an intersection, it can be caused by cars traveling from any number of directions and, sometimes, from all of them."[8] Crenshaw's metaphor is actually a metaphor about the nature and consequences of *intersecting discriminations* supported by structures of power as they operate in heterogeneous spaces to impact people with differing trajectories in different ways. The image is fluid both spatially and temporally: it describes a *circulation network of identity-related effects*.

I contrast discourses about "traffic" metaphors for intersectional positioning as they are used in three different discursive situations:

1. as a source for generative analysis and argumentation for a range of social activists involved in the 2001 World Conference against Racism, Racial Discrimination, Xenophobia and Related Intolerance in Durban, South Africa (hereafter WCAR);

---

8   Crenshaw, "Demarginalizing the Intersection of Race and Sex," 149.

2. as an example of the misrepresentation of the use of the "traffic" metaphor in academic critique by a social scientist who fails to respond fully to the "wicked problem" of subordination addressed at WCAR; and

3. as a misreading repeatedly cited inaccurately and counterproductively by academics caught in a problematic politics of circulation and citation.

Collaborative Discourses to Address Wicked Problems

Before, during, and after WCAR, activist-focused discourses about intersectionality and traffic metaphors circulated in ways responding to the recognition of multiple subordinations as a wicked problem. These discourses exemplify the ways in which wicked problems can provoke people to develop new ways of knowing and being through discursive practices dramatically different from those taken for granted in academic discourses, particularly those in the social sciences.

The complications of audience at conferences such as WCAR are sharply different from those involved in academic discourses, fitting the profile suggested by the theory of wicked problems. For example, WCAR involved over 10,000 governmental delegates attending the UN WCAR and 8,000–10,000 delegates attending the parallel nongovernmental forum (the majority women).[9] Those attending represented and reported back to governments, nongovernmental organizations, and a wide range of groups concerned with human rights. They represented multiple stakeholders seeking to influence decision makers, and included decision makers themselves, all with a wide range of knowledges and opinions.[10] Because WCAR is addressing wicked

9 Maylei Blackwell and Nadine Naber, "Intersectionality in an Era of Globalization: The Implications of the UN World Conference Against Racism for Transnational Feminist Practices — A Conference Report," *Meridians: Feminism, Race, Transnationalism* 2, no. 2 (2002): 237–48; Sylvanna M. Falcón, *Power Interrupted: Antiracist and Feminist Activism inside the United Nations* (Seattle: University of Washington Press, 2016).

10 Falcón, *Power Interrupted.*

problems, there is no definitive test of solutions or objective criteria for testing. Stakeholders are equally entitled to express their judgments about the value of proposed responses to injustice and subordination. How to weight the judgments of stakeholders is, therefore, a political question. In this context, points of entry into discussion of multiple discriminations need to be accessible, focused, and available for practical action. How to create such points of entry are political and rhetorical decisions.

The "authorship" involved in producing preparatory statements, position papers, and presentations for conferences such as WCAR is diffuse, independent, and also collaborative. Preparation for the conference involved numerous preliminary meetings among a wide range of diverse local, national, and international groups developing position statements and other arguments seeking to shift prevailing world-wide public discourses about multiple and compound discrimination. The members of the various groups and their agonists were also stakeholders working through their own conflicting values and arguments in order to contest enduring problems allowed and even fostered by governmental decision makers. An example was the Expert Meeting on Gender and Racial Discrimination held in Zagreb in November 2000, at which law professor and intersectional scholar Kimberlé Crenshaw served as a consultant. Crenshaw's background paper presents an accessible general traffic metaphor to describe the dangers of compound discrimination at the intersection of multiple categories.[11] However, the Report of the Expert Meeting presents a revision of this metaphor without attribution to Crenshaw, as the group collaborated in developing and refining Crenshaw's metaphor for their shared use.[12] The developing and refining of the traffic metaphor is further

11 Kimberlé Crenshaw, "The Intersection of Race and Gender Discrimination," background paper prepared for the Expert Group Meeting, Zagreb, Croatia, November 21–24, 2000.

12 "Report for the Expert Group Meeting: Gender and Racial Discrimination," Expert Group Meeting, Zagreb, Croatia, November 21–24, 2000, United Nations Division for the Advancement of Women (DAW), Office of the High Commissioner of Human Rights (OHCHR), United Nations Development

carried on in the aftermath of WCAR, in reports to and by human rights groups involved in WCAR, sometimes mentioning that their metaphor was "developed by" Crenshaw, other times not mentioning Crenshaw at all. That metaphor is no longer "Crenshaw's" in an academic sense but also part of a general position statement seeking to intervene in the dominant public discourse that insists on treating discriminations as separate rather than intersectional.

Improvising Intersectional Metaphors

The general traffic metaphors introduced in the Report of the Expert Meeting at Zagreb and Crenshaw's background paper were similar to that appearing in Crenshaw's formal conference paper presented at WCAR, "The Intersectionality of Race and Gender Discrimination."[13] The metaphor was manifested in a much more specific and concrete way at a workshop provided by Crenshaw for the gender caucus at WCAR. Reports of the details of the workshop vary, though it appears to have included an introduction to a traffic metaphor, some concrete examples of street names, and probably mention of a many layered blanket of oppression. The various reports created by delegates and brought back to their own social activist groups do not attempt to quote Crenshaw, but summarize and revise her comments, adapting them to suit the particular interests of their own groups. This becomes evident, for example, as different reports provide different names for the examples of thoroughfares with dangerous traffic. For example, according to the report by the Australian National Committee on Refugee Women (ANCORW), "The main highway is 'Racism Road.' One cross street might be

Fund for Women (UNIFEM), http://www.un.org/womenwatch/daw/csw/genrac/report.htm.

13 "Report for the Expert Group Meeting"; Crenshaw, "The Intersection of Race and Gender Discrimination"; Kimberlé Crenshaw, "The Intersectionality of Race and Gender Discrimination," paper presentation, "World Conference Against Racism," Durban, South Africa, August 31–September 8, 2001.

Colonisation Causeway, then Patriarchy Street, Religion Road, Slavery Street, Culture Cul de Sac, Trafficking Way, Forced Migration Road, Indigenous Exploitation Highway, Globalization Street, Caste Road — we could go on naming the town."[14]

According to the report by Asia Pacific Forum on Women Law and Development (APWLD), the streets are "Racism Road, Patriarchy Parade, Sexism Street, Colonization Crescent, Religious Persecution Road, Indigenous Dispossession Highway, Class Street, Caste Street, and so on.... To use this model as an analytic tool, each of the 'Road Names' must be unpacked to explore the origin of the oppression, and the impact of these on women across a range of situations."[15]

The locally inflected "uptake" of the metaphor is evidence of its ability to offer a strategic point of entry for activism and practical action.

With changes from abstract to concrete, with specific varying revisions for different audiences, the traffic metaphor has become part of a repertoire of collective action, perhaps similar to what Charles Tilly likens to improvisational jazz: composers provide an initial line which is taken up by those who improvise in their own ways, in interaction with one another.[16] Sidney Tarrow points out that changes in contentious language are "dialogic" — "the word is half someone else's"; discourses are always multivocal.[17] According to Tarrow, "In ordinary times, elites pos-

---

14 Eileen Pittaway, "Australian National Committee on Refugee Women (AN-CORW) Annual Report," Centre for Refugee Research, University of New South Wales, Australia, 2002, 25, http://www.ancorw.org/2001-2002.pdf.

15 Asia Pacific Forum on Women Law and Development (APWLD), "What is Intersectionality?" in *What Does the WCAR Mean for Asia Pacific Women?* (University of New South Wales: Center for Refugee Research, 2003), 17–20, at 18, http://iknowpolitics.org/sites/default/files/women_human2orights_apwld_part1.pdf.

16 Sidney Tarrow, "Repertoires of Contentious Language," in *The Language of Contention: Revolutions in Words, 1688–2012* (New York: Cambridge University Press, 2013), 8–34.

17 Tarrow, "Repertoires of Contentious Language," 12; Mikhail M. Bakhtin, *The Dialogic Imagination,* ed. Michael Holquist, trans. Caryl Emerson and Michael Holquist (Austin: University of Texas Press, 1981); Mikhail M. Bakhtin, *Speech Genres and Other Late Essays,* trans. Vern W. McGee, eds.

sess power over language, but in critical junctures, ordinary people not only erupt on the stage of history, but also gain the power
to affect the language of contention."[18] Concepts of intersectionality emerged from the arguments of women of color primarily
in the United States but also in Britain and elsewhere. But people
from different nations have different definitions of intersectionality and come together to contest and negotiate these definitions and strategies in order to address wicked problems.[19]

Discursive constructs like "intersectionality" are not epi-
phenomenal when contesting wicked problems, but part of a
complicated set of moves and exchanges. Maylei Blackwell and
Nadine Naber argue: "In order to understand the complex ma-
neuvering in Durban, it is crucial to realize that at the core of
WCAR was a discursive struggle, or a struggle over representation and the power to define, which has been a central feature
of colonial domination and legitimation throughout history."[20]
It appears that the various traffic metaphors for intersectionality and other discussions were successful as points of entry and
points of departure for groups to develop their own arguments
about multiple discriminations, arguments that succeeded in
altering the language of various formal documents emerging
from the conference.[21] Conceptions of intersectionality were effective, not because they remained in the control of elites, but
because they responded dialogically to the needs and concerns
and demands of a wide range of delegates. What makes a metaphor work in thinking through wicked problems — receiving
uptake, guiding analysis and action — is a matter of persuasion,

Caryl Emerson and Michael Holquist (Austin: University of Texas Press,
1986); Michael Holquist, *Dialogism: Mikhail Bakhtin and His World* (London: Routledge, 1990).

18 Tarrow, "Repertoires of Contentious Language," 12.

19 Falcón, *Power Interrupted*.

20 Blackwell and Naber, "Intersectionality in an Era of Globalization," 239.

21 Jennifer Chan-Tiberghien, "Gender-Skepticism or Gender Boom? Poststructural Feminists, Transnational Feminisms and the World Conference
Against Racism," *International Feminist Journal of Politics* 6, no. 3 (2004):
454–84, https://doi.org/10.1080/1461674042000235618; Falcón, *Power Interrupted*.

not scientific accuracy. Steven L. Winter helpfully argues that analogies and metaphors are persuasive not when people judge them to be "sound," but when people find them congruent with or helpful in understanding their world.[22] Apparently the traffic metaphor of intersectionality captured and extended the prior conceptions of social activists at WCAR, opening up useful possibilities that made it persuasive.

At previous UN-sponsored conferences, gender subordination and racism were often treated as if they were separate, mutually exclusive and incommensurable concerns; the 2001 WCAR was the first to include "related intolerances," including the ways that racism intersects with other wicked problems.[23] Workshops on gender were often marginalized, but WCAR "created dialogue around shared oppressions in an international context; and broadened our definition of racism and how racism intersects in its complexities with multiple forms of oppression."[24] As Chan-Tiberghien discloses, at WCAR, the concept of "gender as intersectionality" marked a "paradigm shift" in international human rights frameworks. This move put "the issue of diversity among women at the forefront," marking "the beginning of a new phase of transnational feminist mobilization."[25]

Critical Discourses to Tame Wicked Problems

The collaborative discourses addressing wicked problems such as those surrounding WCAR are distinctly different from academic discourses. As a result, they can be difficult for scholars to analyze and critique. For example, academic critiques assume that statements are put forth by named individual authors or co-authors making formal textual interventions in specialized conversations in their own and related disciplines. These spe-

---

22 Steven L. Winter, *A Clearing in the Forest: Law, Life and Mind* (Chicago: University of Chicago Press, 2001).

23 Chan-Tiberghien, "Gender-Skepticism or Gender Boom?"; Falcón, *Power Interrupted*.

24 Blackwell and Naber, "Intersectionality in an Era of Globalization," 245.

25 Chan-Tiberghien, "Gender-Skepticism or Gender Boom?" 454.

cialized conversations target a particular range of readers with somewhat similar training. Their argumentative purposes speak to the intellectual and political interests of those groups operating within the limited discursive circles of the academy. Scholars trained in this tradition may apply inappropriate criteria and produce inadequate critiques when confronting discourses emerging from collaborative and collective political activist work on wicked problems. I demonstrate here the difficulties resulting when scholarly engagements with the discourse of WCAR and its preparatory meetings fail to distinguish between discourses of the academy and of world-wide activist politics.

The task of discourses in the social sciences is very different than that of discourses attempting to come to grips with wicked problems. Like design, the discourse of social activists focuses on how wicked problems might be addressed, on how to create a future, on what could be. Many social science discourses, in contrast, address "tame problems" with limited solutions, minimizing variables to make what they consider a valid model of reality as it is (or should be). Authorship is linked to a named individual or group of co-authors, not scattered through an enormous range of stakeholders. Perhaps most significant is the issue of authority. In effect, authority in the preparatory meetings and WCAR is shared across stakeholders, who are entitled to hold opinions about wicked problems and how those problems should be defined, conceived, and countered. In contrast, many scholars in the social sciences work to establish themselves as singular authorities, criticizing from their own point of view the discourses of all others — scholars and activists — as if such speakers tried and failed to study tame problems as a scholar in the social sciences might. As an example here, I analyze Nira Yuval-Davis's arguments about the discourses of the preliminary meetings of WCAR and the much revised example of a collaborative metaphor that emerged in a workshop at the gender caucus at WCAR.

Through Yuval-Davis's Eyes

In "Intersectionality and Feminist Politics," Nira Yuval-Davis expresses disappointment with the discourses of one of the preparatory meetings for WCAR — the Expert Meeting on Gender and Racial Discrimination in Zagreb in 2000. She claims that "the analytic attempts to explain intersectionality in the reports that came out of this meeting are confusing," apparently because their discussions of intersectionality differ from one another and appear to confuse "identities" and "structures."[26] Yuval-Davis does not comment on the specifics of audience and authorship that constitute the attempts to address wicked problems at Durban. She disregards the Expert Meeting's intention to address the different concerns, definitions, and positions of thousands of people from a myriad of countries who must negotiate informal and formal discourses at Durban.

Yuval-Davis does not acknowledge the diffuse, independent, and also collaborative nature of authorship involved in creating position papers related to WCAR. She criticizes documents that "came out of this [Zagreb] meeting" without citing the report of the meeting.[27] Of the three documents she cites, only one was closely associated with the meeting, that of Crenshaw — as opposed to the more independent reports of the Australian Human Rights and EOC and the Center for Women's Global Leadership.[28] Yuval-Davis appears to misjudge the discourse situation she is criticizing; she is treating independent social action groups attempting to collaborate to address wicked problems within a

---

26 Nira Yuval-Davis, "Intersectionality and Feminist Politics," *European Journal of Women's Studies* 13, no. 3 (2006): 193–209, at 196, https://doi.org/10.1177/1350506806065752.

27 Ibid., 196–97.

28 Australian Human Rights and Equal Opportunities Commission (EOC), "HREOC and the World Conference Against Racism," 2001, http://www.hreoc.gv.au/worldconference/aus_gender.html; Center for Women's Global Leadership, "A Women's Human Right Approach to the World Conference Against Racism," 2001, http://www.cwgl.rutgers.edu/docman/csw-2001/83-women-s-human-rights-approach-to-the-world-conference-against-racism.

real world context as if their task was to make arguments suitable for academic discourse in the social sciences — a discourse more fraught with contradiction and error than one might suspect. Instead, Yuval-Davis treats this discursive situation as a "tame problem" of definition — to promote as essential her own individually specific and eurocentric set of rules for how intersectionality should be discussed and to hold alternatives up for censure. Everyone makes such errors, though we all try to avoid them, but when they are patterned and predictable, they represent not an individual act but a shared social practice.

The particular instantiation of a metaphor that bridges the contrasting discourses of this analysis appears in Yuval-Davis's text immediately following her claim that the three documents that "came out of this [Zagreb] meeting" are "confusing." There Yuval-Davis argues:

> The imagery of crossroads[29] and traffic as developed by Crenshaw (2001) occupies a central space:
>
>> Intersectionality is what occurs when a woman from a minority group…tries to navigate the main crossing in the city.…The main highway is "racism road." One cross street can be Colonialism, then Patriarchy Street.…She has to deal not only with one form of oppression but with all forms, those named as road signs, which link together to make a double, a triple, multiple, a many layered blanket of oppression.[30]

The block-indented text cited above appears to be yet a third version of the "roads" imagery from reports on Crenshaw's informal workshop. Yuval-Davis dismisses the metaphor as "addi-

---

29 Many white feminist scholars, particularly those in the European arena, fail to acknowledge the specific meanings of Crenshaw's preferred term "intersection" and substitute the term "crossroad." The different implications of the two terms are discussed in Tomlinson, *Undermining Intersectionality,* Chapter 3.

30 Yuval-Davis, "Intersectionality and Feminist Politics," 196.

tive," but does not discuss it further, implying that it contributes to the "confusion" she finds in the three documents.

This moment in Yuval-Davis's argument is a nexus or node in a network of errors, confusions, and misrepresentations. While metaphors of traffic flowing through intersections are found in several of Crenshaw's publications[31] this imagery does not include the material in the block-indented text. While Crenshaw's paper for the Expert Group Meeting (2001) and the Expert Group Report (2000) mention traffic imagery, the imagery is not similar to the block-indented text (the imagery from Crenshaw's presentation at WCAR in 2001 is quoted in its entirety in the note below[32]). There is no imagery of "crossroads" or traffic

---

31 A summary of one of Crenshaw's traffic metaphors appears in the text above. A further traffic metaphor appears in Crenshaw, "Demarginalizing the Intersection of Race and Sex," 149: "Judicial decisions which premise intersectional relief on a showing that Black women are specifically recognized as a class are analogous to a doctor's decision at the scene of an accident to treat an accident victim only if the injury is recognized by medical insurance. Similarly, providing legal relief only when Black women show that their claims are based on race or on sex is analogous to calling an ambulance for the victim only after the driver responsible for the injuries is identified. But it is not always easy to reconstruct an accident: Sometimes the skid marks and the injuries simply indicate that they occurred simultaneously, frustrating efforts to determine which driver caused the harm. In these cases the tendency seems to be that no driver is held responsible, no treatment is administered, and the involved parties simply get back in their cars and zoom away."

32 Crenshaw, "The Intersectionality of Race and Gender Discrimination"; "Report for the Expert Group Meeting." A traffic metaphor also appears in Crenshaw, "The Intersectionality of Race and Gender Discrimination," 11–12: "To use a metaphor of an intersection, we first analogize the various axes of power, i.e., for instance, race, ethnicity, gender, or class, as constituting the thoroughfares which structure the social, economic or political terrain. It is through these avenues that disempowering dynamics travel. These thoroughfares are generally framed as distinctive and mutually exclusive axes of power; for example, racism is distinct from patriarchy, which is in turn distinct from class oppression. In fact, the systems often overlap and cross each other, creating complex intersections at which two, or three or more of these axes may meet. Indeed, racialized women are often positioned in the space where racism or xenophobia, class and gender meet. They are consequently subject to injury by the heavy flow of traffic traveling along all these roads.... This is a particularly dangerous task when the

at all in the other two source documents that Yuval-Davis cites.[33] Thus the implication that the block-indented text represents the essence or entirety of Crenshaw's metaphorical conceptualization of intersectionality through traffic is not accurate; nor could it be said that the metaphor found in the block-indented text occupies "a central space" in the three documents that Yuval-Davis examines, since it appears *in none of them*. In fact, the faux metaphor quotation could never have taken up any space in the discussions and documents *preliminary* to WCAR, since it was *at* WCAR that the informal workshop took place, to be subsequently written up in numerous different ways by stakeholders in attendance.

Yuval-Davis's construction of the sentence introducing and laying out the block-indented text mimics the manner by which scholars would signal that the text is a direct quotation — in this case, from Crenshaw.[34] Numerous scholars have interpreted Yuval-Davis's construction as asserting that the block-indented text is a direct quotation from Crenshaw.[35] Yet it is not a quo-

---

traffic flows simultaneously from many directions. Injuries are sometimes created when the impact from one direction throws victims into the path of oncoming traffic while on other occasions, injuries occur from fully simultaneous collisions. These are the contexts in which intersectional injuries occur."

33 Australian Human Rights and Equal Opportunities Commission (EOC), "HREOC and the World Conference Against Racism"; Center for Women's Global Leadership, "A Women's Human Right Approach to the World Conference Against Racism."

34 Crenshaw, "The Intersectionality of Race and Gender Discrimination."

35 Murat Aydemir, "In Queer Street," *FRAME* 22, no. 2 (2009): 8–15; Murat Aydemir, "Dutch Homonationalism and Intersectionality," in *The Postcolonial Low Countries: Literature, Colonialism, and Multiculturalism,* eds. Elleke Boehmer and Sarah De Mul (Lanham: Lexington Books, 2012), 187–202; Alison Bailey, "On Intersectionality, Empathy, and Feminist Solidarity: A Reply to Naomi Zack," *The Journal for Peace and Justice Studies* 19, no. 1 (2009): 14–36, https://doi.org/10.5840/peacejustice200919116; Alison Bailey, "On Intersectionality and the Whiteness of Feminist Philosophy," in *The Center Must Not Hold: White Women Philosophers on the Whiteness of Philosophy,* ed. George Yancy (Lanham: Lexington Books, 2011), 51–71; Rita Kaur Dhamoon, "Considerations in Mainstream Intersectionality," *Political Research Quarterly* 64, no. 1 (2011): 230–43, https://

tation from Crenshaw at all. The conventional structure is so compelling that few of the scholars quoting and citing the passage mention the endnote following the block-indented text, an endnote that cites as the source of the quotation not Crenshaw, but Indira Patel: "Report of the WCAR meeting as presented by

doi.org/10.1177/1065912910379227; Julie Fish, "Navigating Queer Street: Researching the Intersections of Lesbian, Gay, Bisexual and Trans (LGBT) Identities in Health Research," *Sociological Research Online* 13, no. 1 (2008): art. 12, https://doi.org/10.5153/sro.1652; Ann Garry, "Who Is Included? Intersectionality, Metaphors, and the Multiplicity of Gender," in *Out from the Shadows: Analytical Feminist Contributions to Traditional Philosophy,* eds. Sharon L. Crasnow and Anita M. Superson (New York: Oxford University Press, 2012); Rekia Jibrin and Sara Salem, "Revisiting Intersectionality: Reflections on Theory and Praxis," *Trans-Scripts* 5 (2015): 7–24, http://sites. uci.edu/transscripts/files/2014/10/2015_5_salem.pdf; Rickard Lalander, "Gendering Popular Participation: Identity-Politics and Radical Democracy in Bolivarian Venezuela," in *Multidisciplinary Latin American Studies: Festschrift in Honor of Martti Pärssinen,* eds. Harri Kettunen and Antti Korpisaari (Helsinki, Finland: University of Helsinki, 2016), 149–73; Sabrina Marchetti, *Black Girls: Migrant Domestic Workers and Colonial Legacies* (Leiden: Brill, 2014); Ivona Truscan and Joanna Bourke-Martignoni, "International Human Rights Law and Intersectional Discrimination," *The Equal Rights Review* 16 (2016): 103–31; Elisabeth Tuider, "Ansätze der Geschlechterforschung in Beratung und Coaching" ["Approaches to Gender Studies in Counseling and Coaching"], in *Gender und Beratung: Auf dem Weg zu mehr Geschlechtergerechtigkeit in Organisationen* [Gender and Counseling: Toward a Greater Gender Equality in Organizations.], eds. Heidi Möller and Ronja Müller-Kalkstein (Göttingen: Vandenhoeck and Ruprecht, 2014), 137–54; Anastasia Vakulenko, "Gender and International Human Rights Law: The Intersectionality Agenda," in *Research Handbook on International Human Rights Law,* eds. Sarah Joseph and Adam McBeth (Cheltenham, UK: Edward Elgar Publishing, 2012), 196–214; Luna Vives, "One Journey, Multiple Lives: Senegalese Women in Spain," *ENQUIRE* 5 (2010): 19–38. Dhamoon closely paraphrases what Yuval-Davis provides as block-indented text, but does not identify the source; her citations include two articles by Crenshaw that have no such metaphor, as well as the article by Yuval-Davis that does have the block-indented faux metaphor, it would appear she drew it from Yuval-Davis. Crenshaw, "Demarginalizing the Intersection of Race and Sex," 139–67; Kimberlé Crenshaw, "Mapping the Margins: Intersectionality, Identity Politics, and Violence against Women of Colour," in *The Public Nature of Private Violence,* eds. Martha Albertson Fineman and Roxanne Mykitiul (New York: Routledge, 1994), 93–120; Yuval-Davis, "Intersectionality and Feminist Politics," 193–209.

Indira Patel to a day seminar in London organized by WILPF UK (The Women's International League for Peace and Freedom), November 2001." The metaphor treated by Yuval-Davis as a direct quotation from Crenshaw appears to be an individually-inflected paraphrase included as part of the reports that WCAR participants brought back to their human rights and social action groups. Yuval-Davis does not include Patel in the list of references, though others have specifically cited Patel as the source of this version of the metaphor.[36] Thus Yuval-Davis treats Indira Patel's revised paraphrase of an informal talk that Crenshaw gave in a workshop for human rights and social activists in WCAR as if it were a major claim made by Crenshaw in a scholarly argument about the nature of intersectionality. Yuval-Davis encourages this misimpression by implying that the source of the faux metaphor quotation is actually Crenshaw's "Mapping the Margins" (1994) presented at WCAR, in order to imply that the metaphor is found in Crenshaw's scholarly publications.[37] It is not.

---

36 Yuval-Davis, "Intersectionality and Feminist Politics," 193–209; Asylum Aid, Refugee Women's Resource Project, "Romani Women from Central and Eastern Europe: A 'Fourth World,' or Experience of Multiple Discrimination," Asylum Aid, March 2002, https://www.asylumaid.org.uk/wp-content/uploads/2013/02/Romani-Women-from-Central-and-Eastern-Europe-A-Fourth-World.pdf.

37 Crenshaw, "Mapping the Margins," 1241–99. Yuval-Davis implies that the source of the metaphor she puts in block-indented text is Crenshaw's "The Intersectionality of Race and Gender Discrimination," which she identifies in the reference list as "'Mapping the Margins: Intersectionality, Identity Politics and Violence Against Women of Color,' paper presented at the World Conference Against Racism; at http://www.hsph.harvard.edu/grhf/WofC/feminisms/crenshaw.html." This is an inaccurate citation. Crenshaw's curriculum vita lists her presentation at WCAR as "The Intersection of Race and Gender Discrimination" (2001). "Mapping the Margins" is an article published in the *Stanford Law Review* ten years earlier (in 1991) and subsequently reprinted several times (for example, in 1994 and 1995). The website Yuval-Davis lists is not a site concerned with WCAR. It is hosted by the Harvard School of Public Health (HSPH), in the section for the Global Reproductive Health Forum (GRHF), and the Woman of Color Web (WOC). In any case, "Mapping the Margins" includes no metaphorical language whatsoever to describe intersectionality.

Yuval-Davis does not attempt to defend the notion that a brief passage so pinpoints Crenshaw's thinking that it is not necessary to acknowledge Crenshaw's many complex arguments about fluidity, flexibility, contingency, and both/and thinking. That Yuval-Davis provides no justification for this procedure reveals its function as a rhetorical move of dominant discourse, a discursive technology of power.[38] Robert Stam argues that, "Language and power intersect wherever the question of language becomes involved in asymmetrical power relationships."[39] Asymmetrical power relationships between scholars can be created at the scene of argument by treating isolated comments as the whole of agonists' arguments.

Yuval-Davis dismisses the dialogism and complex efforts to address wicked problems of the activists preparing for and participating at WCAR as "confusing." She casually dismisses the faux metaphor quotation as "additive" (perhaps because there are "layers" of oppression); yet she treats her own "additive" arguments — about "layers" of citizenship — as if she is immune from the same kind of casual dismissals.[40]

Straw-person arguments infuse Yuval-Davis's claims in a way that renders illegible the positions of those she criticizes. For example, she implies that she sees in the preparations for WCAR and particularly in the faux metaphor quotation a disturbing similarity to the Black "identity politics" that she criticized long

---

38 Richard Terdiman, *Discourse/Counter-Discourse: The Theory and Practice of Symbolic Resistance in Nineteeth-Century France* (Ithaca: Cornell University Press, 1985), 61. Terdiman argues that "the inherent tendency of a dominant discourse is to 'go without saying'...the dominant is the discourse which, being everywhere, comes from nowhere: to it is granted the structural privilege of appearing to be unaware of the very question of its own legitimacy. Bourdieu calls this self-assured divorce from consciousness of its contingency 'genesis amnesia'" (61).

39 Robert Stam, "Mikhail Bakhtin and the Left Cultural Critique," in *Postmodernism and Its Discontents,* ed. E. Ann Kaplan (London: Verso, 1988), 116–45, at 123.

40 Nira Yuval-Davis, "Intersectionality, Citizenship and Contemporary Politics of Belonging," *Critical Review of International Social and Political Philosophy* 10, no. 4 (2007): 561–74, https://doi.org/10.1080/13698230701660220.

ago.[41] There she chastises Black British women for thinking they are multiply oppressed because she concludes they do so "mechanically." With no apparent irony, Yuval-Davis contrasts this alleged position of Black women to the celebration of more flexible issues that she and her co-author find when analyzing communities like their own which are "ethnic" rather than "racial." In evoking her previous condemnation of Black identity politics as disturbingly present in the discourse preliminary to WCAR, Yuval-Davis shows no signs of acknowledging the enormous changes in scholarship about identity politics between 1983 and 2006: not least, the recognition that some of the most powerful forms of identity politics are those of white people.[42] These are the forms of identity politics that should be of great concern to feminists, rather than resurrecting critiques of Black identity politics previously used for political and rhetorical purposes, identity politics that lost traction and gained complexity precisely with the development of intersectional arguments.

41 Floya Anthias and Nira Yuval-Davis, "Contextualizing Feminism: Gender, Ethnic, and Class Divisions," *Feminist Review* 15 (1983): 62–75.

42 See, for example, Sara Ahmed, *The Cultural Politics of Emotion* (New York: Routledge, 2004); Kathleen M. Blee, *Inside Organized Racism: Women in the Hate Movement* (Berkeley: University of California Press, 2003); Eduardo Bonilla-Silva, *White Supremacy and Racism in the Post-Civil Rights Era* (Boulder: Lynne Rienner, 2001); Joe R. Feagin, *Racist America: Roots, Current Realities, and Future Reparations* (New York: Routledge, 2001); Ruth Frankenberg, *White Women, Race Matters: The Social Construction of Whiteness* (Minneapolis: University of Minnesota Press, 1993); Charles A. Gallagher, ed., *Rethinking the Color Line* (New York: McGraw-Hill, 1999); Ian Haney López, *White by Law: The Legal Construction of Race* (New York: New York University Press, 1996); George Lipsitz, *The Possessive Investment in Whiteness: How White People Profit from Identity Politics* (Philadelphia: Temple University Press, 1998); Karyn McKinney, *Being White: Stories of Race and Racism* (New York: Routledge, 2004); Charles W. Mills, *The Racial Contract* (Ithaca: Cornell University Press, 1999); and David R. Roediger, *The Wages of Whiteness: Race and the Making of the American Working Class* (London: Verso, 1991).

I Heard It through the Grapevine

It is evident that Yuval-Davis is an unreliable source about Crenshaw's arguments and metaphors.[43] Scholars who rely on unreliable sources create their own unreliable arguments. Most of those who repeat Yuval-Davis's faux metaphor quotation attribute it to Crenshaw and treat it as a metaphor appearing in a published scholarly argument. Some do not criticize it; many use it as a basis for criticism of the concept of intersectionality formulated notably by Black American feminist scholars. As is common in critiques of intersectionality, most assume that Crenshaw has presented only one metaphor, and that her entire argument about intersectionality is completely encapsulated by that metaphor, so that dismissing the metaphor can make dismissal of intersectional theorizing by women of color a simple, efficient process.

Sabrina Marchetti, for example, uses the "faux" metaphor from Yuval-Davis's quotation of Indira Patel to argue:

Initially, in 1989, the US scholar Kimberly (sic) Crenshaw suggested the following image of the black woman at a crossroads, saying:

Intersectionality is what occurs when a woman from a minority group…tries to navigate the main crossing in the city….The main highway is "racism road." One cross street can be Colonialism, then Patriarchy Street….She has to deal not only with one form of oppression but with all forms, those named as road signs, which link together to make a double, a triple, multiple, a many layered blanket of oppression.

Later on, in Europe, scholars preferred images such as that of the "kaleidoscope" (Botman, Jouwe and Wekker, 2001),

---

43 Yuval-Davis, "Intersectionality and Feminist Politics"; Yuval-Davis, "Intersectionality, Citizenship and Contemporary Politics of Belonging."

or that of "intersecting boundaries" (Anthias & Yuval-Davis, 1983) in order to go beyond Crenshaw's simpler model of the multiple oppressions, which had already received much criticism in the US (Davis, 2008).[44]

Marchetti continues Yuval-Davis's pattern of multiple errors. Not only does she not include any of Crenshaw's publications on her reference list, but she even misspells Crenshaw's name. Furthering the notion that Black women speak only for Black women, her introduction to the faux metaphor quotation says it is an image of "the black woman at the crossroads," when the faux metaphor quotation itself, immediately following, says "a woman from a minority group." While seeing Crenshaw only through Yuval-Davis's text, Marchetti nonetheless assumes that the faux metaphor quotation from Patel's report is the same found in Crenshaw's "Demarginalizing the Intersection of Race and Sex," even though the false source provided by Yuval-Davis is actually "Mapping the Margins."[45] Perhaps because Marchetti sees Crenshaw through the eyes of Yuval-Davis and other European scholars, she is not aware that Crenshaw has a different traffic metaphor developing a complex theoretical argument about the politics of both/and, and sameness/difference, embedded in complex discussions of civil rights law and sharing points of connection with the positions of many poststructuralists.[46] Instead, Marchetti relies on a trope endemic to European critiques of intersectionality: American Black feminists are simplistic in their thinking and their concern for "oppression," while Europeans have improved the concept of intersectionality with superior thinking.[47]

---

44 Marchetti, *Black Girls,* 22. Quoted material within Marchetti is Yuval-Davis, "Intersectionality and Feminist Politics," 196.

45 Crenshaw, "Demarginalizing the Intersection of Race and Sex."

46 Ibid.

47 Barbara Tomlinson, "Category Anxiety and the Invisible White Woman: Managing Intersectionality at the Scene of Argument," *Feminist Theory* 19, no. 2 (2018): 145–64; Barbara Tomlinson, *Undermining Intersectionality:*

Marchetti also indulges in a problematic claim shared across the Atlantic: the assumption that the use of any race or ethnicity-related term or metaphor other than "intersectionality" represents a studied criticism or invalidation of it. This is a logical leap intended to increase the extent of what can be taken to be negative criticism of intersectionality. Marchetti's citation of Botman, Jouwe, and Wekker (who used the word "Kaleidoscopic" in a title) does not indicate that the authors have repudiated the term "intersectionality"; for example, in Gloria Wekker's most recent book, *White Innocence: Paradoxes of Colonialism and Race,* Wekker frequently uses the terms "intersection," "intersectional," and "intersectionality."[48] Further, Anthias and Yuval-Davis were not in a position to "prefer" "intersecting boundaries" to "intersectionality" because the latter term was not available in 1983: the article in which Crenshaw presented her formulation of the term was published six years later.[49] In fact, Yuval-Davis uses "intersectionality" today, as in the titles "Intersectionality and Feminist Politics" and "Intersectionality, Citizenship and Contemporary Politics of Belonging," obviating the entire line of argument.

Anastasia Vakulenko uses the "faux metaphor" that Yuval-Davis quoted from Indira Patel to argue that

> Crenshaw's own metaphor to explain intersectionality is that of the crossroads:

> > Intersectionality is what occurs when a woman from a minority group...tries to navigate the main crossing in the city....The main highway is "racism road." One cross street can be Colonialism, then Patriarchy Street....She has to deal not only with one form of oppression but with all forms, those named as road signs, which link together

---

The Perils of Powerblind Feminism (Philadelphia: Temple University Press, 2019).

48 Gloria Wekker, *White Innocence: Paradoxes of Colonialism and Race* (Durham: Duke University Press, 2016).

49 Anthias and Yuval-Davis, "Contextualizing Feminism."

to make a double, a triple, multiple, a many layered blanket of oppression.

Accordingly, an individual is treated as a composite of (discrete) identity elements such as gender, race....This is problematic precisely because it seems to defeat the very point of intersectionality — that one strand of identity (gender) cannot exist in isolation from others.[50]

Vakulenko, like Yuval-Davis and others, misunderstands the polysemic and flexible nature of metaphor and its multiple meanings — reading metaphor through a hegemonic lens as limited to mapping one territory, rather than acknowledging the role of metaphor in offering a series of snapshots and differing points of view to clarify various aspects of theory for social activists. Neither Crenshaw nor Patel and the other reporters from WCAR argue that identity elements begin discretely; Vakulenko cites Wendy Brown and others who have criticized multidimensional theorizing as if it required such arguments without noticing that their claims are radically under argued — providing little evidence that scholars hold such positions.[51] Vakulenko could establish a more robust understanding of Crenshaw's arguments if she closely examined Crenshaw's arguments in "Demarginalizing the Intersection of Race and Sex" or the actual text of "Mapping the Margins" that Vakulenko falsely cites as the source of the faux metaphor quote.[52]

---

50 Vakulenko, "Gender and International Human Rights Law," 206–7. The passage supposedly from Crenshaw, cited by Vakulenko, is mistakenly referred to in Vakulenko's text as "Crenshaw, 'Mapping the Margins,' Harvard School of Public Health, http://www.wcsap.org/Events/Workshop07/mapping-margins.pdf at 9 December 2008." But it is important to note, again, that this is a false reference.

51 Tomlinson, *Undermining Intersectionality*, provides extensive evidence about the problems of argument and evidence characterizing the widely-cited critiques of intersectionality on which Vakulenko relies.

52 Vakulenko's citation of the source of the metaphor, like that of Yuval-Davis, is structured to imply the metaphor is in a published scholarly text, "Mapping the Margins," as noted above in note 48. However, Vakulenko's citation

Intersectionality Telephone

This discourse uncritically re-citing and re-circulating careless academic critiques of intersectionality treats important political and intellectual tools as "fodder" for something like the childhood game that Americans call "Telephone." In Telephone, the first player originates a phrase and whispers it to the next person down a line of players; players successively whisper what they believe they have heard to the next player until finally the last player announces to the entire group the statement that he or she may have heard. The game of Telephone is explained on Wikipedia: Errors typically accumulate in the retellings, so the statement announced by the last player differs significantly, and often amusingly, from the one uttered by the first. Some players also deliberately alter what is being said in order to guarantee a changed message by the end of it.

The entertainment provided by the childhood game of Telephone rests on the difference between the original statement and the final representation of it. Re-citing and re-circulating careless critique serve to evaluate effective tools for antiracist analysis according to the standards of fidelity provided by Telephone. But the originating argument is treated as if no longer available to be compared with the changes developed through the game of Telephone. The game of Intersectionality Telephone is not particular to individual authors, but symptomatic of white feminist critiques of intersectionality. The game authorizes and naturalizes denigrating and dismissing without acknowledging the purpose, the precision, and the context of originating arguments. Critics often focus so closely on their own disciplinary concerns that they lose sight of *other people's* disciplines, interests, and needs. Intersectionality Telephone allows critics

---

is inaccurate. The website WCSAP is provided by the Washington Coalition of Sexual Assault Programs, which has affiliations with the Harvard School of Public Health. The citation appears to be for an event that used "Mapping the Margins" as a source for discussion. This cannot be the source of the faux metaphor quotation; "Mapping the Margins" includes no metaphorical language whatsoever to describe intersectionality.

frequently to treat *any object of analysis* as if the only proper criteria for judgment are those authorized by their own discipline. In consequence, concepts directed to problems of law or literature or human rights activism are judged as failed attempts at, for example, sociology. The game of Intersectionality Telephone substitutes hearsay and careless citation for the precise, rigorous development of the concepts and tools desperately needed to counter wicked problems.

Part III

CULTURAL PRODUCTIONS

11

Pleasure as an Imperative (for Black Femmes) in 5 Acts

Ebony P. Donnley

I. Act Natural

i command you to feel good
i command you to feel good
i command you to feel good
break the trancy cadence typical of pseudo spiritual guru mira-
cle mumbo jumbo that's nothing remotely like the saccharine
self-help for justified skeptics, agnostic cynics who didn't know
that all the God that's left here on this earth on this dreary day
in the blood red dirt somewhere in america
is in they/them
in she/her. any pronoun
a name they don't know
can't pronounce correctly
won't say

Pants not fitting
Caretaker to old white lady who can't open her own corner store
bought parfait, both sitting on the bench outside the Bean and I
just want to talk to you
I want to talk to her

DOI: 10.21983/P3.0250.1.14

"What happens when your pants don't fit?"
I'd imagine she'd say,
"Wear them anyway"
Because you have to
Live life like you play the bass
Another occult figure in my origin story of how black women
peopled the earth
so sweet, self-effacing even,
saying yes cus we dont/havent gotten to know my/our NOs yet,
saying no like no means death—an advanced directive for the
young and disaffected
Tiarah Pouyah
Joyce Quaweay
I'm charged to write about human death and make it poetic.
Til this day, more than 64,000 black women have gone missing
in the United States
scant coverage for the poor
or rich
now just a pointless schism, a pointed criticism of both,
none matter the day after you never made it home

II. Ack Up

when they put my little brown body in a box
a wooden box is where my body will go
i will continue to say thank you from the bottom of this box
i will end well
i will be gracious
niced and polited out of life and even now i'll be less transgres-
sive in my behavior
a corpse smacking its lips and contorting its neck, talking shit
mid rigor mortis
from a bloated mass of formaldehyde
once a grandmother, a mother, a patron at the shop in Fort
Greene, the last vestiges of black anything over there, sitting in
her wheelchair, hair slicked down close to her scalp, listening to

an obscure trap song by rihanna about shopping in paris throwing bands.
Lovely, underneath the drier station that looks like the astronaut helmet tattooed on a brown guy's wrist on a visit to new york to see her girlfriend whose skin is brown too, thank God. I prayed for such skin.
i want to talk to her too
not rihanna
not my lover
but this woman in her chair in Fort Greene getting her hair done and i just wish she would notice me
i strike up conversation with every black woman i see

i'm trying to stop writing about death
I have to grasp, oxymoronically, the Buddhist tenant of impermanence that discourages grasping, discourages longing the indelibly finite as veiled suffering at its core, unfettered like his namesake, I convince myself to celebrate having already died, rather than grasp at the primordial finite — this life
So many of us have already died
Enough to fill an entire museum
Enough to fill every museum in America
I can't keep up with the faces or the names
Alas, impermanence is not imperative
Like pleasure is

III. Act Now

I've been to the meadow and the creek where there was no water
where there was no lead in said water
where that rhyme scheme could not possibly make sense to a single audience in a developed country in the 21st Century
i've been to the prairies of old towns deserted with old folks who still consider dessert
presents for christmas
cake foods named after
the pontified dead

i've been to the nail shop and salons
filled with Sunday Saints pontificating over pompadour fades in
preparation for well deserved sin to be had on Saturday
well deserved
long overdue
pleasure

this poem could end right here in black

In East Oakland, at a quaint middle school on one of the posher
blocks that intersect International Avenue, several small children are seated in a large dining room, possibly adjacent to a
kitchen that houses an industrial-sized freezer, a pair of micro-
waves and an antique faux-porcelain gas stove blackened from
the pinguid resin that accompanies feeding bleeding chickens to
black children who'll die soon too
not in a pool of their own blood — like poultry
but because school lunch is now the first and last meal of the day
and possibly, of their lives
themselves
each other
each one an omnipresent apparition to a disheveled orchid carpel,
a wrought iron laurel whose innermost whorl we call ovaries
hardened from one too many millers after her seed was bore and
couldn't grow no more
i'm speaking of her daughter who is now in highland hospital
cross-pollinating with diabetes patients awaiting amputation on
the corner of a ward that
feels eerily similar to the block where she was once posted, sup-
planted, in front of Lee's 99 cent store
waiting for savings
like corporations
like hoes who can't no more, precisely the type of death that this
world enjoys
Her mother can't wait til she also dies — an easier way to justify
why she sleeps the entire day, a slumber not nearly as metaphorical as it seems

just plain old ass not having a reason for breathing, much less
staying awake in the kind of darkness that a cis man would be
afraid of
a supreme darkness that feels nostalgic,
like we're a part of it
I'm writing about writhing
in pleasure

is it just me or are you melting too?

IV. Acting Lessons

Is the ocean black?
Does it wear bowties? Does it milly rock at the Blue Flame on
snapchat
O' Oshun
Did it go topless at Afropunk leaving outdated perceptions of
illness in its wake? Do the waves ride together and vibe together
to Badu, and debate her occasional, off-kilter misogyny and her
love for us and for money and our devotion to her regardless
Eyes glistening, don't know if we listening or submitting
Donny Hathaway on highway 1 laughing the whole way down
Brain awash with filthy water even when it knows that holy requires only permission
Is the ocean of a visage of Her teachings, a God with a vagina
that only weeps in diegesis, only speaks in laymen Jesus
Living on a prayer and surviving on a diet of frozen pizza
she is dying to meet you
O' Oshun
she is dying to meet you
does the ocean
effortlessly give to those who only take, is it chipped fingernail
polish and not giving a fuck
The ocean has no mechanism to support our survival
The sound never stops
water hitting the shore

like a thousand Tibetan monks chanting a dirge in 6/4 time for
me, like 32 St. Bernard parishioners
second line for me, the timbre
Never gets tired
Never stops for the comfort of someone else
The ocean does what it does
Because that's all it's there to do
It's not here for our enjoyment

V. Tired of Actin'

I want white people to know that they confer the benefits and
magnanimity of a black love ethic everyday we choose emotional intelligence or spiritual intuition or timidity or fear or
paralysis or whatever and not burn this bitch to the ground and
write the names of all the people who've died in soot on your
door frames of your houses, and your gates, instead of these
generous, thoughtful and oft well written open letters to closed
coffins, *poetic musings* and dense, academic rants in these status
boxes in a fit of emotional exhaustion

a song of song for the mangroves that house no bird species,
much less cages
we are not palm trees
we do break
bending is commendable but some of us do break
it is okay to break
it is okay to be bent to an unrecognizable shape
it's okay if you're not okay

rightly do i love you

Draw me after you, Mercedes, Keyonna, Diamond,
Shante…let us run

> where you pasture your flock,
> where you make it lie down at noon;

a flock of shorn ewes,
    come up from the washing, black and holy
    though many among them have lost their young,

Dee Whigham
Rae'lynn Thomas
Say her name for it is oil poured out
Her name is oil poured out;

a sachet of myrrh
    that lies between my breasts.
Picture India Clarke covered in a cluster of henna blossoms
    in the vineyards of Engedi.

i really wish this was an ode to black girls, from pure sin to gnostic text —
talking nasty and ratchet from the same orifice from whence the 8 octave range came and hands that threaten to rewrite the magna carta
black femmes
i didn't intend for this to be worship,
but a deep longing for a call to arms,
for us to lock ours
an Audre-esque amalgam of mythology, teetering on the precipice of dreamscape and legends of watermelon women before me mistaken for men so i could at least know there was a template
for the experience of being in a barbershop, looked upon like a lamb shorn by sheep just as black as me who ask, with faded nape and razor line like mine across their heads, if i want to be a man, that this type of cut would look more feminine
that ask me if i'm male or female, to which i reply woman but really mean neither, then with a sigh of relief at bus stops and corner stores and farmer's markets, say,
"whew, i thought you were a guy
"can i have your number?"
this was all prior to the binding

working through the weeping while he tells me to wait because
he's almost there
and i let him keep moving because mangroves never really float
to shore,
never reach nowhere

12

How Does Cultural Criticism "Work" in the Age of Antiracist Incorporation?

Felice Blake

*There's a whole cultural phase of revolution that deals
with art — it deals with song, it deals with everything
about the people that the people produce.[1]*
— Akinsanya Kambon, Former Sacramento Lieutenant of
Culture, Black Panther Party

Of all the reactions I heard to the outcome of the 2016 US presidential election, the most vexing one for me was, "I can't wait to hear the music that comes out of this!" The widely covered news about the struggle to hire bands for the 2017 US inauguration *did* seem to indicate that the music was not on the then president-elect's side. Even still, the conversations about "the music" made my head spin: enthusiasm about the anticipated music; romantic ideas about how the best songs come out of struggle; cultural memories of James Brown shouting that he was "Black

---

1   Akinsanya Kambon, interview with the author, Goleta, CA, November 14, 2016. Thanks to Malena Blake Kleiven for her unique insight about K-Pop and BTS and their ARMY. All errors are the fault of the author.

DOI: 10.21983/P3.0250.1.15

and proud;"[2] and the perception that younger musicians and rap artists are part of the Black Lives Matter[3] generation. These comments, I first thought, buried Black suffering under what often looks like exclusively *consumer*-cultural appreciation for Black expressivity.

But the association between "good" Black music and "progressive" politics is not simply an overused stereotype. There is, as we know, a historical relationship between Black liberation struggles and Black cultural expression. Black artists and intellectuals have long described the relationship between Black creativity and Black inclusion, whether for better or for worse. Black cultural expression has been a site where people (Black or non-Black, intellectuals or everyday folk) contemplate the diverse meanings of and obstacles to freedom and liberation.[4] Such perspectives are as much about political culture as they are about cultural politics, or the existing conditions for the emergence of various cultural practices and products, as well as their circulation in public discourses about race and representation. As such, Black cultural criticism and Black expressive culture have also been about engaging the spirit of a moment in relation to what we thought *in and about* the past, and in terms of what we're *calling for or anticipating* in the future. The Movement for Black Lives has certainly impacted public discourse about racism, violence, and policing, but in the era of the 45th US president, are we awaiting the "sorrow songs" of the new millennium?

It is safe to say that we *have* had the music — and it has been amazing! James Baldwin famously wrote in 1955 that, "It is only in his music, which Americans are able to admire because a pro-

---

2   James Brown, "Say It Loud – I'm Black and I'm Proud (Part 1)," writ. James Brown and Alfred Ellis, *A Soulful Christmas,* King Records, 1968.

3   #BlackLivesMatter was created by activists Alicia Garza, Patrisse Cullors, and Opal Tometi in response to the acquittal of neighborhood watch coordinator George Zimmerman for the killing of Trayvon Martin, an unarmed Black American teenager in 2012. See http://blacklivesmatter.com/about/.

4   See George Lipsitz, *Dangerous Crossroads: Popular Music, Postmodernism and the Poetics of Place* (New York: Verso, 1994) and Herman Gray, *Cultural Moves: African Americans and the Politics of Representation* (Berkeley: University of California Press, 2005).

tective sentimentality limits their understanding of it, that the Negro in America has been able to tell his story."[5] Historically, such protective sentimentality depended upon narrow definitions of blackness as sexually pathological, cyclically impoverished, hopelessly criminal, and musically masterful. The same presumptions of Black inferiority reinforce the popularity of Black expressive culture, and especially Black popular music, in the (post)-Obama era as well. The election of the US' first African American president fueled the public representation of the nation's belief in the commitment to antiracism — a shaky presumption about US democracy and its development since the post-World War II era.[6] However, sentimentalist racial fantasies[7] about blackness encourage mass publics to applaud displays of Black economic mobility, aka "success," without addressing how Black exclusion makes the American dream possible or serves as a trusty scapegoat for either White American dreams or national nightmares. Dominant representations of blackness celebrate stylized performances of Black thuggery as the "real" voice of the streets because of the overdetermined association between blackness, poverty, and criminality. Protective racial fantasies produce images of "black-on-black" love and its limited "ride-or-die" spirit because we lack a shared grammar about the importance of Black intimacy to Black struggle and liberation. The dialectics between Black poverty and wealth, Black criminality and respectability, and Black sexual pathology and sexual desirability in popular cultural representations incorpo-

---

5   James Baldwin, "Many Thousands Gone," in James Baldwin, *Notes of a Native Son* (Boston: Beacon, 1955), 19–34, at 24.

6   See Howard Winant, *The New Politics of Race: Globalism, Difference, Justice* (Minneapolis: University of Minnesota Press, 2004), Jodi Melamed, *Represent and Destroy: Rationalizing Violence in the New Racial Capitalism* (Minneapolis: University of Minnesota Press, 2011), and Chandan Reddy, *Freedom with Violence: Race, Sexuality, and the US State* (Durham: Duke University Press, 2011).

7   On "racial fantasies" see Paula Ioanide, *The Emotional Politics of Racism: How Feelings Trump Facts in an Era of Colorblindness* (Stanford: Stanford University Press, 2015).

rate Black cultural products in order to contain them within the existing racial hierarchy.

This containment through incorporation safeguards the dominant American public from an understanding of the complexity of Black expressivity even as they celebrate the music. As Stuart Hall argues, such appropriations are not merely about capitalizing on cultural representations of blackness, but about creating an image of racial progress by commercializing Black difference.[8] They present a distorted and ultimately deceitful depiction of racial progress and racial strife simultaneously *because of* presumed Black difference. As other authors in this collection elaborate, antiracist incorporations of Black popular culture sever Black cultural products from the complexity of Black creativity. Antiracist appropriations fetishize Black commodities (or even Black people as commodities), while repressing the epistemologies, cosmologies, and imaginations that generate them. We've had the music, but the attempt to engage it through appropriation and incorporation keeps us from ever *hearing* it, and thus perpetually thirsting for the next album to drop.

Black popular culture is a contradictory space. Although the "popular" in Black popular culture is meant to anchor such expressions in the experiences of Black communities from which they draw their inspiration and strength, the mainstreaming of Black cultural production *as* US popular culture is not separate from US ascendancy as a world power and focal point of global cultural production and circulation.[9] The recognition and/or fetishization of Black cultural expression have also resulted in *some* Black cultural workers' access to and control over the means of producing mass culture in an era of global media conglomeration[10] and antiracist incorporation. These conjunctures — the dominant position of Black popular culture nationally and its circulation globally, as well as the antiracist

---

8   Stuart Hall, "What is This 'Black' in Black Popular Culture?" in *Black Popular Culture,* ed. Gina Dent (Seattle: Bey Press, 1992), 21–37, at 21–33, 24.

9   Ibid., 26.

10 See Tricia Rose, *The Hip Hop Wars: What We Talk About When We Talk About Hip Hop* (New York: Basic, 2008).

appropriations of Black culture and the development of Black creativity — shape the cultural politics through which Black cultural criticism engages popular culture. Thus attention to antiracist incorporations asks how the music speaks in the context of appropriation and how cultural critics approach these evolving, improvisational strategies. Such a critical method can illuminate the framework of oppression *and* articulate a politics of possibility simultaneously. Rather than seeking "good" representations and receptions of Black culture, this article considers a variety of cultural workers and work, and how they negotiate the contradictions of popular culture and the depiction of blackness. First, I discuss the antiracist incorporation of Black expressive culture. Second, I engage Antonio Gramsci's term "interregnum" to describe the tensions and paradoxes embedded in the process of incorporation itself. Finally, I provide examples of how Black music continues to inspire important cultural work today and generate new paths for cultural criticism. Attending to the ongoing and irresistible desires to wait for *and listen to* the music provide an opportunity for considering how antiracist cultural criticism works.

Hard of Hearing: Antiracist Incorporation

> *As a revolutionary artist my job was basically making sure that the art and the culture was relevant to our struggle. We'd go to parties and the music — if they had music that was reactionary — we had to go "oh, nah you can't play that." We had to play shit that was mostly Curtis Mayfield stuff!*[11]
> — Akinsanya Kambon, Former Sacramento Lieutenant of Culture, Black Panther Party

Fifty years after the founding of the Black Panther Party, Akinsanya Kambon (née Mark Teemer) and former Sacramento Lieutenant of Culture and Emory Douglas, Minister of Culture, still emphasize the importance of Black music to the revolu-

---

11 Kambon, interview with the author.

tionary spirit. In fact, both artists continue to stress the value of Black popular culture as a whole to the development and dissemination of the Panther vision and collectivity. While studying at City College in the Bay Area of California, Douglas was actively involved in the Black Arts Movement. It was due to this capacity that Bobby Seale and Huey Newton sought to work with Douglas; and he joined the Black Panther Party in January 1967, just three months after its inception. Art was always part of the original vision for the Party and figured prominently in the Panther newspaper. The numerous photographs and artworks featured within addressed the issue of illiteracy among impoverished and working class Black people by enabling them to learn and participate through observation. Black art and culture also played invaluable roles in the development of the newspaper and of the Black Panther Party itself. As Douglas describes, "readers" could perceive "how the Party was going from one phase into another by looking at the artwork," and "in many cases, you could take any one of the 10-Point Platform Program of the Black Panther Party and see that in the art at any given time."[12] The people were not waiting for the music, but actively engaged in its production and circulation.

The powerful relationship between Black cultural production and Black struggle continues in the subsequent decades of counterrevolution against the organizing, mobilizations, and transformations of the 1960s and 1970s. Neoconservatism, the War on Drugs, the War on Terror, the shrinking welfare state, militarized policing, and mass incarceration in subsequent decades echo the concerns of a previous generation, but do so in an era that celebrates Black popular culture above all others. According to the latest Nielsen ratings, hip hop music has become the most popular music genre in the US — more popular even than rock and roll.[13] Black music-making has been the

---

12 Emory Douglas, interview with the author, Goleta, CA, November 14, 2016.
13 Patrick Ryan, "Rap Overtakes Rock as the Most Popular Genre Among Music Fans: Here's Why," *USA Today*, January 3, 2018, https://www.usatoday.com/story/life/music/2018/01/03/rap-overtakes-rock-most-popular-genre-among-music-fans-heres-why/990873001/.

vanguard of the popular cultural revolution, producing leaders, innovators, and visionaries that have influenced all other forms of Black cultural production. Although Black music-making is key to understanding Black vernacular culture, Black fiction, fashion, and art, among others, it has also achieved institutional inclusion and representation in the post-Black Power era. Black cultural workers from Nobel-Prize-winning author Toni Morrison (the only US woman to receive the honor), to the late graffiti artist *cum* neoexpressionist Jean Michel-Basquiat are regularly described with superlatives by critics, scholars, and fans around the world. Basquiat has also set the record for any US artist for the $110.5 million sale of his 1982 painting *Untitled*, the sixth most expensive painting ever sold at an auction. Art dealer Jeffrey Deitch, described as an expert on the artist, states that Basquiat is "now in the same league as Francis Bacon and Pablo Picasso."[14] Of course, in 2008 the US elected its first nonwhite president in the history of the country. Regular footage of him playing basketball or quoting rapper Jay-Z while brushing metaphorical dirt from his shoulder buoyed President Barack Obama's popularity. What is the relationship between political culture and cultural politics in a context that destroys Black lives, communities, and institutions while elevating Black expressivity, even if those expressions critique racial, sexual, and economic injustice?

In his book *Cultural Moves*, Herman Gray interrogates dominant cultural institutions' incorporation of Black cultural products, despite those hegemonic spaces' abiding and deep ambivalence about Black cultural presence.[15] Although such recognition marks a shift in the historic pattern of excluding and/or distorting the representation of blackness, he questions if the recognition and representation by mainstream institutions should still serve as a focus of cultural politics or provide a measure of ra-

---

14 Robin Pogrebin and Scott Reyburn, "A Basquiat Sells for 'Mind-Blowing' $110.5 Million at Auction," *New York Times,* May 18, 2017, https://www.nytimes.com/2017/05/18/arts/jean-michel-basquiat-painting-is-sold-for-110-million-at-auction.html.

15 Gray, *Cultural Moves,* 15.

cial progress. Ambivalence, obsession, or outright disgust can characterize the dominant public's response to Black presence in social, educational, and political spaces as well. Consider, for example, the stark contrast between Toni Morrison winning the Nobel Prize for literature and three of her novels appearing on "most challenged book" lists in 2006, 2012, 2013, and 2014, according the American Library Association.[16] Celebrating Toni Morrison's creative work as proof of US racial progress while censoring her novels, and most often texts by historically aggrieved authors, point to the contradiction of Black popular culture *as* US popular culture that disrupts traditional ideologies about racial integration and American democracy. There's also the discrepancy between the popularity of the image of the first Black first family, and the cynical non-apologies from elected officials for circulating representations of the Obamas as primates during his eight years as US president.[17]

What about the distinction between the importance of hip hop music to US popular culture and Michael David Dunn's murder of Jordan Davis in 2012 for allegedly playing Chicago rapper Lil Reese's music too loudly in the parking lot of a Florida gas station? Some of us remember the 1992 trial against Ice-T and his rock band Body Count because of their song "Cop Killer" due to the state of emergency following Los Angeles Police Department officers' beating of Rodney King in March of 1991

---

16 "Top Ten Most Challenged Books Lists," ALA *Office for Intellectual Freedom,* http://www.ala.org/advocacy/bbooks/frequentlychallengedbooks/top10.

17 Dan Johnson, then-Kentucky-Republican-state-House-candidate, won his seat in the November 2016 election. Calling his posts satire and denying that he is a racist, Johnson refused to apologize for Facebook posts that depicted President Obama and the first lady Michelle Obama as monkeys. Mayor Beverly Whaling of West Virginia resigned her position in 2016 following uproar over her comments on a Facebook post that anticipated Melania Trump as the new first lady because she was "tired of seeing a [sic] Ape in heels," referring to then-First Lady Michelle Obama. California Republican and elected member of the Orange County Republican Central Committee Marilyn Davenport apologized for her "unwise behavior" in sending a group email that included an image of a family portrait of chimpanzee parents and child with President Obama's face superimposed on the young chimp to Republican committee members in 2011.

and the acquittal of officers Stacey Koon, Theodore Briseño, and Timothy Wind in 1992.[18] Although he was pressured to retract the critique of state-sponsored violence and to censure the articulation of rage about police violence, most know Ice-T from his various roles as a police officer from television programs like *Law and Order svu, Chicago pd, New York Undercover,* or the police detective in the film *New Jack City* (dir. Mario Van Peebles, 1991). In these various examples, incorporation functions to neutralize counterhegemonic critique. The unlivable conditions that racial and gendered injustice produce become not only palatable, but entertaining, through antiracist incorporation.

Even still, Gray points out that "the successful 'occupation' of and use of institutional cultural spaces and the political claims that emanate from them complicate rather than simplify the very notion of black cultural politics."[19] Black cultural production — its incorporation *and* its popularity — becomes a site for political disputes over representation, meaning, and the valuation of blackness as a cultural expression. It is in this way that even the contradictions of Black popular culture in the present, despite the efforts at sanctioned incorporation and "pure" entertainment, become sites for interrogating the relationship between dominant recognition and daily racial terror and between the development of radical epistemologies and the protections of sentimental engagement. In other words, the very contradictions that emerge through the mainstream recognition of Black popular culture presents critical opportunities to question the very cultural and political terms of order that structure cultural institutions and dominant discourses about race, creativity, and representation in the complicated space of incorporation.

---

18 See George Lipsitz, "The Hip Hop Hearings: The Hidden History of Deindustrialization," in George Lipsitz, *Footsteps in the Dark: The Hidden Histories of Popular Music* (Minneapolis: University of Minnesota Press, 2007), 154–83.

19 Gray, *Cultural Moves*, 14.

The Interregnum and Morbid Projections of Blackness

Antonio Gramsci's conception of "interregnum" characterizes the dialectical and dialogic spaces Black cultural production occupies. The contradictions that impact the conditions for Black expression and how we analyze it demand attention to antiracist incorporation as a unique modality of racism. He writes:

> That aspect of the modern crisis which is bemoaned as a "wave of materialism" is related to what is called the "crisis of authority." If the ruling class has lost its consensus, i.e. is no longer "leading" but only "dominant," exercising coercive force alone, this means precisely that the great masses have become detached from their traditional ideologies, and no longer believe what they used to believe previously, etc. The crisis consists precisely in the fact that the old is dying and the new cannot be born; in this interregnum a great variety of morbid symptoms appear.[20]

Gramsci's description of the interregnum speaks to the monetized valuation of Black popular culture, a wave of materialism (or "bling," for example) that presumes individualism and self-interest alone motivate the intellectual and creative will — or that racial politics can be explained simply by how much money a film, album, magazine cover, or scholarly manuscript can fetch if it features the lives, experiences, and perspectives of non-White people. Is life only credit and debt? Gramsci points to how this materialism conceals the crisis of the ruling class, that it's lost its consensus and rules coercively instead. Sanctioned, and often championed, violence against vulnerable communities functions in tandem with antiracist incorporation and examples of Black exceptionality, especially in entertainment and cultural production. These examples of excellence circulate as proof of

---

20 Antonio Gramsci, *Selections from the Prison Notebooks,* ed. and trans. Quintin Hoare and Geoffrey Nowell-Smith (London: Lawrence and Wishart, 1971), 276.

racial progress, further legitimating the violence against those considered non-normative and unassimilable. Perhaps this is the reason why the Movement for Black Lives, one more recent instantiation of the Black liberation movement, is so inspiring to Black cultural creators and critics, for this mobilization has demanded that mass publics pay attention to state violence and coercion as a brutal sign that the old is dying and violently resistant to the new being born. The interregnum thus manifests in morbid symptoms, deferred dreams, and partial wish fulfillment. In this, the longing for the music and the desire for new "sorrow songs" take on new meanings.

In the new millennium, for example, Black cultural incorporation actually demonstrates how a coerced or "respectable" allegiance to definitions of antiracism betray democratic promises. The popularity of Black expressive culture has rarely won elections, as Hillary Clinton learned in 2016 despite rapper Jay Z's and songstress Beyoncé's public appearances, performances, and endorsements on behalf of the Democratic presidential candidate. Twenty-two years earlier, Clinton's husband, President Bill Clinton, signed the 1994 "Violent Crime Control and Law Enforcement Act" that increased the penalties for crime and increased funding for "substantially" higher police presence in us communities and the technology to control them.[21] Jay-Z released his first and highly celebrated album *Reasonable Doubt* in 1996.[22] With references to the xenophobic film *Scarface* scattered between the songs, in the track "Dead Presidents" for example, he mocks the misguided pursuit of wealth as protection in a rapidly expanding police state. Having sold over 100 million albums since then, he is now one of the best-selling musicians of all time.

---

21 H.R. 3355, "The Violent Crime Control and Law Enforcement Act of 1994," https://www.congress.gov/bill/103rd-congress/house-bill/3355/text. See especially "Title I" (12–21): "The purposes of this title are to — (1) substantially increase the number of law enforcement officers interacting directly with members of the community ("cops on the beat")" (12).

22 Jay-Z, *Reasonable Doubt,* prod. Damon Dash, Roc-A-Fella Records, 1996.

President Bill Clinton also signed the 1996 Personal Responsibility and Work Opportunity Act (aka the Welfare Reform Act) that ended the guarantee of cash assistance for children in poverty, created a 5-year lifetime limit for receiving support, and required heads of households to find work within two years.[23] These dramatic new policies depended upon the public's perception of welfare recipients as poor Black mothers, and they trafficked in representations of Black people as sexually irresponsible, socially abject, and politically expendable. Beyoncé's rise to fame began with her participation in the group Destiny's Child with whom she helped develop and commodify an image of contemporary Black female independence: heteronormativity, sexual self-confidence, sanctioned-expressions of vulnerability, and performances of economic autonomy. In 2014, and on the heels of global economic recession, President Obama signed legislation authorizing an over $8 billion cut to food stamp benefits. In 2016, Beyoncé performed during the Pepsi Super Bowl Halftime Show in Silicon Valley, less than an hour away from where the Black Panther Party formed in 1966, flanked by Black female drill-team dancers clad in leather bodysuits, curly afro wigs with black berets on top, and waving Black leathered fists in the air. She didn't sing "Mississippi Goddamn" or "I Hate the Capitalist System," but "Formation," a song featuring the voices of New Orleans YouTube personality Messy Mya and "Queen of Bounce" Big Freedia. Beyoncé's track and music video champion "conspicuous consumption" and sing "bitch" into a term of empowerment, while directing the world's attention to the Black belt and Black Lives Matter mobilizations. Her halftime show stands in for the movement and activism with all the props of symbolic resistance, including musical mastery. As a solo artist, she is one of the best-selling artists in music history.

Jay-Z and Beyoncé have taken a stake in, and have been staked by, the traditional means of production. Their popularity has increased their wealth, access to production and distribution

---

23 Dorothy Roberts, *Killing the Black Body: Race, Reproduction, and the Meaning of Liberty* (New York: Vintage, 1997), 202.

channels, and control over the representation of race, gender, and Black popular culture. But this also means that they are also trained in neoliberal lessons in neocapitalism and performance. Expanding the channels for commerce and advertising through new medias and technologies, for example, made Beyoncé's sixth album *Lemonade* (2016) a success on economic, technological, and racial fronts. *Lemonade* is a visual album (each song accompanied by an extended music video) and a concept album (whereby each track contributes to an overall collective expression) that debuted through cable television (HBO) and international, online commercial outlets like Amazon Music, the iTunes Store, and her husband Jay Z's multinational streaming service Tidal. Apart from making music products available to a global audience, these various production and distribution channels provide the veneer of individual choice by producing the individual as a unique consumer of the objects and technologies that reflect their projected "lifestyle." As Jodi Melamed argues, neoliberal versions of multiculturalism abstract race and in place of reference to it specifically use the term "difference" as a way of coding the Beyoncé brand and its consumers for insertion into neoliberalism.[24] Radiating fierce independence and musical mastery, Beyoncé appears as the object and director of the public's gaze upon *her*. Her carefully curated image and haunting lyricism bring together the questions "Why can't you see me?" and "You're the love of my life" that echo across songs from the album *Lemonade* and its visual representations of the performer. At once, Beyoncé projects mastery and vulnerability, sensuality and sensitivity, rage and reason as a specifically Black performance that is also for sale.

Black popular culture is contradictory, but is it that Beyoncé projects ambiguous representations of blackness onto the public, or that *we* want *her* to be *everything we need and want her to be*? Returning to Gramsci's concept of the interregnum, we recall that morbid symptoms and projections emerge in the dying of an old regime and the struggle for the "new" to be born — for

---

24 Melamed, *Represent and Destroy,* 176.

change. In cultural criticism, this refers to the war of maneuver and the struggle for hegemony. Morbid symptoms in popular culture can be perceived in the love of Toni Morrison's international recognition and the hatred for her novels and in the fetishization of gangsta rap music and the murder of unarmed young Black men. Is Beyoncé embracing the desire for designer handbags or wondering if they will keep her afloat in the proverbial flood recently symbolized as Hurricane Katrina and the context for the video "Formation" from *Lemonade*? What might it say about the desire for things (even Black people as objects, performers, or brands) in the midst of the destruction of Black life? It is like asking Black people, still, to market integration, reject their own pitch, yet profit from their ideas remade into white property. It doesn't make sense.

And yet it's still important to remember the significance of why culture mattered then and matters now to Black artists and intellectuals in relation to Black performance and politics. As Stuart Hall asked in 1992, "what sort of moment is this in which to pose the question of black popular culture?" He continues:

> These moments are always conjectural. They have their historical specificity; and although they always exhibit similarities and continuities with the other moments in which we pose a question like this, they are never the same moment. And the combination of what is similar and what is different defines not only the specificity of the moment, but the specificity of the question, and therefore the strategies of cultural politics with which we attempt to intervene in popular culture, and the form and style of cultural theory and criticizing that has to go along with such an intermatch.[25]

Dominant appropriations of Black cultural expressions persist today in ways similar to that of the past. But the struggle for liberation, and thus its cultural soundtracks and expressions,

---

25 Hall, "What is This 'Black' in Black Popular Culture?" 21.

do too. In the next section I consider how contemporary artists work despite antiracist incorporation.

Working from Noun to Verb

> *You wanna see a dead body?*
> — Pusha T (feat. Kendrick Lamar), "Nosetalgia"[26]

New York Times music critic Nate Chinen, like many other music journalists, ranked Kendrick Lamar's "Alright" as the best song of 2015. He acknowledges that the "song's defiantly hopeful refrain became a rallying cry at Black Lives Matter protests, but the verses harbor a more internal struggle — and some of Kendrick Lamar's most inspired showboating as a rapper."[27] This perspective retreats from the examination of "Alright" in relation to Black Lives Matter mobilizations in order to pursue a "morbid" fascination with the rapper's presumed inner turmoil and musical mastery. This "othering" of Lamar in relation to the music critic's own subjectivity points to the protective sentimentality that James Baldwin describes. Nathaniel Mackey similarly argues that, "other is something people do, more importantly a verb [rather] than an adjective or a noun."[28] Thinking about othering in artistic media and in our society more broadly allows Mackey to illustrate how movement and mobilization can be shifted from "verb to noun" through "the erasure of black inventiveness by white appropriation."[29] These critical analyses of racializing and appropriative tendencies also mean that Black

---

26 Pusha T featuring Kendrick Lamar, "Nosetalgia," writ. Terrence Thornton, Kanye West, Dominick Lamb, Anthony Khan, Kendrick Duckworth, Scott La Rock, Lawrence Parker, Homer Banks, Carl Hampton, Raymond Jackson, Trevor Horn, and Malcolm McLaren, *My Name Is My Name,* Good Music/Def Jam, 2013.

27 Jon Pareles, Ben Ratliff, Jon Caramanica, and Nate Chinen, "The Best Songs of 2015," *New York Times,* December 15, 2015, http://www.nytimes.com/2015/12/15/arts/music/the-best-songs-of-2015.html.

28 Nathaniel Mackey, "Other: From Noun to Verb," in *Jazz Among the Discourses,* ed. Krin Gabbard (Durham: Duke University Press,1995), 76–99.

29 Ibid., 77.

cultural workers have long thought about both content and form as part of the racial imposition on creativity as they *work* to make their art move.

For example, Kendrick Lamar begins his featured section of Pusha T's song "Nosetalgia" by asking, "Ya wanna see a dead body?" The accompanying music video features the two rap artists strolling down residential streets of Compton, California. The artists reflect on their seemingly long involvement in selling cocaine and Black pain: "20 plus years of selling Johnson & Johnson / I started out as a baby face monster" Pusha T admits to open the song. Lamar, in his articulation, reflects on a childhood with "Troubles on my mind, / I still smell crime / My little brother crying." The song features an intraracial and intergenerational dialogue to confront the paradoxes of the drug trade and the entertainment industry. On the one hand, opportunities for economic survival and status elevation emerge from both pursuits. Lamar confronts his father, an orignial drug dealer himself, through his lyrics: "He said 'son, how come you think you be my connect?' / Said 'pops, your ass is washed up with all due respect' / He said 'well nigga, then show me how it all makes sense' / Go figure, motherfucker, every verse is a brick / Your son dope, nigga / Please reap what you sowed nigga." Lamar links his poetry ("every verse") to an illicit commodity ("a brick" or a package of cocaine). Through the song and his reflection on his family of origin, Lamar is able to establish himself as superior to his father professionally and creatively: "I was born in '87, my grand daddy a legend / Now the same shit that y'all smoking is my profession." Despite Lamar's youthful bravado, the song also reveals how the fracturing of relations can be an opening for vulnerability and thus form the bases for transformation. A son's knowledge of a father's weakness becomes the opportunity to critique the mask of masculinity and grieve the pain behind it. The two rappers' errant wandering through the neighborhoods of Compton further intensifies the longing and search for "home" the song conveys. The "nose" in "Nosetalgia" links the drug trade to the nostalgia for a home that never was, but will be and now is in the song.

The realist narratives Pusha T and Kendrick Lamar share about their memories of home and their proverbial fathers express the pain over the fracture of intimate relations between Black people and especially in racialized conceptions of gender in the meaning of survival. Lamar's haunting question, "Ya wanna see a dead body" also challenges the terms through which he or his father could be seen. "Nosetalgia" does not seek to reify social death, but to question the preoccupation with dead Black bodies in the news and in popular cultural representations. Reanimation through redefinition better indicates Lamar's unique approach to engaging how Black people imagine their own *processual* relationship to the representation of blackness as we see in his dialogue with Pusha T and their fathers. Lamar is therefore able to bring the complex material and creative experiences that shape Black expression into view and to life.

This attention to movement, to refusing the status of nouns, has become a priority of many contemporary Black artists like Lamar. I've been reiterating throughout this essay that Black cultural production accompanies radical movements for liberation. In that way, it also remembers histories of struggle and its pleasures with a difference. For example, we know that the linked Black Power and Black Arts movements meditated on the long history of the Black Left as well as Civil Rights discourses and strategies even as they negotiated their unique circumstances and developed a vision of liberation. The Movement for Black Lives also understands itself in relationship to the long struggle for Black liberation even as it exposes the exploitative, homophobic, and sexist terms upon which Black lives are rendered disposable. The rallying cry "Black lives matter" indicts racist violence while affirming and embracing Black life. In this way, the movement also helps bring into crisis the authority of the ruling class, or what Cedric Robinson calls a "racial regime," hostile to its exposure.[30] Moving from noun to verb, this emphasis on

---

30 Cedric Robinson, *Forgeries of Memory and Meaning: Blacks and the Regimes of Race in American Theater and Film Before World War II* (Chapel Hill: University of North Carolina Press, 2007), xii.

traversing collective histories of struggle reveal the "work" of Black radicalism. This, too, is the Black in Black popular culture.

The Movement for Black Lives refracts the creative impulses that hip hop, Black art, fashion, studies, histories, and criticism have uniquely captured global attention. For example, we can't help but be excited by the worldwide phenomenon that is South Korean popular culture! Broader than the slightly disparaging label of "K-Pop" and its sometimes appropriative engagement with a wide variety of musical and visual genres and styles, Korean popular culture maintains a profound connection to Black music culture. K-Pop's youth, subcultural vibes and negotiations of intergenerational conflict and trauma find expression through the familiar sounds and fashion associated with R&B and Hip Hop music, but global K-Pop phenomenon also demonstrates a particular understanding of Black culture as "culture." As Sunaina Maira[31] argues in her analysis of South Asians, South Asian Americans, and cultural appropriation, the terrain of culture is a site for negotiating relations of power in the context of labor migration patterns, global shifts in the political economy, and processes of racialization. Cultural production has to do with the relations of cultural production and the nuances of lived experience.

In the realms of culture and consumption, Black expression, especially Hip Hop music and youth subculture, has offered an alternative means of gaining status in a post-industrial economy through the performance of urban cool associated with Black and Latino youth.[32] Maira describes how South Asian American youth subculture in New York City combined British-born remix music with hip hop sounds to allow "ideologies of cultural nostalgia to be expressed through the rituals of clubbing and dance music."[33] In other words, their engagement with Black cultural expression depended upon stereotypical associations

---

31 Sunaina Maira, "Henna and Hip Hop: The Politics of Cultural Production and the Work of Cultural Studies," *Journal of Asian American Studies* 3, no. 3 (October 2000): 329–69, at 333, https://doi.org/10.1353/jaas.2000.0038.

32 Ibid., 334.

33 Ibid.

between blackness and "cool" in the context of global economic and political transformations.

North and South Korea maintain unique relationships to the US in terms of immigration (Hart-Cellar Immigration Act 1965), militarization (US/Korean entanglement in the post-World War II era), and in US post-Cold War representations of evil (the figure and presumed threat of North Korean Supreme Leader Kim Jong-un). The various depictions of North, and by contrast, South Korean culture have turned to US blackness for entry into the discussion of global politics from the vantage point of cultural currency. From *Saturday Night Live*[34] skits about the profound relationship between Supreme Leader Kim Jong-un and former professional US National Basketball Association player Dennis Rodman to critiques of K-Pop artists' appropriation[35] of US Black culture to develop a thriving commercial industry, attention to race, culture, and politics accompanies the formation of contemporary Korea.

A large quantity of the most influential contemporary South Korean musicians borrow or appropriate Black music styles and the culture associated with them. In the early 1990s, South Korean artists Seo Taiji and the Boys incorporated gangsta rap and breakdance into songs like "Come Back Home."[36] When the group dissolved, former band member Yang Hyun-Seok started YG Entertainment, one of South Korea's largest record labels. Seo Taiji and their involvement with hip hop reflects a broader wave of Korean artists using hip hop music and culture directed towards Korean youth.

Kwon Hyuk, better known as Dean, is another South Korean artist who developed his unique sound through his engagement

---

34 "C-Span North Korea Cold Open," *Saturday Night Live* sketch, *NBC*, April 6, 2013, https://www.nbc.com/saturday-night-live/video/c-span-north-korea-cold-open/n35029

35 Suk-Young Kim, *K-Pop Live: Fans, Idols, and Multimedia Performance* (Stanford: Stanford University Press, 2018), 29.

36 Sterling Wong, "Black K-Pop Fans Come Out of the Closet," *Daily Beast*, August 31, 2014, http://www.thedailybeast.com/black-k-pop-fans-come-out-of-the-closet.

with R&B and rap. Epik High, another hip-hop group hailing from Seoul, was the first band from the country to ever play Coachella. Heize and CL (née Lee Chae-Rin) are South Korean female rappers who have strong international following. Korean American rapper Jay Park from Seattle, has had a prominent international career in the multiple countries. Consider also the global phenomenon known as the band BTS. This group develops albums, like *Dark & Wild* (2014) and *Wings* (2016), modeled after the "old school" hip hop mixtape — including intros, outros, and skits between songs. Performing most of their songs in Korean, BTS has been catapulted into international fame by their unmatched international fan following and was the most Tweeted-about celebrity of 2017.[37] These, and many other, popular South Korean artists credit collaborations with Black producers, choreographers, and style-makers for the development of their work. Missy Elliot, Kanye West, and will.i.am are just a few of the high-profile collaborations that have helped shape South Korean popular culture in addition to Black choreographers like Jay Black.[38]

The unique role that Black culture and music play for Black people in the struggle for racial justice is significant, but Asian American musical traditions of resistance falsely seem like a relative absence. Laura Pulido uses the term "racial differentiation" to describe how politically, socially, and culturally constructed differences impact how specific groups may experience racism and perceive other groups in the racial order.[39] The perceptions of Black people as the most oppressed and their histories of resistance struggles as the most radical lend subcultural credibility to creative expressions that seek to engage Black aesthetics. Asian artists' engagement with hip hop and other forms of Black cultural production can certainly reproduce racial stereotypes

37 Rania Aniftos, "BTS Is the Most Tweeted-About Artist of 2017, Plus More Twitter Year-End Data," *Billboard,* December 5, 2017, https://www.billboard.com/articles/news/8055112/bts-most-tweeted-artist-in-2017.

38 Wong, "Black K-Pop Fans Come Out of the Closet."

39 Laura Pulido, *Black, Brown, Yellow, and Left: Radical Activism in Los Angeles* (Berkeley: University of California Press, 2006), 4.

and fetishistic performances, but they can also disrupt the terms of order. The popular band collective EXO, for example, was a South Korean-Chinese boy band who sang in Korean and Mandarin, and eventually in gender-neutral lyrics on the album *Universe* (2017). The band, however, was rocked by internal lawsuits over the differential treatment between Korean and Chinese members. Indie band Hyukoh, formed in 2014, features front man Oh Hyuk, the son of university professors who resided in various parts of China and Korea. The band performs songs in Mandarin, Korean, and English while commenting on these cultural influences and geopolitical spaces in songs like "Bawling."

In 2014, the Modern Sky Festival, which debuted in China in 2017, held its first event in Central Park in New York City. In 2017, the festival took place in Santa Anita, California, eyeing large Chinese student populations at southern California colleges and universities.[40] The Los Angeles lineup included Hyukoh and the Chinese hip hop group HHH. The global success of South Korean K-Pop group BTS is due largely in part to their extraordinary fan-base, known as ARMY. During the press conference for their new album *Love Yourself: Tear,* leader and main rapper for the group Kim Namjoon (RM) explained why the Korean word *naega* (meaning "I") was being censored at live US performances and radio play. Having received backlash for his own use of the so-called "n-word," BTS spokesman and rapper Namjoon's acknowledgment of the violence associated with the term was significant enough that the group would censor a word so vital to the Korean language and rap performance.[41] The extraordinary and growing popularity of South Korean popular culture emerges during an era increasingly attentive to US foreign, immigration, and affirmative action policy debates, even as these musicians negotiate the contradictions and ten-

---

40 Chris Kissel, "Modern Sky, a Music Festival from China, Comes to California This Weekend," *LA Weekly,* September 19, 2017, http://www.laweekly.com/music/modern-sky-festival-brings-chinese-bands-xtx-and-re-tros-to-southern-california-8649697.

41 "'Fake Love' Press Conference," *YouTube,* May 23, 2018, https://www.youtube.com/watch?v=zItARBqdqhY.

sions within their own global and local networks. BTS was the first K-Pop group to speak at the United Nations. Speaking to UNICEF's "Generation Unlimited" the band used the opportunity to discuss their "Love Myself" campaign, which opposes youth violence, and the #SpeakYourself to focus on education and the necessity for each of us to acknowledge and be humbled by the complexity of our individual identities, for better or worse.[42] The many thousands of student protesters who called for the ouster and formal indictment of South Korean President Park Geun-hye and the global focus on North and South Korean politics further indicate how new generations around the world continue to question the status quo.[43] Embracing Black cultural influences and re-imagining gendered performances, K-Pop music and its visual representations bring together sources like anime, rap, and urban stylings to contest state power nationally and internationally. These contestations also occur through frameworks that don't re-center US, incorporated, antiracist discourses into the analysis of the complex negotiation that takes place within and between aggrieved communities. Consider, for example, the fact that BTS performs mainly in Korean, despite their international fanbase and US recognition. The growing popularity for such contemporary, remixed, and diasporic Asian/African urban sounds remind us not to wait for the music, but to listen differently.

These local and global connections allow us to look critically at the work of Toni Morrison, Kendrick Lamar, Hyukoh, and BTS and the work taking place on our own streets. If our only objects of analysis circulate in the so-called mainstream, then we remain tied to the false promises of integration and inclusion. As we have seen, antiracist incorporation can also be a

---

42 Bard Wilkinson, "K-Pop Band BTS Tells World Youth to 'Speak Yourself' at UN," *CNN*, September 25, 2018, https://www.cnn.com/2018/09/24/asia/bts-un-korea-intl/index.html.

43 Chloe San-Hun, "Tens of Thousands March in Seoul, Calling for Ouster of President," *New York Times*, November 14, 2005, https://www.nytimes.com/2015/11/15/world/asia/antigovernment-protest-seoul-south-korea.html.

modality of oppression that leaves us as dead nouns in the end. Mainstream incorporation often peddles a disembodied version of inclusion that distances expressive work and culture from the communities who motivate and inspire them.

Local actors have also developed ways to occupy cultural institutions and to challenge the othering of Black radical cultural politics. One organization, the Bronx Documentary Center (Bronxdoc.org) has become such a center of local self-activity in New York City. The Bronx Documentary Center (BDC) opened in 2011 as a nonprofit gallery with a mission to grow. Director and founder Michael Kamber is a photojournalist who traveled globally photographing war and conflict. Having resided in the Bronx, he dreamt of creating an educational space in the south Bronx that would offer residents exposure to and education about high-quality documentary work. Although it started as a small afterschool program on photography for junior and high school age students, the BDC has now served thousands of students and provided an artistic and educational space visited mostly by people from the Bronx. As a gallery and an educational center, the BDC hosts twelve to fourteen exhibitions annually as well as multiple events for and in the community. The BDC has the only black-and-white darkroom in New York City not located on a university campus as well as the only photo book library in the city. Many of these volumes come from donations to the center. As a meeting space for community organizations in the Bronx, the BDC has also sponsored the Gentrification Conference annually since 2013. The BDC not only employs Bronx residents, but trains and encourages them to tell their own stories as well.

The BDC hosts regular Friday evening classes and meetups that allow photojournalists the opportunity to speak about their work for an adult audience. These events also give participants the chance to show their own work and to receive constructive feedback from established photographers. From these Friday sessions, participants organized themselves into the Bronx Photo League (BPL), a name chosen in honor of the New York Photo League of the 1930s — 50s. Many of these photographers are not

Figure 1. "The Storm Before the Calm." Simpson Street subway stop, the Bronx, New York. Photo by Rhynna Santos; used with permission.

formally trained, but self-taught and committed to the type of local documentation and expression the BDC promotes. In January 2016, sixteen members of the BPL formalized the Jerome Avenue Workers Project (jeromeaveworkers.com) to document and celebrate the workers and trades of people on Jerome Avenue, one of the New York City's few remaining working-class neighborhoods.

The South Bronx is commonly known as the birthplace of hip hop music and stereotypically perceived as a center of concentrated poverty and crime. Nevertheless, NYC urban planners began plans to rezone Jerome Avenue to clear the way for new housing construction. The proposed new buildings would charge rents according to a $71k median income despite the fact that the median income for current residents is approximately $23k. Similarly, the billboards promoting the "Piano District" that real estate developers put in place sought to create a cultural shift in how people perceive the Bronx. Regardless of the defeat of the suggested name "SoBro," the efforts to change the South Bronx to the Piano District sought to capitalize on the history of piano-making during the 1800s in the US when the area was a center for piano production. Looking towards Brooklyn, Bronx residents began to organize against the impending threat of gentrification.

The Jerome Avenue Workers Project used documentary photograph and journalism to present the people who live along Jerome Avenue. Kamber decided to use Hasselblad cameras, vintage German film cameras, to unify the project among the photographers and to "photojournalistically" capture timeless portraits of these workers. Learning to use the apparatus required education, training, and cooperation among the photographers. Ultimately, the BPL produced a book and website featuring these extraordinary photos as a way to document this historic avenue and to inform people in the neighborhood about the proposed rezoning. For example, Isabel Khalife, featured in one of Santos's pieces for the collection, Came to the Bronx 24 years ago from Ponce, Puerto Rico in search of a better economic future. She has worked at the 99 Cents USA store as a cashier for the last two years and financed her two son's high school and university education through her earnings. Rather than being reduced to another commodity in the store, Khalife and her lived experiences of Jerome Avenue come to life in the photograph and in a new representation of the Bronx. The Jerome Avenue Project

Figure 2. Isabel Khalife, 99 Cents USA, the Bronx, New York. Photo by Jerome Avenue Workers Project, used with permission.

created opportunities for creativity, storytelling, and education for artists and community members as well.

Rhynna Santos, a Puerto Rican Bronx resident and member of the BPL explains how her participation in the project also meant engaging personally with a variety of people from the neighborhood. These experiences have fueled her development as a photographer and the curator of the popular Instagram feed @everydaybronx. Featuring the work of street and documentary photographers, the feed attempts to tell a more complex about everyday life in the Bronx.

Through her engagement with the BDC, Santos has also developed as a photographer with a unique point of view about the

Figure 3. "Stratford Avenue," @EverydayBronx (Instagram). Photo by Rhynna Santos, used with permission.

vibrant cultural life of the Bronx. Instead of the dissociation of struggle from representations of struggle, these cultural actors speak *to* aggrieved communities and not simply *of* their experiences. They ask, "what is your story" and engage in the work of collectively developing strategies to tell it. They create art collectively and question why they've been excluded from learning formally about art or learning how to think of themselves as art. They gain knowledge from community and at the same time keep learning how to see them, how to re-present them, and how to see them again.

In her portrait of Nusaiba Martha Guerrera, Santos captures the unique cultural dialogues, conflicts, and social critiques

Figure 4. Nusaiba Martha Guerrera, the Bronx, New York, @Everyday-Bronx (Instagram). Photo by Rhynna Santos, used with permission.

that reflect the burrough. A Bronx native, Guerrera stands in her mother's "botanica," a store specializing in Santeria religious products. Her parents immigrated to the US from Cuba in the early 1980s. Although she grew up in her mother's Santeria religion, Nusaiba converted to the Muslim faith in 2011. She used to interpret for Spanish-speaking clients at her mother's store during religious consultations. After her conversion to Islam, Ms. Guerrera no longer felt comfortable working as an interpreter because Santeria worships more than one god. Her mother's unwillingness to rely on other interpreters caused a significant financial decline in the family's botanica. Nusaiba, a former navy sailor, is now pursuing a Master's degree in education at City College with the goal of becoming a professor of religion. After her conversion she says, "now I feel like I am walking on solid ground." The community sees itself in the community as the art of the community and a community of artists.

In the article "A Daughter Documents Her Father" Rhynna Santos provides to the world candid black-and-white photographs and a brief entry into the world of her father Ray "El

Figure 5. Webster Avenue, the Bronx, New York, @EverydayBronx (Instagram). Photo by Rhynna Santos, used with permission.

maestro" Santos. A legendary Puerto Rican musician, composer, conductor, arranger, teacher, father, and Bronx resident, his biography includes study at the prestigious Juilliard School, twenty-eight years of teaching at City College in New York, and "performances with the Big Three – Tito Puente, Machito, and Tito Rodriguez."[44] Santos was a musician whose musical epiphany came through Coleman Hawkins and his expression of "Body and Soul" on tenor sax. But Hawkins's example of pursu-

44 David Gonzales, "A Daughter Documents a Giant of Latin Salsa and Jazz," *New York Times,* October 30, 2018, https://www.nytimes.com/2018/10/30/lens/a-daughter-documents-a-giant-of-salsa-and-latin-jazz.html.

ing one's own path was El maestro's model for his daughter, and in turn brought her to the Bronx Documentary Center.

If we prepare ourselves to listen, we don't need to keep waiting for the music. What would the music sound like then?

13

If a tree falls in the forest…

Daniel Hershel Silber-Baker

[This volume] contends with the very real problems people are facing in communities when their testimonies are refused, inverted, or incorporated toward agendas that further their oppression

If a tree falls in the forest,
and everyone is there to see it —
but everyone said that falling
was a thing of the past; that tree falling didn't exist anymore
does racism make a sound?

The graveyards of tree and elephant trunks say yes
The people who gather
Sankofa say
Black Lives Matter say yes

Say vigil *every* time a tree falls in the forests called home
hold spiritual space
each mourning
upon becoming the sun

DOI: 10.21983/P3.0250.1.16

14

Nahenahe:
The Sound of Kanaka Maoli Refusal

Kevin Fellezs

Nahenahe is the Kanaka Maoli (Native Hawaiian) term for "soft, sweet, melodious," and is the term most often used to describe the aesthetic ideal for Hawaiian slack key guitar, or *kī hōʻalu,* a Hawaiian fingerpicking open-tuning acoustic guitar tradition, with roots in the *paniolo* (Hawaiian cowboy) ranch culture of nineteenth century Hawaiʻi.[1] In this essay, I challenge the stereotyping of softness as acquiescence or worse, cowardice, sweetness as weakness or naiveté, and melodiousness as the sound of the tritely familiar or perfunctorily conventional. Hawaiian music's central *nahenahe* aesthetic is often overdetermined as *merely* soft and gentle, incapable of expressing force or registering gravitas. How might Hawaiian slack key guitar or Hawaiian musicking more broadly be heard as offering alternatives

---

1   The literal translation for *kanaka maoli* is "true people," but is used to indicate "Native Hawaiian." All Hawaiian definitions are taken from Mary Kawena Pukui and Samuel H. Elbert, *Hawaiian Dictionary: Hawaiian–English, English–Hawaiian,* rev. and enlarged edn. (Honolulu: University of Hawaiʻi Press, 1986).

to conventional notions of the ways in which music signifies action, agency, and authority? How might Hawaiian musicians perform "native refusal," a concept borrowed from Audra Simpson meant to designate the Native Hawaiian "refusal" of settler colonialist logics, including white supremacy and racism?[2] I understand settler colonialism in Hawaiʻi as mobilizing racist policies since the nineteenth century in order to lay claim to Hawaiian territory, dispossessing Native Hawaiians, while using Hawaiian culture to promote the colonialist project as a benign effort. In a decolonizing move, I focus on the ways in which the nahenahe aesthetic catalyzes a soft and gentle yet powerful, forceful sounding presence in antiracist struggles.

Hawaiian slack key guitarists aim for *nahenahe,* seeking a balance between delicacy and flexibility. *Nahenahe* is the affective register deeply connected to the particular *ʻāina* (land, earth) of a song, usually signaled in its *moʻolelo* (story, history) and discovered through its relationship to the *ʻohana* (family) with the *kuleana* (responsibility) to preserve and perform it. Part of that attention to geographical particularity is the result of slack key's "disappearance" during the Hawaiian Kingdom (1795–1898) and US Territorial (1898–1959) periods in which slack key moved "underground" as Hawaiian culture was suppressed by white New England missionaries and US American businessmen ensconced in the political life of the Hawaiian Kingdom as advisors and legislators.[3] The tradition was kept alive by *ʻohana* jealously guarding tunings and repertoire though this almost led to its disappearance by the late 1960s (there are still *ʻohana* songs,

---

2   Audra Simpson, *Mohawk Interruptus: Political Life Across the Borders of Settler States* (Durham: Duke University Press, 2014).

3   The years 1893–98 were years in which politicians such as Sanford Dole and Lorrin A. Thorston, emerging from the *haole* sugarcane oligarchy (largely built from the ranks of New England Protestant missionaries and their descendants), worked to annex the Kingdom of Hawaiʻi through state-like entities they controlled, the Provisional Government of Hawaiʻi (1893–94) and the Republic of Hawaiʻi (1894–98). In 1898, they forcibly overthrew the Hawaiian Kingdom with the support of US military, entering the US Territorial period.

performed only at informal family gatherings, unrecorded and uncirculated beyond such gatherings).

If slack key's power — affective, proactive, effective — comes from the way that it *sounds,* then what *is* the *sound* of slack key? To answer, I will begin with a short discussion of the *nahenahe* aesthetic and its relationship to the *kī hōʻalu* tradition, focusing on the Hawaiian slack key guitar because of its role in the Hawaiian Renaissance period (1964-1980), a time when young people in Hawaiʻi revived traditional Hawaiian arts, crafts, and language use, largely by re-connecting to an older generation of Native Hawaiian artists and artisans.[4] I then turn to musician and activist George Helm as a way to think about Native Hawaiian cosmological understandings of human relations with the *ʻāina,* which is an agentive force, not a commodity or property subject to human domination. I conclude with a meditation on the ways in which soft music such as Hawaiian slack key guitar sounds out against racism by challenging the assumption that difference is always marked as threatening or antagonistic. Slack key offers the possibility of resisting racism by welcoming collaboration as an alternative to meeting difference with a desire for dominance or extermination.

* * *

Softness in musicking is doubly marked as sweet, gentle, serene, often associated with spirituality or solemnity, and just as often, with silence or silences. Soft has been a term used to describe genres and styles as varied as ambient, downtempo, chill, bossa nova, smooth jazz, new age, easy listening, MOR (middle of the road), soft rock, psychedelia, singer-songwriter, and folk/folk rock. The category, soft rock, was a marketing term used in

---

4   I date the Hawaiian Renaissance beginning with the publication of John Dominis Holt's *On Being Hawaiian* in 1964 and ending with Gabby Pahinui's death in 1980, although most of the activities associated with the Renaissance occurred in the 1970s. This period is sometimes referred to as the "Second Hawaiian Renaissance" in recognition of the "First Hawaiian Renaissance" initiated by Mōʻī David Kalākaua (1836–1891).

the 1970s to mark the merging of pop, folk, and rock with the former two terms modulating the latter — in distinction to the more aggressive sounds of contemporaneous "hard" rock. Soft rock musicians' apolitical stance was allegedly signaled by their introspection and focus on personal expression, rather than more social concerns.[5] Art music categories such as minimalism as well as liturgical or religious music from medieval Gregorian chant to Zen monks' *honkyoku* (shakuhachi or vertical bamboo flute music) have all been perceived, described, or marketed in terms synonymous with soft.

Music produced by ensembles as varied as the Necks, Kafka's Ibiki, and the Philip Glass Ensemble has been described as soft, consonant, and static, the latter quality further delinking activity from the soft. Individuals as different in aesthetic approach from one another as Pauline Oliveros, Bon Iver, Stefan Micus, Brian Eno, and Enya produce musicking categorized and represented in terms synonymous with softness, gentleness, and the ethereal. The category, women's music, which gained widespread use when the record label, Olivia, began producing recordings of artists such as Meg Christian in the 1970s, was described as soft despite the musicians' protestations in their music of gender and sexual norms (and could be used to argue for the effectiveness of soft music in progressive movements, as well). Due to the gendering of softness as female — and therefore associated with being weak and emotional — the music of female artists as varied as Janis Ian, Carole King, Joni Mitchell, Laura Nyro, Rhiannon Giddens, Valerie June, Sarah McLachlan, and Sade are often described as soft, personal, intimate. Soft is one of the

---

5   For example, Stephen Holden, in his *Oxford Music Online* entry (https://doi. org/10.1093/gmo/9781561592630.article.49243), defines soft rock as "A term invented in the early 1970s to describe acoustic folk-rock and other tuneful, soothing types of popular music that use electric instruments. James Taylor, Neil Young (the early recordings), and Cat Stevens typify the folk element in soft rock; in Los Angeles the pop-rock groups Bread and the Carpenters made polished, soft-rock recordings that the music industry designated 'middle of the road'. *The term is now applied broadly to quieter popular music of all sorts that uses mild rock rhythms and some electric instruments in songs of the ballad type*" (emphasis added).

textures of "indigenous" musical signification throughout new age and the retro-lounge-exotica music genres, especially in the attempts to evoke a misty-eyed view of extinct tribes, lost in prelapsarian fantasies of innocent savages "dwelling in nature" and, in the case of Hawaiians, evoking a gentle, indolent people blessed with a childlike innocence, even at their most lascivious. The links between the feminine and the native are many: both are emotional rather than intellectual, weak rather than virile, naïve rather than worldly, soft rather than hard.

I freely concede the point that soft and its adjectival cousins are not the only terms used to categorize the entirety of these various musickings, and that the distinct terms not shared by the generic markers or individual artists I list above may have more significance than any shared (or similar) traits predicated on an idea of musical softness. Rather, I use softness as a keyword to tease out the ways softness and corollary terms such as smooth, sweet, and gentle articulate social relations in which norms are not merely inverted but are subverted, even perverted. I am writing my essay in the wake of the 2016 US presidential election in which racism and white supremacy was an explicit part of Donald Trump's appeal. I seek to reconsider the ways in which the soft, gentle musicking of Native Hawaiians prefigure and sound out social relations antithetical to the racist logics invoked in Trump's campaign, countering with the soft and gentle sounds of *kī hōʻalu*, which, importantly, stake these political claims in Kanaka Maoli rather than Eurocentric terms.

Listening to Hawaiian music as an agentive soft music enables us to hear guitarist George Helm use a performance of Hawaiian standard, "Hiʻilawe," to fuel Kanaka Maoli opposition to the continued denigration and commercial appropriation of their culture, a foundational slab in the construction of the US militourism industrial complex in Hawaiʻi.[6] The militourism

<hr />

6   Kathy E. Ferguson and Phyllis Turnbull, *Oh, Say, Can You See? The Semiotics of the Military in Hawaiʻi* (Minneapolis: University of Minneapolis Press, 1999); Vernadette Vicuña Gonzalez, *Securing Paradise: Tourism and Militarism in Hawaiʻi and the Philippines* (Durham: Duke University Press, 2013); Kyle Kajihiro, "The Militarizing of Hawaiʻi: Occupation, Accommodation,

industrial complex rests on an ideological base of colonialism aided and abetted by white supremacy and articulated through settlers, a conjuncture brought into high relief as Japanese Americans assumed political and business control of Hawai'i politics and trade in the 1950s.[7]

Partner to the tourist industry's interest in representing Hawai'i as a paradiscal escape from modernity, sociologists such as Robert Park championed Hawai'i's mixed-race population as the perfect case example of American multiculturalism *avant la lettre*.[8] Park argued that the racial and ethnic mixture of Hawai'i resulted in a tolerance for difference and a model for American assimilationist ideals, an idea that was used to promote Hawai'i statehood. Yet underlying those idyllic conditions Park describes is the illegal US takeover of Hawai'i in 1893, as Manifest Destiny spread across the Pacific. The interests of US capitalists in Hawai'i were standing, *haole* annexationists argued, on the sanctioned foundation of American democracy, capitalism, and (Protestant) Christianity, which they coupled to their construction of Native Hawaiians as a naturally affectionate and welcoming people, allowing for a blossoming of mixed race social harmony to prevail. As I suggest, however, this view ignored Native Hawaiian genocide and land dispossession and the dire circumstances faced by labor immigrants induced in part by the political and economic motives of *haole* landowners.

A final preliminary note: Hawaiian music in its most commercial and available forms was early associated with musical kitsch, an "ethnic" novelty music for early twentieth century popular music audiences. Since the post-Territorial period (1898–1959) and the rise of the militourism industrial complex in Hawai'i, the music industry in Hawai'i has focused on pro-

---

and Resistance," in *Asian Settler Colonialism: From Local Governance to the Habits of Everyday Life in Hawai'i*, eds. Candace Fujikane and Jonathan Y. Okamura (Honolulu: University of Hawai'i Press, 2008), 170–94.

7   Asian Settler Colonialism: *From Local Governance to the Habits of Everyday Life in Hawai'i*, eds. Candace Fujikane and Jonathan Y. Okamura (Honolulu: University of Hawai'i Press, 2008), 170–94.

8   Robert Park, *Race and Culture* (Glencoe: Free Press, 1950).

ducing music for tourists rather than the much smaller local market.[9] Furthermore, Lisa Kaheleole Hall notes:

> The kitschy transformation of Hawaiians and Hawaiian culture [means] that unlike other stigmatized groups in the United States, Hawaiians are not feared, even though, with our warrior history, our popular image could easily have been different. Instead, our friendliness has been a major selling point for the tourist industry for more than a century, possibly because the death toll from colonization was so one-sided.[10]

The tourism industry promotes an image of Native Hawaiians as always welcoming, their aloha spirit imbuing them with an innate hospitality and generosity that ignores a long history of Native Hawaiians battling non-Hawaiian encroachment in the islands in conventional ways.[11] But as Hall suggests, the legacy of Hawaiian warriors has been long forgotten, replaced by the laconic yet hypersexualized beach boy and *hula* maiden who embrace all *malihini* (strangers) into their welcoming arms. The gruesome cannibals of Cook's apotheosis have long been softened by the feminization of Hawaiian culture as it has been transfigured into the inviting brown *hula* maiden.[12]

Both the fearsome Kanaka Maoli warrior and the rough riding *paniolo* of slack key lore have largely disappeared from his-

---

9 Similar to music markets everywhere, with the rise of digital downloading, the local music industry has had to re-define its role; however, the tourist trade remains the primary market for the music industry in Hawai'i. Elizabeth Tatar, *Strains of Change: The Impact of Tourism on Hawaiian Music* (Honolulu: Bishop Museum Press, 2012).

10 Lisa Kaheleole Hall, "'Hawaiian at Heart' and Other Fictions," *Contemporary Pacific* 17, no. 2 (2005): 404–13, at 409, https://doi.org/10.1353/cp.2005.0051.

11 Noenoe K. Silva, *Aloha Betrayed: Native Hawaiian Resistance to American Colonialism* (Durham: Duke University Press, 2004); Haunani-Kay Trask, *From a Native Daughter: Colonialism and Sovereignty in Hawai'i,* 2nd edn. (Honolulu: University of Hawai'i Press, 1999).

12 Elizabeth Buck, *Paradise Remade: The Politics of Culture and History in Hawai'i* (Philadelphia: Temple University Press, 1993); Heather A. Diamond, *American Aloha: Cultural Tourism and the Negotiation of Tradition* (Honolulu: University of Hawai'i Press, 2008).

torical memory and popular representation. Yet even in warfare, Kanaka Maoli modeled a distinct way of staging conflict. An annual period, observed from October through March, known as *Makahiki,* was a time of spiritual renewal and celebration of the harvest in which war was outlawed. This lull in warfare allowed the *ali'i* (chiefs) to circuit their islands to receive tribute as well as participate in various festivities and activities such as hula and surfing.[13]

* * *

Hawaiian music of any style rarely registers as abrasive even to non-Hawaiian ears unfamiliar with the music. Innocuous, pleasant, even simple perhaps, but it would take a highly contrary pair of ears to find slack key guitar, for example, "noisy" or "disturbing." In contrast, I want to suggest that slack key guitar's *nahenahe* sound is oppositional precisely because it offers an alternative to settler colonialist logics by softly announcing its presence, quietly opposing the racialized hierarchies articulated in social relations in which *haole* and Local (non-Hawaiian, non-*haole* residents), particularly Japanese Americans, dominate Hawaiian social and political life.

Can we hear *nahenahe* as a Hawaiian call for strategies of beauty and gentleness voiced from within a general cultural tendency toward inclusion sustained by a reciprocal set of obligations? Conversely, can we argue that in the contemporary metropolitan soundscape, *noise* is non-threatening, quotidian, even banal?[14] Noise or noisy music as the sound of the "shock of the new" is anything but, with noise reiterating a now-barely registered buzz, oblivious to its own complacency and reactionary

13 Kame'eleihiwa Lilikalā, *Native Land and Foreign Desires: Pehea La E Pono Ai?* (Honolulu: Bishop Museum Press, 1992); Patrick V. Kirch, *Shark Going Inland Is My Chief: The Island Civilization of Ancient Hawai'i* (Berkeley: University of California Press, 2012).

14 Jacques Attali, *Noise: The Political Economy of Music,* trans. Brian Massumi (Minneapolis: University of Minnesota Press, 1985).

position.[15] Noise just as readily reproduces forms of dominance and power as of resistance and opposition, its sounding out just as often reactionary as progressive.[16]

By contrast, *nahenahe* offers listeners alternatives rather than excesses, gently persuasive rather than aggressively argumentative. I do not wish to be misunderstood: There is a place for both noise artist Merzbow (né Akita Masami) and Hawaiian slack key guitarist Charles Philip "Gabby" Pahinui. More pointedly for this essay, Merzbow's animal rights activism is the sort of visible political action comparable to George Helm's activities, which I discuss below (to be clear: Helm is not recognized as a slack key guitarist). Sonically, Hawaiian musicians are invested in a *nahenahe* aesthetic and are uninterested in wielding power by dominating a listener with decibels and velocity. Rather, the *nahenahe* aesthetic invites listeners to explore compassionate, dialogical possibilities through its merging of six voices — each individual string of the guitar an independent part within a larger harmonious ensemble — into a family, or 'ohana, of resonating bodies in sync yet independent, sounding out the nature of open tunings.

Open tunings, as the name suggests, allow for the strings to reverberate harmoniously when struck together without fretting, unlike standard tuning. We might also think of open tuning as free, liberated, uninhibited, yet amicable, consonant, empathetic. It is not without its tensions — slack key guitar does not simply offer anodyne sonic pabulum for it emerged from the agonistic world of the rural Hawaiian, unlikely to be swaddled in anaesthetizing material comfort despite over a century of iconography displaying languid Hawaiian natives. These native lives of material ease are used to convince us of Hawaiians'

---

15 Theodor Adorno, *Aesthetic Theory*, trans. Robert Hullot-Kentor (Minneapolis: University of Minneapolis Press, 1997); Barry Shank, *Political Force of Musical Beauty* (Durham: Duke University Press, 2014).

16 Susan Fast and Kip Pegley, eds., *Music, Politics, and Violence* (Middleton: Wesleyan University Press, 2012); *Dark Side of the Tune: Popular Music and Violence,* eds. Bruce Johnson, Martin Cloonan, and Derek B. Scott (Burlington: Ashgate, 2013).

unconditional love, a simple but good-hearted people with a preternatural proclivity for musicking.

Nahenahe is not a romantic return to Nature or "the folk," that space of unsullied *communitas* often ascribed to rural folk music. While slack key may have its origins as a rural music, formed in the hardscrabble ranch culture of nineteenth century Hawaiʻi, the music is anything but roughhewn.[17] It is a uniquely Hawaiian blend of Spanish instrumentation, Protestant hymnody, and Native Hawaiian rhythmic and melodic sensibilities enfolded within an oral culture that extensively employed *kaona*, or hidden meanings, in song texts. Slack key's early history is obscured by its oral transmission and folk practice, meaning, the music circulated largely outside the circuits of the Hawaiian music industry with little of a popular audience outside of the islands and provoking little interest from scholars. Hawaiian music enjoyed a brief period of interest for continental US popular music audiences in the first decade of the twentieth century. By the second and third decades, Hawaiian music was a popular music genre little to do with traditional Hawaiian musicking, which was assumed to have largely passed away, leaving *hapa haole* (literally, half foreigner[18]) to represent Hawaiian music to

17 There is a form of music distinct from slack key guitar that emerged from the Hawaiian ranch culture of the nineteenth and early twentieth century termed "*paniolo* music," which sounds very similar to the contemporaneous "cowboy songs" of North America.

18 *Hapa haole* is literally "half foreigner," but is used to categorize Hawaiian-themed popular music that is based on continental US popular music forms. As noted in the text, since most of this music was composed in the early twentieth century in attempts to cash in on the Hawaiian craze of the time, the songs follow vaudeville and Tin Pan Alley forms rather than traditional Hawaiian *mele* (chant) or hula forms. For a more detailed investigation of the *hapa haole* song phenomenon, see Charles Hiroshi Garrett, "Sounds of Paradise: Hawaiʻi and the American Musical Imagination," in *Struggling to Define a Nation: American Music and the Twentieth Century* (Berkeley: University of California Press, 2008), 165–214; Elizabeth Buck, *Paradise Remade: The Politics of Culture and History in Hawaiʻi* (Philadelphia: Temple University Press, 1993); and George Kanahele, "Hapa Haole Songs," in *Hawaiian Music and Musicians: An Encyclopedic History*, rev. ed., eds. John Berger and Joanna Kanahele (Honolulu: Mutual Publishing,

non-Hawaiian audiences. Eventually, *hapa haole* gained enough historical patina to enjoy a kind of survivor's victory.[19]

In any case, slack key guitar does not *sound* like conventional ideas regarding the ways in which protest or opposition *should* sound. *Nahenahe* is offered up by guitarists to describe slack key so often that it has become a cliché of interviews and artist profiles. Like any generalization, one easily finds counterexamples: Sonny Chillingworth's virtuosic "Whee Ha Swing," which is a showcase tune for slack key artists to display their chops (technical skills); Keola Beamer's neoclassical arrangement of "Hi'ilawe"; or Ozzie Kotani's studied arrangements of Queen Lili'uokalani's music on his 2002 recording, *To Honor A Queen* (*E Ho'ohiwahiwa I Ka Mo'i Wahine*). These counterexamples reflect other facets of slack key, however. "Whee Ha Swing" is a tour de force that portrays the exuberant *paniolo* ranch culture and slack key's resonance with bluegrass and other country and western repertories that emphasize rural virtuosity with its competitive macho sensibilities (think, rodeos) that is both good-natured and evidence of difficult "hard country" lives.[20] Beamer and Kotani, on the other hand, give notice to slack key's inherent aesthetic value in terms more widely held in the broader musical world external to Hawai'i. Granted, these counterexamples do not register as "oppositional" or "resistance music" to most ears any more than the standard, "Hi'ilawe," though I want to continue to suggest that *nahenahe* is an aesthetic resistant to dominant understandings of musical value and beauty *because*

2012). For a study that recuperates *hapa haole* song from its critics, though with important qualifications, see Akio Yamashiro, "Ethics in Song: Becoming Kama'āina in Hapa-Haole Music," in *Cultural Analysis* 8 (2009): 1–23; https://www.ocf.berkeley.edu/~culturalanalysis/volume8/vol8_article1.html.

19 For reasons of space, I am less concerned with this larger history of Hawaiian music here.

20 Aaron Fox, *Real Country: Music and Language in Working-Class Culture* (Durham: Duke University Press, 2004). While not a slack key song and therefore outside the scope of this study, George Helms's version of "Hawaiian Cowboy" with his virtuosic yodeling, conjure another ready comparison between Hawaiian and western US "cowboy" music.

it offers a vision of the world which privileges gentleness, empathetic interpersonal interaction, and representational modesty.

Nahenahe remains the core aesthetic, counterexamples notwithstanding, and it is easy to hear the sweet, gentle quality in a majority of recordings and performances. There are other remarkable acoustic guitar traditions such as *flamenco,* some forms of the blues, the Celtic traditions of the British Isles and France, the guitar traditions of the South Asian Sub-Continent.[21] These guitar cultures are conceived as acoustic guitar traditions hardwired to specific communities, and though, for instance, the blues and other folk guitar traditions share a number of identical open tunings with slack key, any similarities among the guitar traditions fall away before *nahenahe.* By comparison, the unhurried tempos of slack key accentuate the tradition's gentle rhythmic pulse in contrast to the blues or *flamenco.* Where Hawaiian rhythms are supple, the blues and country music offer more energetic rhythmic pulses built for dances quite distinct from *hula.* These guitar traditions are often entangled in notions of the dangerous yet erotically appealing subaltern; slack key music, unlike most traditions, offers a far gentler seduction with its promise of an erotics of languid pleasure, if wrapped in similarly primitivistic cloth.

Living within an oral culture, Hawaiians accept that words convey more than they denote, and that multiple meanings and interpretations accompany any spoken word. Words are also spoken through the *ea* or breath, an important spiritual concept for Kanaka Maoli, giving spoken words an importance beyond surface meanings. Correspondingly, Hawaiians are often circumspect in their verbal communication and direct confrontation is often avoided. It is one reason *kaona* is so widely practiced. Traditional Hawaiian pedagogy, especially for slack key, entails a "no questions" attitude by *kumu* (teachers). The

---

21　There is no space here, even restricting ourselves to presenting a list, to be anything near comprehensive, but there are innumerable string instrument traditions, including those of the oud, banjo, quattro, tiple, shamisen, koto, sitar, violin, cello, gambola, and of course, "classical" guitar.

us American disposition to "speak one's mind" is at odds with Kanaka Maoli understandings of communication in which the unspoken saturates every conversation with meaning beyond the merely verbal.

* * *

But sometimes candor is precisely the order of the day despite the possibility of confrontation. The Hawaiian Renaissance (1964–80) was a time in which "a movement spearheaded by a new form of Hawaiian music that was, at the same time, emergent in its ideological implications, residual in its ties to traditional forms, and oppositional in its challenges to the political, social, and cultural assumptions of the dominant mainland-created ideology," energizing young Hawai'i musicians, activists, artists, and hula dancers in efforts of Hawaiian cultural preservation, innovation, and legitimation and slack key was part of the musical sound of the era with Gabby Pahinui, Atta Isaacs, and Peter Moon.[22] Groups such as the Sunday Manoa, Hui Ohana, and the Makaha Sons of Ni'ihau were formed by young Hawaiian musicians looking to older traditional Hawaiian music for sources and inspiration while updating those traditions and songs by mixing in elements from contemporary popular music. As George Lewis points out, even the band names reflect a turn away from the types of group names then dominant such as the Hawaiian Surfers, the Maile Serenaders, or the Waikiki Beachboys in order to emphasize a number of political stances emergent at the time: The importance of place and the 'āina and the use of the Hawaiian language.[23]

---

22 George H. Lewis, "Style in Revolt: Music, Social Protest, and the Hawaiian Cultural Renaissance," *International Social Science Review* 62, no. 4 (1987): 168–77, at 172, http://www.jstor.org/stable/i40088381; George Hu'eu Sanford Kanahele, "Hawaiian Renaissance Grips, Changes Island History," *Ha'ilono Mele* 5, no. 7 (1979): 1–9.

23 For a critical assessment of these musicians' Hawaiian language use, see Amy Ku'uleialoha Stillman, "Young Composers Have Trouble with Hawaiian," *Ha'ilono Mele* 4, no. 7 (1978): 6–7.

Along with the renewed interest in *hula kahiko* (ancient *hula*), *oli* (chant without dance), use of Hawaiian instruments such as the *'ulili* (gourd rattles), *'uli'uli* (gourd or shell rattles), and the *ipu* (gourd drum), slack key signified traditional Kanaka Maoli culture, emerging from the protected enclaves of once-secretive *'ohana*. Keola Beamer's 1973 publication of the first slack key method book coincided with the era's resuscitation of traditional Hawaiian culture. Given Gabby Pahinui's stature in the Renaissance period, there was renewed interest in slack key, reflected in his invited participation in the Hawaii Music Foundation's first fundraising concert in 1972, which was also Hawai'i's first concert devoted exclusively to slack key.

Younger musicians followed the template laid down by a group formed in the early 1960s by Gabby Pahinui and *'ukulele* virtuoso Eddie Kamae named the Sons of Hawaii, which openly incorporated contemporary forms of popular music and state-of-the-art record production techniques with traditional repertoire while singing in the Hawaiian language and grafting popular music elements with an ear tilted toward traditional Hawaiian aesthetics and concerns. Even when composing original music using rock as its main musical referent, the use of the Hawaiian language by Renaissance-era bands signaled a turn away from the tourist trade. The focus was on solidifying Hawaiian cultural norms and establishing solidarity or, in Hawaiian terms, re-establishing the *'ohana*.

* * *

The link between Hawaiian music and Hawaiian political activism can be most clearly drawn in the life of George Helm. A *leo ki'e ki'e* (falsetto) singer and guitarist, Helm helped form the Protect Kaho'olawe 'Ohana (PKO), a group of young Hawai'i activists dedicated to reclaiming the island of Kaho'olawe from the US Navy, which had been using the island for live ordinance exercises, including missile testing, beginning in 1941. PKO was inspired by a group called the Aboriginal Lands of Hawaiian

Ancestry or ALOHA, formed to reclaim territory for Hawaiians.[24] Helm, along with Kimo Mitchell, hoped to get arrested when they attempted to land on Kahoʻolawe, an illegal act at the time, as a way to draw media attention to the issue.[25] Helm was a key figure in articulating *aloha ʻāina* (love of the land) as a foundational concept in the Hawaiian sovereignty movement before his untimely death in 1977.

The only extant recordings of Helm performing music are culled from live performances in 1976 at the Gold Coin, a restaurant where Helm held a regular gig, released posthumously the following year on two separate recordings by the venue's owner, Richard Wong. Originally planned as nothing more than private recordings without any intention to release them publicly, the recordings contain a number of anomalies. For example, many tracks begin after the start of the song or end before the song has finished. However, Wong managed to capture some of Helms's song introductions in which he describes the history of a song's composition or the meaning of the lyrics — the songs' *moʻolelo* — revealing the depth of his knowledge and concern for Hawaiʻi even when entertaining diners at a restaurant. Remembered today more for his activism than his musicking, it is fitting that the only surviving record of his expressive *leo kiʻe kiʻe* vocals and dexterous fretboard fingerwork also presents him as a politically conscious Native Hawaiian.

However, the Renaissance was not welcomed by everyone in the Native Hawaiian community, with some viewing activists such as George Helm, Walter Ritte, Bumpy Kanahele, and others as either individuals more interested in self-promotion than in solving the dire material conditions faced by the Kanaka Maoli community or upstart rabble rousers without a clear agenda or plan beyond "making trouble." At the time, Helms and Walter Ritte's occupation of Kahoʻolawe was initially op-

24 Norman Meller and Ann Feder Lee, "Hawaiian Sovereignty," *Publius* 27, no. 2 (1997): 167–85, https://doi.org/10.1093/oxfordjournals.pubjof.a029904.

25 *Hoʻihoʻi Hou: A Tribute to George Helm and Kimo Mitchell,* ed. Rob Morales (Honolulu: Bamboo Ridge, 1984).

posed by the Hawaiian Civic Clubs, which had taken out ads against the PKO actions (the members of the Clubs would eventually change their minds and support the PKO and the ideology of *aloha ʻāina*).[26] Hiʻilawe, the waterfalls, seemed to be receding even as "Hiʻilawe," the song, became a prominent standard among young slack key artists.

* * *

On 3 January 1976, Helm along with eight others, organized a landing on the island. Arrested almost immediately after they landed, PKO was organized to begin reclamation of the island and to stop the Navy missile testing, arguing that the island was sacred to Kanaka Maoli. The Navy finally relented and allowed for a small party of Hawaiians, including Helm, to perform religious rites on the island on 13 February 1976. Helm disappeared, along with fellow activist Kimo Mitchell, on 7 March 1977 in a failed attempt to land on Kahoʻolawe for a third time, but his catalytic work in shaping the PKO and his public advocacy for the reclamation of Hawaiian lands renewed Kanaka Maoli attempts to regain political and territorial sovereignty.

Helm observed the softness of Hawaiian protest, declaring:

Hawaiian music reflects the attitudes toward life and nature. *These are basically clean protests and not harsh,* for example, "Kaulana Nā Pua," but with a deep hidden meaning. Unfortunately, modern Anglo-Saxon reasoning cannot truly appreciate the deep meaning of a song such as "Kualana Nā Pua." Many of the Hawaiian songs that are now openly played were once hidden from those who were not of the culture. Many of the songs now openly express, if one understands the words, the language — pain revolution; it's expressing the emotional

---

26 George H. Lewis, "The Role of Music in Popular Social Movements: A Theory and Case Study of the Island State of Hawaii, USA," *International Review of the Aesthetics and Sociology of Music* 16, no. 2 (1985): 153–62, at 157, https://doi.org/10.2307/836774.

reaction the Hawaiians are feeling to the subversion of their life style. *It's an immediacy of feeling.*[27]

Critical of both the Bishop Museum's "mummification" of Hawaiian culture and the Polynesian Cultural Center's "commercial preservation," Helm called for a vibrant, living Hawaiian cultural revolution, emphasizing the spiritual outlook of *aloha 'āina,* a concept rooted in Native Hawaiian cosmology in which the *'āina* is a living entity as a source of human life. Helm is also referencing *kaona* here — "if one understands the words" — as a means of bridging musical and political meanings to an "immediacy of feeling."

Toward the end of the documentary film, *Kaho'olawe Aloha 'Āina* — George Helm (dir. Pahipau and Joan Lander, 1977), Helm defends the notion of *aloha 'āina* against those characterizations at a public rally in front of the 'Iolani Palace, declaring:

It's very important that we get together. We got to shed off a lot of the images that have been thrown on top of us by newspapers, by television. We just want one thing to talk to you folks about. This is a seed, today, of a new revolution. And we not talking about da kine like the Pilgrims came ova' heah and run away from England, go wipe out the Indians, y'know, and call this America and celebrate two hundred years with firecrackers. *The kind of revolution we're talking about is one of consciousness* — the consciousness, awareness, facts, figures. And like Walter [Ritte] said, "We're going to the 'Iolani Palace to make *ho'o pupū* [make a stand with] to our *kupuna* [ancestors], yeah? Our *ali'i.* We hope to put somebody back in deah. We serious! We gotta think this way, we gotta talk that way because that's the only facts that allow for change. And change is synonymous to revolution. And revo-

---

27 Kimo Turner, "George Helm and the 'Language — Pain Revolution,'" *Ha'ilono Mele* 2, no. 6 (1976): 2–3, at 3 (emphasis added). Cf. Amy Ku'uleialoha Stillman, "'Aloha Aina': New Perspectives on 'Kaulana Nā Pua,'" *Hawaiian Journal of History* 33 (1999): 83–99.

lution comes from the word, revolving, turning in and out so that you have something better, better to live with. And we say again, we want to get rid of that image — radicals — we don't know what that word means but I know a lot of people get turned off by us. Not giving us a chance. You know, we not getting our kicks doing this. This is the beginning. After this, *pau* [finish]! We're going down to something else. What we're looking for is the truth. The truth, the truth, the truth, the truth. *Aloha nō.*

Disavowing the image of the radical, Helm argues that the truth is on the side of the Native Hawaiians. After two centuries of settler-colonialism, Helm argued that Hawaiians needed a change of consciousness — a change in thinking and feeling, a transformation of ideological and instinctual reflexes.

After his impassioned speech, Helm and some of his compatriots begin singing "Hawai'i Aloha." If this were to occur today, the audience would begin to hold hands and sing along, perhaps swinging their arms in unison rhythm with the singing. However, even at the height of the Hawaiian Renaissance, only a handful of people seem to be singing along and no one is holding hands. Most of the audience stand motionless, merely listening. Thirty years later, in a 2007 YouTube video of Iz (Israel Kamakawiwoʻole) performing the song, the audience — young, old, men, women, children, *tūtū* (elders) — quickly jump to their feet, form a human chain of linked hands, and sing along with the star, gently swaying to the rhythm (I have been a part of countless Hawaiian music performances which end this way). The difference in reception and the performance of *ʻohana* in the latter version speak to the impact of the Renaissance. The effects would take some time to ripple out but as the 1980s saw an increase in Japanese and other non-Hawaiian investment in resort developments and increasing numbers of tourists, Hawaiian activists and their sympathizers renewed efforts to highlight

Hawaiian territorial rights into the set of issues covered by the term, the Hawaiian sovereignty movement.[28]

Scholars such as Joyce Linnekin critique such constructions as *aloha ʻāina* as inventions, convenient truths that subordinate groups formulate in response to their debased condition.[29] However, the hegemon's construction of superiority and moral rectitude is also deeply rooted in invention. In other words, both are constructing rationales, defenses, and covers for either the maintenance or the usurpation of the status quo. Again, it is the *moʻolelo* that inform slack key songs with its revolutionary, decolonizing sensibilities. The *nahenahe* sounds of slack key, similar to lyrical *kaona,* especially in a time when noise or direct lyrics are conventionally thought to convey protest, subvert our modern understanding of oppositional or "protest music."[30]

Helm performed repertoire we might readily call traditional Hawaiian folk song but many of his most enthusiastic performances are of *hapa haole* songs. Helm notes in this essay's opening epigraph that the value of musicking is in its ability to catalyze individuals into collective action, and his song selections indicate a similarly non-dogmatic open-eared approach to Hawaiian song. Still, despite being a folk hero of the Hawaiian

---

28 Lilikalā Kameʻeleihiwa, "Preface: The Hawaiian Sovereignty Movement," in *Islands in Captivity: The Record of the International Tribunal on the Rights of Native Hawaiians,* eds. Ward Churchill and Sharon H. Venne, Hawaiian language edn. (Cambridge: South End, 2004), xvii–xxvii; Lewis, "Style in Revolt."

29 Richard Handler and Jocelyn Linnekin, "Tradition, Genuine or Spurious," *Journal of American Folklore* 97, no. 385 (1984): 273–90, https://doi.org/10.2307/540610; Jocelyn S. Linnekin, "Cultural Invention and the Dilemma of Authenticity," *American Anthropologist* 93, no. 2 (1991): 446–49, https://doi.org/10.1525/aa.1991.93.2.02a00120; Paul Lyons, "Questions about the Question of 'Authenticity': Notes on Moʻolelo Hawaiʻi and the Struggle for Pono," in *Native Authenticity: Transnational Perspectives on Native American Literary Studies,* eds. Deborah L. Madsen (Albany: State University of New York Press, 2010); Trask, *From a Native Daughter.*

30 Even the discussion of *mele kuʻe,* literally "songs of resistance," in the latest edition of *The Encyclopedia of Hawaiian Music and Musicians,* focuses on the lyrics rather than the musical sound. Much of the music of *mele kuʻe* can be said to conform to the *nahenahe* aesthetic.

Renaissance and possessing beautiful vocal and guitar talents, Helm's commercially available musical legacy is reduced to Wong's bootleg quality recordings.[31]

Soft Power

It is in considering a softness underlying *nahenahe* — and by extension, readers can listen for other examples readily drawn from the constellation of genres, performative and aesthetic properties, artists and ensembles I describe or list earlier — that I want to conclude my remarks.

We will end by listening to two tracks from "Gabby" Pahinui and Leland "Atta" Isaac's duet recording, *Two Slack Key Guitars* (Tradewinds 1969). The liner notes begin: "Slack key guitar cannot be adequately described, compared or analyzed. As Hawaiian as *limu* [algae, traditional Hawaiian food staple], it could almost be called an emotion poured from the very soul into the instrument." With this in mind, we begin with the initial track, "I'm-A Livin' On-A Easy," sometimes used as an alternate title as "A-Livin' On A Easy" is printed as a subtitle on the cover of the recording, below a photograph of Isaacs and Pahinui performing on their guitars while sitting on the grass beneath a shade tree, cane weave hats atop their dark black hair and smiling faces, yellow leis 'round their necks, both men sporting matching bright red and white Hawaiian shirts, dark slacks, and bare feet.

Placing "I'm-A Livin' On-A Easy" at the beginning of the album establishes the mood for the rest of the recording. The song is a playful first-person soliloquy on the unfettered joys of unemployment, homelessness, and, least convincingly, bachelorhood. A paean to the carefree ways of a footloose beach boy, the cover image of two middle-aged men as happy-go-lucky layabouts reinforces the idea of Hawaiians as childlike people whose

---

31 According to ethnomusicologist Amy Kuʻuleialoha Stillman, Helm has a total of 62 unique tracks spread out over 88 total tracks on the four commercial recordings available — two on vinyl and two CD compilations. See http://www.amykstillman.wordpress.com/2011/07/19/crunching-data-the-music-of-george-helm-a-true-hawaiian/.

lives of ease in paradise are fulfilled by the simple joys of good song, strong drink, and human companionship.

I want to suggest an alternate hearing/reading, however. Native Hawaiian priorities challenge the tenets of acquisitive capitalism, bourgeois social norms, and settler-colonialism, and representations such as the *Two Slack Key Guitars* cover hint at, if in exaggeratedly comic ways (at the expense of Hawaiians), alternative lives desired by harried tourists, middle-class office workers, and cosmopolitan elites. In the songs of *Two Guitars,* we witness aurally the attraction of Kanaka Maoli attitudes toward labor, the distinctions between the public and the private, and, most significantly, we hear the ways in which Local Hawaiʻi culture, characterized by a relative casualness to social difference, cultivates that casualness through *a constant attention to difference* rather than a denial of its presence.

Hawaiʻi is distinctive in the US for more than the level of militarization or that it is officially bilingual, recognizing both English and Hawaiian. Hawaiʻi is the only state in which *haoles,* whites, and *haole*-ness, whiteness, are made visible in ways that are familiar to people of color from the continental US.[32] To *haoles,* this feels like a spotlight is being thrust on them. To their brown- and black-skinned neighbors, this double consciousness, to sample W.E.B. Du Bois's formulation, this self-knowledge of the disjunct, contradictory, and negative ways in which one is perceived while working out the ways in which one's subjectivity can be lived is trans-generational, a piece of living passed on through the scrim of white supremacy, and no less frustratingly infuriating for remaining unavoidable.

Our final song, "Wahine Uʻi E," is a playful two-step dance number, for which the original liner notes describe: "Atta [Isaacs] and Gabby [Pahinui] are at their best using the give and take, you-play-one-I-play-one system. Instrumental." Perform-

---

32 Judy Rohrer, *Haoles in Hawaiʻi: Race and Ethnicity in Hawaiʻi* (Honolulu: University of Hawaiʻi Press, 2010); Judy Rohrer, *Staking Claim: Settler Colonialism and Racialization in Hawaiʻi* (Tucson: University of Arizona Press, 2016).

ing the social "give and take" of Native Hawaiian culture, the two guitarists perform as a single performer capable of performing on two guitars simultaneously, only modified by the number of bars given to each guitarist throughout the song's progress. The track provides the ideal of *nahenahe,* a collective ideal, with an easy, relaxed virtuosity in which seamless collaboration is a privileged aesthetic criterion. The first full band chorus locates the far-fetched, by which I mean to call on George Lipsitz's use of a wave's long fetch as a metaphor for the histories of connections related through vernacular song with the Caribbean travels of Kanaka Maoli sailors sounded out in the rhythm guitar hinting at calypso and reggae strumming patterns.[33] "Wahine U'i E" is a true duet requiring both guitarists to retain an individual voice while contributing to the two-guitar rendition of the song's central theme, sharing the responsibility of conveying a coherent melody. The entire recording ensemble is largely a family affair. Besides the two guitarists, Isaac's father, Alvin, performs on the 'ukulele, with uncle Norman on bass and Harold Hakuole on rhythm guitar.

While there is a sweet, gentle sound, the song is anything but solemn. We can hear the dance roots of the music from the beginning with Atta Isaacs's solo guitar introduction. It captures the feeling of a social dance, a collective celebration expressed through joined individual efforts. It is a song meant for movement for a community rooted to a particular place. It is a song for a community willing to open its arms to *malihini* (strangers) but always with a sense of mutual obligation and reciprocity. The comfortable lilting of the underpinning rhythm feels unhurried though energetic, never wavering throughout the entire performance, inviting listeners to dance or sway in time.

* * *

---

33 George Lipsitz, *Footsteps in the Dark: The Hidden Histories of Popular Music* (Minneapolis: University of Minnesota Press, 2007), vii–viii; James Revell Carr, *Hawaiian Music in Motion: Mariners, Missionaries, and Minstrels* (Urbana: University of Illinois Press, 2014).

In conclusion, I want to suggest that the *nahenahe* aesthetic, which is often characterized as narcotic, even by some of its practitioners can be thought of as a sounding out against settler-colonialist logics by "acting softly," that is, by thinking of agency not only through bold, "loud and hard" acts but through quieter, less volatile ways as well. Perhaps we might think of "soft agency" through the metaphor of water. Water has two fundamental ways of leveraging power. One way is patient. Water simply drips on the same spot, forever. Eventually, whatever the drops are hitting bear an ever-expanding cavity, slowly worn away with the patient drooling of water. The other way is for enough water to gather together to overwhelm: from individuals drowning to entire settlements disappearing in the wake of tsunami or floods to assisting earth and wind in mudslides and hurricanes. Water is often imagined as benign, but it carries the potential for death even as it is necessary for life.

Softness often uses a sly stratagem of patient corrosion — think, again, of the relationship between water and mineral, the soft liquid eventually working the hard mineral into sandy softness. Soft music almost imperceptibly reshapes materiality. Soft music is not anodyne or "safe" but intensely introspective while simultaneously active, alert, sensitive to the larger ambient context, enfolding itself in its narrowest cracks and crevices, enlarging the space it occupies with geologic tenacity.

Nahenahe as expressed in the buoyant "Wahine Uʻi E" suggests defeating racism is possible through a relentless but patient demonstration of powerfully soft, aggressive gentleness, generous outpourings of love (a topic worth its own paper), and happiest when others are sharing in the *jouissance* expressed by the two guitarists sharing the melody. Hawaiian slack key guitarists' musickings are forceful, agentive, and, refusing life within the colonial matrix, confront it with a seductive blend of exuberance and quiet charm, presenting a world of social relations in which differences are visible, even of *haoles,* and in which encounters of difference are not automatically confrontations but are transformed into moments of collaboration.

Like the slow drip of water, the efforts of the poorly funded PKO eventually paid off. In 1980, a consent decree was signed between the US Navy and PKO mandating the Navy to begin restoration of the island to its pristine state through soil conservation, revegetation, and goat eradication. In 1990, President George Bush banned the bombing of Kahoʻolawe. The Navy would eventually cede the land back after they attempted to thwart the federal court judgment by failing to comply with the order to clear the island of any remaining ordinance, dragging its feet in clearing the island and finally evacuating, but leaving approximately twenty-five percent of the land uncleared. It would take until 2004 before the island was deemed clear of enough unfired ordinances, or unexploded bombs, to accede the island completely over to the State of Hawaiʻi. However, there has been little effort to restore Kahoʻolawe to its pristine state, ostensibly because of the amount of live ordinances still on the ground but also a consequence of the lack of funding from the State to complete the task.

Still, the lessons to learn from the soft songs of the Kanaka Maoli are heard/seen most clearly if one turns around in the way ancient Hawaiians imagined their relationship to temporality, to walk backward in order to learn from the past, which we can now see clearly behind/before us, while not rushing into the future, behind us now, in a largely unknown unfolding. Turned around in this way, we can hear George Helm, Gabby Pahinui, Atta Isaacs, Fred Punahou, Leonard Kwon, Auntie Alice Namakelua, Keola Beamer, and countless others, performing their *nahenahe* songs in a gathering wave pitched toward the scales of the world. To do this soft work, we need only be relentless and patient, each of us a drop in the continuous wearing away of racism and racist ideology, awaiting the chance to join other drops in a transformative tsunami.

15

Gangland Wonderama

YDS

I.

reel recording
in a wonderama
spooled from Unknown
and coiled round loins,
in the guts,
a projection
of every last house addicted to shatter
because Unknown hurts so bad
everything from it
becomes Everything you believe
and belief keeps you safe
even when beliefs make you sick,
addicted and reeled to
your own worthlessness.

II.

Awoke and her stars were cold,
in tight coils.
Nothing to do but warm them to music
An artifact of burning lack

DOI: 10.21983/P3.0250.1.18

That coal music
Always playing
"remember / we wore masks / to bring the light down / against
the locks bored into us / brought the light down, like lips, like
keys / brought it down and it looked like…"

III.

Masks around
The Artifact and parlor
Remarked how fortune lit this
Feature or that
But never spoke to it
Nor to each other

IV.

She prays God still finds her
Amidst all her lost fires
rising into valleys in the night sky
smuggles them in pictures from days past
four cold corners to a frame
so when she woke
nothing to do but warm the muse
the coal unwrapped
that black

V.

Lives culture certain winds,
like valleys
shepherd through a howl.
The kids' are lonely shapes
Which no fist or inquiring heel
Of lover's palm
could rightly dimension
encrypted in coil

but holler into the howl
and it will holler back,
reveal scale and shape in attitude
coal mosaic
myth imprinted onto pavement
fashion dance out that
lust over lack
lady you could chain that
loop that and pose it
lady art a totem
articulating, uncoiling
through the theatres
they say
are not war
a little too loudly

VI.

Vibe birthed out voice, uncoiled that
How you sing
when you can't
they said you too ugly to
but you clamor out the trench
dug in your back when they nailed "too"
there for good
so you talk like
the words might run away
with your pain
and when they do
you stand up straight
talk like words
might carry more than them little letters
something more than they said
you would ever do cuz you're too
and how it feels when folks form behind your words
yours?
can you own a feeling alone? An idea?

the fact we all already felt it?
what vein long ago opened bestride us

VII.

She woke in the parlor
where trenches began
a casketeering dance.
Seeing
blood indicates body and
body, land
a continent in their common rupture
asks
"Do we be a vein?"

VIII.

What then
when
you live inside
the unnamed
murder weapon

IX.

Looking
for bodies
muse warm and running fire
down the vein.
It stirs her through poses,
what has
and has to come,
grips her by the trench
where out pours the murders of the hundred girls of her
all too, too, too
stark in the affront of her burning lack
and still blessed.

Looking for bodies
eyes on vibes

X.

You go around
looking for bodies
vibe eyed and silent but for disagreeing
metals ferrying you
on muffled explosions.
you have a hand that unfolds into flags
you have a hand palming more metal disagreements
you are a modern nation in motion
leave the boys cut behind you like daisies
looked just like you
speculate you did a favor
as revolver wound
like planets in their own chambered rounds
body for body after body
you theorize
bullets as screaming flotsam of the Unknown
meeting overboard bodies yelling out the same
maybe bringing both to shores
of somewhere actual
somewhere Known

XI.

you theorize
time.
rounds, reports as tectonic groans
of scape settling in the wake of those
who leave behind enough Known land
to hold them when time comes
to turn around and die.
the kids
with hands that tree ragged cuneiform

bodied in tangram
uncorporable glyphs
in a wonderama
that isn't,
that isn't

XII.

What is body but
record of what should
never happen again,
lives you
can never resume
corrupted saves, pictures of you
your portrait round the dinner table
anchoring down the
love who prays
she is not next
to be thrown headlong overboard
and set the night afire.
She theorizes what is a stone
but locked light
and what is a body but a breathing stone
what is in breath
but what is in the flesh:
howls and
trenches,
the body's bread and text.
folded round
a single doom
in the horizon

XIII.

May all the coal
totems uncoil its name

XIV.

reel recording out the

Part IV

RACIAL JUSTICE PRAXIS

SOCIAL JUSTICE

16

This Is Just to Say

Dubian Ade

This Is Just to Say
Colonizer
You will not wake up
Tomorrow morning
Forgive me
I can't promise that
Your transition will be painless
Ours will not be either
More importantly
The people have been watching
For a very long time
Soon they will be looking
At themselves

Facebook Message I
You are
a tired contradiction.
You say things will get better
"like they always do"

I hand you the bones
Of my ancestor.
"well, that's in the past"

DOI: 10.21983/P3.0250.1.19

I pick up my weapon:
"Sir. Remember Dr. King!"

OK.

Dr. King would have wanted
Me
To live.

November 22, 2014
When I was 12-years-old,
I played cops and robbers
With my toy gun see!
He didn't think twice before he shot me

PO(S)TUS
The worst part about all of this
Is not that he is orange
Or a white supremacist
Or a sexual predator
A raving misogynist
Or yuge ass-wipe bastard.

The worst part is
You will never admit
He is you.

Look at you.
When millions of voters
Baptized their hands in whiteness
Were you not sitting in a chair
Made of skulls in the living room
whispering "I have never seen anything more American"?

August 9, 2014
I was 18-years-old
There were 7 or 8 bullets

Bled for 3 to 4 hours
They haven't put the fire out yet

Odu
The time table for revolution
Bends in on itself
It is very simple:

The bird turning back in on itself
Is the revolution

It is very simple:
The face looking into its reflection
In the water
Is the revolution

It is very simple:
The slave turning into dust
Is the revolution.

Who remembers the meaning of this oracle?

Another Day in KKKourt
Your honor,
What are the stuff
Judges are made out of?

Room of silicon. White studio audience.
Laugh track.

"We find officer Daren Wilson…" <laughs>
<laughs>
Cue lights.

Cut.

Here
It is here where it happened.
Where black boys
Became the roses laid on the curb
And the people
Became the straw that broke the nation's back.
Babylon aint got much long left.
And
if you think we came here to protest
you aint seen shit yet.

They pretend as though
They don't hear the people coming
They see us speaking to each other
That's when they start running
This collective recognition
We hold like ammunition
Communication with the people
Who will listen.

When our blood spilled
Onto the concrete
This became our street
Where our feet buckled at
Failed police indictments
And winced at state-sanctioned bombs
Dropped on Palestine
43 students murdered in Mexico
And a twelve-year-old slain
In Ohio

Yet, it is here where it happened
Right here
In this spot
Where the First Nations fled
From the scorched earth
And America was birthed in

A miscarriage.

It is here where it happened.

July 13, 2015
My ears are still ringing
After he told me "I will light you up"
Now alone on the cold wet floor
I can hear the prison guards talkin

Forgetting
Aint nothin surprise us
down here no mo'.
The other day
I seen white men
Come down the street
With torches
yelling: "blood and soil"
They weren't skinheads.
Or white-hooded shadow
Paper tigers blowing down the street.
Na.
They were the white men
Who drive sports cars
And say things like "well, actually."
And everyday Merica gasps
Like it was suddenly born again.
Na
Nothing surprise us down here
No mo'.

Charleston
In South Carolina
When a white man
Walks into a church
And asks you if this seat
Is taken

You will look down to pick at your cuticles
And say "no"
Knowing he don't look right
But with a warmness
Like southern cookin
In the summer.
Because Jesus lives in the heart
And everybody have to meet him
Sometime.

In KKKourt Again
"Case number 2342 step forward"
<laughs>
Defendant staring as Black slave
In leg and arm shackles.
Behind wax dolls with assault rifles.
"and eh… how do you plead"
<laughs>
Not guilty your honor
<laughs>
Defendant taken out of kourt room

End credits.

April 12, 2015
Throw me into the back of a police van
Using my spine as an air freshener hanging
from the windshield, my life a bumper sticker.
Hoping that I will die before you parallel park

Facebook Message II
Yes, all cops.
All of them.
I did not stutter.

The state
Pays all the pensions.

August 1, 2016
My son says they are trying to kill us
But they wont get through this door
Baby I promise. History is made of
Women like me who say "enuf is enuf"

Egun Speak Through
The ancestors
Live out their
Vengeance
Through me
My eye red from their blood
If they could see me now
They would say
"Boy! We aint gots no tim fi waste"

17

The Logic of "Illogical" Opposition: Tools and Tactics for Tough Times

George Lipsitz

The *Antiracism Inc.* project addresses what seems like a clear contradiction. Antiracism is frequently proclaimed but rarely practiced. Civil rights laws have been on the books for a half century. Government agencies, private businesses, and educational institutions present themselves as committed to equality and justice. People of color have come to occupy positions of power and prestige in many areas, including the highest offices in government. Yet racial oppression and suppression continue in the form of ever expanding racial wealth and racial health gaps, in the disproportionate exposure of people of color to multiple forms of premature death, and the relegation of members of aggrieved racial groups to polluted poverty stricken neighborhoods and to jails, detention centers, and prisons. Rather than ushering in a new era of human liberation, the changes of the last half-century have simply produced a new system of racial subordination.

Malcolm X used to say that if they can't beat you, they'll join you, but when they join you, they lead you down a path

DOI: 10.21983/P3.0250.1.20

you never intended to follow.[1] The solutions crafted by people in power in response to the freedom movements of the twentieth century did not meet the radical demands of insurgents, but instead channeled them toward reformist ends. The superficial surface embrace of antiracism stems from assumptions that racism is aberrant, irrational, individual, and intentional, when in fact it is structural, systemic, collective, and cumulative. Civil rights laws, diversity programs, and the elevation of darker faces to higher places enable individuals to object to overtly racist impediments to upward mobility and full citizenship, but they keep in place systems of collective racial rule. As Chandan Reddy eloquently explained at several meetings of Antiracism Inc., the co-optation of antiracism by capital and the state relies on a narrative that divides communities of color into binary opposite categories of exceptionality and disposability. A few members of an aggrieved group can win a modicum of inclusion by performing an exceptionality that marks them as different from and better than the rest of the members of their group. Their partial inclusion requires the abandonment of others. The exceptionality of the individual reinforces the disposability of the masses.

This logic of co-optive antiracism encourages members of aggrieved groups to perform normativity, to internalize the logic of neoliberal racialized capitalism in order to advance themselves as individuals. Sociologists who study social movements argue under these conditions that aggrieved groups can only make gains when they express their desires in dominant terms, when their frames are aligned with the hegemonic forces in society.[2] Yet at the grassroots, social movement groups recognize

---

1   George Breitman, ed., *Malcolm X Speaks* (New York: Pathfinder Press, 2017), 120.

2   David A. Snow, E. Burke Rochford, Jr., Steven K. Worden, and Robert D. Benford, "Frame Alignment Processes, Micromobilization and Movement Participation," *American Sociological Review* 51, no.4 (1986): 464–81, https://doi.org/10.2307/2095581. David Snow, Robert D. Benford, Holly McCammon, Lyndi Hewitt, and Scott Fitzgerald, "The Emergence, Development, and Future of the Framing Perspective: 25+ Years Since 'Frame Alignment,'" *Mobilization* 19, no. 1 (2014): 23–45.

and reject the terms of this bargain. In Los Angeles, houseless activists fight for *less* rather than more policing, arguing that police intervention creates more problems than it solves. In New Orleans, Students at the Center (SAC) adamantly refuse to coach students to perform better on standardized tests, teaching them instead to realize their potential as leaders of their community. In San Diego, the Environmental Health Coalition (EHC) rejects plans to redevelop Latinx neighborhoods as profitable sites for polluting businesses and insists instead on green development planned and implemented by community residents. In Houston, Project Row Houses (PRH) mobilizes residents of the Third Ward ghetto to resist gentrification, to oppose policies that will increase property values in their neighborhood at the expense of its historical character, to remain in the area rather than accepting cash offers to leave. In Oakland, Asian Immigrant Women Advocates (AIWA) rejects campaigns focused on securing outside political and financial support in favor of the Community Transformational Organizing Strategies, which seek to develop the long-term capacity for leadership among low-wage, limited-English speaking immigrant women workers.

The campaigns waged by these community organizations are race-based but not race-bound. They begin with attention to the ways in which racism crafts a linked fate for aggrieved communities of color, but they also recognize racism as a mechanism of capitalist suppression and oppression. They express what might seem like illogical forms of opposition. They do not think their interests will be served adequately by conforming to the dominant logics of reward and recognition that guide prevailing political and economic policies. They believe that having a greater police presence in their midst, coaxing some students to get higher scores on standardized tests, attracting polluting businesses to impoverished neighborhoods, selling their homes but losing their community, or winning back stolen wages by stepping back and letting others direct the struggle will not help them in the long run. They seek to change the society that oppresses them, not simply sign up for greater inclusion in it.

The seeming illogic of these strategies of opposition appears as well in their insistence on treating race as a sense of group position rather than as an embodied attribute of individuals. From the perspective of most policy makers, politicians, planners, and researchers, the conditions these groups protest all seem clearly to be primarily issues of social class that are only incidentally, ecologically, or tangentially racialized. Yet these social movement organizations insist that housing insecurity, educational inequality, environmental pollution, gentrification, and gendered low-wage labor are all steeped in racial subordination and exploitation. From their perspective, capitalism is a racial as well as an economic system. They refuse to separate the struggle for class justice from racial justice, gender justice, and language justice. They are *always* antiracist, but never *only* antiracist. In their eyes, racism is always intersectional. It is *ever* present, but *never* present only by itself. They refuse to conform to the logic of liberal multiculturalism that configures racism narrowly as an amalgam of intentional, individual, and aberrant acts, as isolated injuries and exclusions based on skin color and phenotype. Instead, they conceive of racism as systemic, structural, collective, and cumulative. No one has to burn a cross or utter a racial epithet to relegate people of different races to different places, to consign entire populations to disproportionate vulnerability to displacement, dispossession, and deportation. Racism manifests itself in patterns of police stops, frisks, arrests, and beatings. It skews opportunities and life chances and makes people of color excessively vulnerable to homelessness, foreclosure, eviction, overcrowding, and predatory lending. It justifies and excuses pervasive practices of labor exploitation and wage theft. It looms large at the point of production in determining which workers will become targets of sexual harassment and language discrimination. To these organizations and their constituents, homelessness, educational inequality, environmental racism, gentrification, and gender and language discrimination are the logical consequences of a system of racialized capitalism — that rather than forging a working class united round the common experience of economic exploitation, capitalism instead creates a world riddled with a seemingly endless array of diverse forms of differentiation. These groups reject the logic that limits struggles for racial justice merely to the removal of overtly and expressly racist impediments to upward mobility, and instead follow a logic that leads to the creation of new democratic practices, processes, and institutions. As john a. powell and Caitlin Watt observe, in this society, race is "not about skin color, but about the production of group identity with the power to exclude, control and benefit."[3] Thus, struggles against racism are always about more than just race, while any meaningful effort to increase collective capacity for democratic living requires an antiracist frame.

Each of these race-based, but not race-bound, organizations draws on the specific resistance traditions of particular aggrieved racial collectivities for their philosophies, practices, tactics, strategies, and critiques. Their politics are expressly antiracist, but they reject narrow racialisms. Their struggles are rooted in the specific resistance traditions of their racialized groups, but they seek to cooperate rather than compete with others similarly aggrieved. Los Angeles Community Action Network (LACAN), Students at the Center (SAC), and Project Row Houses (PRH), all emerge from and resonate with what Cedric Robinson has termed the Black Radical Tradition, a tradition that is not exclusively Black. LACAN and SAC see themselves as descendants of the Black Panther Party and the Free Southern Theatre. The EHC reflects the continuing relevance and power of historical struggles by Mexican American *mutualistas,* the Chicano/a movement, and community feminism. AIWA evidences the enduring ability of a pan-ethnic Asian American Identity to serve as common ground for people of different national origins, languages, and religions, while at the same time emphasizing the sometimes-suppressed importance of language, immigrant status. and gendered labor exploitation to the pan-ethnic formation.

---

3   john a. powell and Caitlin Watt, "Negotiating the New Political and Racial Environment," *Journal of Law in Society* 31, no. 11 (2010): 31–69, at 45.

It has been important for LACAN to foreground the racial dimensions of housing insecurity. Black people make up only about ten present of the population of Los Angeles, but they account for as many as three-quarters of Skid Row residents.[4] Nationwide, Black families are seven times more likely than white families to be houseless.[5] Houselessness on Skid Row has been caused by long histories of expressly anti-Black acts of private discrimination and public policies that have channeled assets that appreciate in value to whites while relegating Blacks largely to means-tested public housing. Decades and centuries of racial zoning, restrictive covenants, racial steering, blockbusting, mortgage redlining, urban renewal, and other discriminatory practices make housing insecurity an especially important feature of life for African Americans.[6]

LACAN recognizes that race-bound problems require race-based solutions. They draw on the local Black resistance tradition in their work. One of the group's leading activists, General Dogon, spent eleven years in a California state prison where he was mentored by fellow inmates, especially an intellectual and activist known by the name Magic who was revered by other prisoners for having been an associate of George Jackson, cofounder of the Black Guerilla Family inside the walls of Soledad Prison.[7] Dogon entered prison as a drug addicted bank robber and gang leader; he emerged from incarceration as a member

---

4   "The Safer Cities Initiative is a Failed Policy: End Human Rights Violations and Build Housing Today," Lamp Community and the Los Angeles Community Action Network, cangress.wordpress.com/tag/los-angeles-community-action-network/.

5   Jeffrey Selbin et al., "California's New Vagrancy Laws; The Growing Enactment of Enforcement of Anti-Homeless Laws in the Golden State," *SSRN,* June 24, 2016, 4, https://papers.ssrn.com/sol3/papers.cfm?abstract_id=2794386##.

6   Melvin L. Oliver and Thomas M. Shapiro, *Black Wealth/White Wealth: A New Perspective on Racial Inequality* (New York: Routledge, 1997); Patrick Sharkey, *Stuck in Place: Urban Neighborhoods and the End of Progress Toward Racial Equality* (Chicago: University of Chicago Press, 2013).

7   "The Panther of Skid Row: General Dogon," *FRANK151,* http://frank151.com/general-dogon/; Lisa "Tiny" Gray-Garcia, "From Skid Row to your Overpriced Condo: Po' Folks Resisting Removal," *San Francisco BayView Na-*

of the Black Guerilla Family committed to fighting for social justice. Living on parole on Skid Row, Dogon witnessed incessant harassment of houseless people by law enforcement officers and private security guards instructed to clear the area of people whose presence would be an obstacle to development. Local Black Panther and activist Bilal Ali advised Dogon to emulate the Community Alert Patrol created by Black militants in the 1960s to monitor the police. Using clipboards and cameras, Dogon and other area residents worked with LACAN to create the Community Watch Program to monitor racial profiling, harassment, and nuisance arrests.[8]

The legacies of the Black Guerilla Family, the Community Alert Patrol, and the Black Panther Party inform the contemporary activism of LACAN. Similarly, the group draws on critiques mounted by Fannie Lou Hamer, Huey P. Newton, and others during the 1960s and 1970s of the limits of a narrow civil rights perspective. They cite the Universal Declaration of Human Rights proclaimed by the United Nations in 1948 in declaring the right to a decent home and living environment as an inalienable human right. Emphasis on human rights as well as civil rights opens the possibility of exposing housing policy in Los Angeles to potential allies overseas. LACAN activist Deborah Burton traveled to Geneva, Switzerland in 2010 to testify at a United Nations tribunal to call attention to and put a human face to what she described as "the ongoing and massive violation of the human right to housing we face in the United States and in my home city."[9]

Like the Black Power movement of the 1960s, LACAN creates parallel institutions that expose the failures of dominant institutions to meet human needs and provide members of aggrieved groups with opportunities for democratic participation in de-

---

tional Black Newspaper, November 26, 2012, http://sfbayview.com/2012/11/from-skid-row-to-your-overpriced-condo-po-folks-resisting-removal/.

8 Ibid.

9 Jordan T. Camp, "The Housing Question: An Interview with Mike Davis," in *Freedom Now!,* eds. Jordan T. Camp and Christina Heatherton (Los Angeles: Freedom Now, 2012), 82–91, at 91.

termining their own destinies. In addition to the Community Watch program monitoring policing, LACAN runs a nutrition workshop and a community garden that are attuned to the health needs of impoverished people, many of whom are struggling with recovery from addiction and alcoholism while living in a food desert. Other parallel institutions of LACAN include the Downtown Women's Action Coalition that enables women to meet every other week to diagnose and discuss the particularly gendered indignities and abuses they suffer from houselessness and to devise collective solutions to their individual problems. The organization publishes its own newspaper, runs an attractive and informative website, stages hip hop concerts, puts videos online, and organizes an array of events, activities and clubs dedicated to deepening social cohesion and mutual recognition among residents. Civil rights campaigns by LACAN entail marches, demonstrations and non-violent civil disobedience. Grassroots creativity permeates these actions. In one instance, demonstrators wearing plastic handcuffs marched through the downtown streets under banners that proclaimed their demand for "House Keys, Not Hand Cuffs." In addition to dramatizing the folly of spending money to lock people up when they were simply locked out of opportunities to live in decent dwellings, the march also evoked and inverted eerie resonances of the nineteenth-century slave coffle that made a spectacle of parading chained Africans through city streets as a way of emblematizing Black subordination and the power of the white gaze. During another direct-action protest against the cruel but routine seizures by police officers of the abandoned shopping carts that houseless people convert into closets, forms of shelter, and vehicles for transporting their belongings when ordered to "move along," General Dogon customized a cart by painting it orange and black, installing rear view mirrors, and equipping it with a battery-powered sound system. He uses similar creativity to transform bicycles abandoned in vacant lots and dumps into stylized "lowrider" bicycles for use by downtown residents.

The Black Resistance Tradition of New Orleans similarly informs the work of Students at the Center. Classroom exercises deploy the Story Circle pedagogy devised by the Free Southern Theatre in its work with the Student Nonviolent Coordinating Committee in the 1960s. Students studying theater at Tougaloo College in Jackson, Mississippi wanted to bring theater into the freedom struggle emerging around them. They staged performances of *Waiting for Godot* and other works from the Euro-American tradition, but worried that plays relevant to the life circumstances of the sharecroppers and laborers they hoped to reach had not yet been written. They set out to write and commission such works, but they also recruited audiences to be authors through the story circle method. They would convene a discussion among community members and cultural workers. Participants were asked to sit in a circle and speak consecutively about something on their minds, about something that happened to them that day, about something they desired or something they feared. Each participant had to listen carefully and make a statement that recognized the concerns of the previous speaker. From the group discussion, the cultural workers would craft a play that they would have the entire group perform. After the performance, actors and audience members engaged in collective conversation and reflection on the play. When the Free Southern Theatre established its headquarters in New Orleans, local arts activists brought this pedagogy into classroom instruction at local high schools. Students gather each day for eighty-minute SAC classes that follow this pedagogy bequeathed to them by the Black freedom struggle. The students read a wide range of challenging works by canonical authors (Edwidge Danticat, Mark Twain, Virginia Woolf) and write two-paragraph responses connecting the readings to their own lives. Students volunteer to read their paragraphs out loud to the class and then pick two of their classmates to respond and comment.

Just as the ensemble format of the Black music from New Orleans known popularly as "Dixieland" combined individual virtuosity with collective accompaniment and improvisation, SAC classes produce individually authored essays attuned to a collective conversation. These essays grace a series of student authored books published under the aegis of SAC. Available for free online, these books include *The Long Ride* in which students reflect on their relationship to the 1896 Supreme Court case of *Plessy v. Ferguson* which was initiated at a train station located in the Ninth Ward neighborhood where many of the students live. Both the continuities and ruptures of Black life are delineated and analyzed in student writing about past slave rebellions and contemporary mass incarceration, or about their parents' experiences with *de jure* Jim Crow segregation and their own existence in a thoroughly racialized society that purports to be post-racial.[10]

Project Row Houses does its work in the first neighborhood in Houston occupied by free Blacks after emancipation from slavery. The restored El Dorado ballroom where many PRP public gatherings take place faces Emancipation Park, an expanse of land seized and developed by newly freed people at a time when all other public parks in Houston were off-limits to them. The shotgun houses that PRH has been renovating and celebrating since 1994 comprise an enduring presence of an African form of architecture ingeniously reconfigured to meet the exigencies of existence in America. The idea of restoring and honoring row houses initially came to Rick Lowe, one of the seven artists who founded PRH, from the paintings that John Biggers made depicting these houses and especially the women who lived in them as pillars of strength supporting and sustaining the entire Black community. Lowe moved to Houston at a time when city officials considered the row houses to be embarrassing eyesores that needed to be torn down. Armed with the insights permeating the paintings of John Biggers, however, Lowe and his fellow artists discerned value in undervalued edifices. Fresh coats of paint created bright contrasts between the walls of the dwellings and their copper roofs gleaming in the Houston sunlight. Houses positioned close together enabled front porches and sidewalks to function as common community spaces, while small decorations provided dramatic counterpoint to the uniformity of the

---

10 *The Long Ride,* 2nd edn. (New Orleans: Students at the Center, 2011), http://www.sacnola.com/thelongride/.

buildings' design. When Lowe and the other artists began work renovating and redecorating abandoned row houses, people from the area poured forth to help. Individuals with histories of unemployment, substance abuse, and incarceration found meaningful work to do with others. People struggling with illness, poverty, and broken families found common ground and connections that brought out their creative abilities. Discovering value in undervalued things and places proved to provide a path toward discovery of the value residing in undervalued people.

LACAN, SAC, and PRH are always pro-Black, but never only Black. Houselessness, educational inequality, and neighborhood development in the United States require taking anti-Black racism into account. Yet a narrow racialism by itself cannot create the new kind of social charter necessary for a democratic, decent and dignified shared existence. Latinx and white people are a prominent presence inside LACAN's mobilizations. Vietnamese students in New Orleans write about their similarities and their differences from the Black students. Project Row Houses needs alliances and affiliations with Latinx people living in and around the Third Ward to fend off white gentrification. All three groups have attracted allies, advocates, attorneys, and artists who are not Black yet play vital roles in strategic mobilizations. For all three groups, being race-based does not entail being race-bound. For them, race is a matter of culture and condition rather than color, a question of politics rather than of pigment. Their organization and mobilization does not flow from histories of separate bloodlines, but rather from recognition of the dire consequence and somber responsibilities emanating from uneven but shared histories of bloodshed.

The Environmental Health Coalition in San Diego (EHC) mobilizes as a multiracial, multilingual and multinational organization grounded in the historical practices, processes, and politics of the Chicano/a movement and community feminism. Meetings, signs, slogans, and publications carefully balance Spanish and English. The organization communicates its ideas and aspirations through mural art, silkscreen posters, and musical performances that draw on the traditional signs and symbols of Mexican and Mexican-American radicalism. They foreground gender in their organizing by recruiting working class women to become *promotoras* — neighborhood health experts, teachers, and organizers. As individuals, the intersectional challenges these women face from economic marginality coupled with domestic centrality can be overwhelming. As organizers and mobilizers of a community coalition, however, they can do together what they lack the resources to do separately. Working as *promotoras* offers women visible public roles, promotes the development of leadership skills, and creates spaces where women can encounter each other and work together as defenders of their community rather than simply as mothers, wives, daughters, or sisters.

The neighborhoods where the EHC works are treated by urban planners and city officials like diseased limbs that need to be amputated in order to save the rest of the body. Urban renewal and development projects constantly target impoverished areas filled with pollution for destruction and replacement for more profitable uses. Yet in public policy, and often even in medicine, this logic of amputation produces the very problems it purports to prevent. As Patricia J. Williams argues, abandoning poor people and the places in which they live does not make cities healthier or safer.[11] Zones of concentrated pollution produce sick people who need costly medical care and become unable to work. As sacrifice zones become unlivable, desperate people try to flee, but their very desperation then makes them vulnerable to predatory slumlords who charge high rents for dilapidated buildings that are poorly maintained. Amputation does not contain slums, it merely multiplies them. In order to improve their own living conditions, EHC activists find themselves compelled to challenge the logic of amputation that renders them and the places where they live valueless and therefore disposable. They need to find value in undervalued places and the undervalued people who live in them. They have to mobilize, organize, ed-

---

11   Patricia J. Williams, *Seeing a Color-Blind Future: The Paradox of Race* (New York: Noonday, 1998), 11.

ucate, and agitate to make improvement of their conditions a priority of entire cities, counties, and regions. Through organizing and activism, EHC members and allies in National City secured adoption of the Westside Specific development plan, an effort to do city planning from the bottom up based on the EHC's #healthyhoods initiative. Their victory led to the closing of polluting businesses and produced more parks, pedestrian paths, and open spaces, but it also called for priorities and programs based on promoting the health of the whole body (politic) rather than amputating its most imperiled part through plans for affordable solar power and other forms of green development.

The activism of the EHC draws directly on the traditions of resistance and affirmation of the Chicano/a movement. Yet the roster of the group's activists, staff, and allies include men and women of different races with origins in many different places around the world. Dealing with an ecosystem, an economy, and a social formation that traverses both sides of the US–Mexico border precludes any kind of narrow nationalism. Serving a constituency created by a global shake-up that spans several continents in an area penetrated by capital from around the world requires attention to dynamics of difference as well as solidarities of sameness. Seeking to be part of a larger movement for social as well as environmental justice entails invention of new forms of democratic deliberation, debate, and decision making.

Through its formulation of the pan-ethnic identity of the "Asian Immigrant Woman," AIWA attempts to turn negative ascription into positive affirmation. As the group's instructional unit on Asian migration to the US reveals, immigrants to the US from Asia encounter the continuing consequences of centuries of anti-Asian beliefs and practices that lump together Chinese, Korean, Japanese, Vietnamese, Filipino, Thai, and other national groups as interchangeable and forever foreign "Asians." AIWA members teach each other about the Chinese Exclusion Act of 1882, the Gentleman's Agreement with Japan in 1907 and the 1924 Immigration and Naturalization Act. Members learn how US wars in Asia and investments in newly industrializing countries led to changed immigration policies that allowed admission of war brides and refugees, and gave special preference to skilled workers, wealthy individuals, and families seeking reunification. These histories of immigrant exclusion become the basis for discussions about where today's immigrants live, what jobs they can secure, and how they are treated at work, and why employers presume that they can easily exploit and control workers on electronics and garment assembly lines who are, as one manager described them, "small, female and foreign."[12]

AIWA's ideology and practice emerged from collaborative work uniting Asian immigrant women advocates with veterans and inheritors of the Asian American movement. Yet the group has never viewed the plight of Asians as separate from the workings of white supremacy against all aggrieved communities of color. This perspective is especially important in contemporary California where Asian immigrants interact constantly with Black and Latinx people. Lessons about language discrimination provide a generative context for addressing the specific grievances of Asian immigrants without erasing the broader contexts from which they emerge. AIWA's instructional unit on language discrimination delineates how enslaved Africans found their native tongues banned because whites feared rebellions and understood English as a useful tool for controlling, exploiting, and degrading the people they held in bondage. The unit then describes how Native American students forced to attend boarding schools were required to use English and prohibited from using, learning, and developing tribal languages. The unit goes on to detail how English became the official language of the southwest even though Spanish served as an official and popular language in many parts of the region. In this unit, the focus is not on the narrow identities of the injured but on the broad scope of the injury. The obstacles that limited-English speaking women workers experience where they live, work, and play in the US are treated by AIWA as part and parcel of a long history

---

12 Karen Hossfield, "Hiring Immigrant Women: Silicon Valley's 'Simple Formula,'" in *Women of Color in US Society*, eds. Maxine Baca Zinn and Bonnie Thornton Dill (Philadelphia: Temple University Press, 1994), 66.

of conquest, colonization, enslavement, and empire. A separate unit on Latinx immigration tells a story of displacement, dispossession, and deportability, while a lesson on civil rights locates Asian Immigrant Women as the heirs to Rosa Parks. They feel a special affinity with Parks, a seamstress and garment worker whose self-activity proved crucial to mobilizing a mass struggle that changed the racial order in the US in many ways including helping produce the very alterations in immigration law that enabled mass migration from Asia after 1965. Like the Environmental Health Coalition, Project Row Houses, Students at the Center, and the Los Angeles Community Action Network, Asian Immigrant Women Advocates mobilize on the basis of race-based premises that do not entail becoming race-bound.

The forms of opposition advanced by the Los Angeles Community Action Network, Students at the Center, the Environmental Health Coalition, Project Row Houses and Asian Immigrant Women Advocates can appear illogical because they reject short term concessions structured in dominance that will enact long term harm, and they insist on viewing class and gender oppression as constitutive elements of racialized capitalism. Another seemingly illogical dimension of their work stems from their insistence on procedural as well as distributive justice.[13]

Distributive justice concerns the allocation of resources, opportunities and life chances available to members of different groups. As antiracist organizations, these five groups all seek a more equitable distribution of resources. Racial subordination in the US has always been about property as well as pigment, about assets as well as attitudes. By every available measure, racialized communities suffer from the absence of distributive justice. Houseless people living on the streets of downtown Los Angeles, Black students in New Orleans, immigrants residing in sacrifice zones near the US–Mexico border in San Diego, residents of Houston's Third Ward, and low wage limited-English

---

13 Julie Sze et al., "Defining and Contesting Environmental Justice: Socio-natures and the Politics of Scale in the Delta," *Antipode* 41, no.4 (2009): 807–43, https://doi.org/10.1111/j.1467-8330.2009.00698.x.

speaking immigrant workers in Oakland suffer tremendously from the white opportunity hoarding and exploitation enabled by the possessive investment in whiteness. Yet within a structurally racist society, the feasible forms of distributive justice logically offered to aggrieved groups remain structured in dominance. Poor people can get better police protection only if it will lead to "cleaning up" an area like Los Angeles' Skid Row that can then be targeted for redevelopment. Schools in New Orleans can get sorely needed funds if they adhere to regimes of standardized testing that establish educational settings as sites for profitable returns on investment for designers and marketers of tests and modules designed to coach teachers and students through the tests. They can reward a few students as exceptional, thereby excusing the abandonment of the larger number of students deemed disposable. Jobs and business activity can come to areas of south San Diego, but only in the form of firms that make the area a concentrated locus of polluted air, water, and land. Residents of Third Ward neighborhoods in Houston that are starved for capital because of decades of restrictive covenants, mortgage redlining, racial zoning, transit racism, and predatory lending can sell their homes profitably when low land prices and subsidies for developers promote gentrification, but because they must then seek new shelter in an artificially constricted racist housing market, their temporary gains do not translate into valuable assets that can be passed down across generations. Asian Immigrant Women Advocates can win an occasional victory for distributive justice by staging a boycott that secures back wages for victims of wage theft. Yet this victory comes by forcing them to step back from the key goal of developing their long-term potential for collective and accountable leadership. These victories for distributive justice are real, important, and necessary, but they are not sufficient. They do little actually to redistribute wealth, power, and opportunity, and they ultimately serve to frustrate grassroots desires and demands for procedural justice.

Procedural justice concerns the processes through which decisions are reached, the ability of individuals and groups to participate in democratic deliberations about the decisions that

affect their lives. It entails seeking not only the fruits and benefits of collective mobilizations but what Nancy Fraser terms
"participatory parity" in shaping and waging those struggles.[14]
In a society where people with property and political power ex-
ert disproportionate influence, where rationalized and bureaucratic power works to make solving social problems a matter of
technical expertise and efficiency rather than of negotiating differences and courting political agreement, most people exercise
little to no control over the key decisions that affect them. Pas-
sivity and powerlessness plague members of all social groups,
but they are especially deleterious to aggrieved, exploited, and
racialized people whose interests and aspirations are the most
likely to be left out of elite decision making. Antiracist social
movement organizations raising seemingly illogical forms of
opposition, however, fight for processes of collective participation. They argue that houseless people who own little or no
property have every right to inhabit the city and help determine
its future. They recruit high school students to write about the
conditions they encounter in their everyday lives, to participate
in social movement mobilizations, to learn how to find something left to love in themselves and in others in their community
in the midst of oppressive circumstances that can make people
unlovable. They train working-class Latinas to be health *promotoras* — teachers and activists working within community
networks to resist environmental racism and grassroots urban
planners. They turn abandoned shotgun houses into works
of art and in the process create a community that is an ever-
changing living sculpture. They carve away space for women to
meet each other and teach each other in an organization where
they are no longer defined solely by traditional gendered roles as
mothers, daughters, wives, and sisters and to think about what
society would look like if it could tap the experience, ability, and

---

14 Nancy Fraser, "Social Justice in the Age of Identity Politics: Redistribution,
Recognition and Participation," in Nancy Fraser and Axel Honneth, *Re-
distribution or Recognition? A Political Philosophical Exchange* (New York:
Verso, 2003), 7–109.

knowledge of the eyewitnesses to empire, war, migration, language discrimination, sexual harassment, and low-wage labor.

The Logic of Neoliberal Multiculturalism

These grassroots race-based but not race-bound social movements have emerged in opposition to the ways in which neoliberal capitalism and liberal multiculturalism have transformed the terms of racial recognition and subordination. Antiracist struggles by aggrieved groups in the twentieth century succeeded in rendering as politically illegitimate (albeit still widely practiced) the express and overt forms of racial discrimination and segregation that prevailed in the era of industrial capitalism. Being politically illegitimate, however, does not mean that they do not remain in force. The National Fair Housing Alliance estimates that more than four million acts of racially motivated housing discrimination take place every year, even though the Fair Housing Act outlawed such behavior a half century ago. More than sixty years after the Supreme Court's ruling in *Brown v. Board,* schools remain separate and unequal. The one-hundred-and-fifty-year-old promise of the 1866 Civil Rights Act that all persons under the jurisdiction of the United States have the same rights as white people to make contracts and conduct business is still not honored in practice.

Yet the artificial austerity, economic restructuring, evisceration of the social wage, and capital flight attendant to neoliberalism requires a new and revised racial order. A system that seeks to give capital unlimited mobility and power needs to make market identities seem like the only ones that matter. It needs to traverse traditional racial barriers in recruiting workers and consumers from all around the world. Managing a multinational, multilingual, and multiracial world entails incorporation of local differences into a fully linked and integrated global system that is undermined by impediments based on artificial, arbitrary, and irrational considerations rooted in race. To establish and maintain political legitimacy, this system needs to have some dark faces in high places, to have Barack Obama directing drone strikes in Afghanistan, Colin Powell and Condoleezza Rice championing the war in Iraq, John Yoo and Alberto Gonzalez administering regimes of torture and abandonment of *habeas corpus* and due process, to place John B. King in charge of the privatization of public schools, and to authorize Eric Holder and Loretta Lynch to break up immigrant families through mass deportation policies. Through a relentless focus on the individual, and a ruthless suppression of the social, neoliberalism represents race as a private and personal attribute, not a structured system of group advantage and disadvantage. It thus transfers antiracism from the public sphere to the realms of private experience. It proposes technocratic and therapeutic approaches to collective political problems. In the process, it justifies and excuses the cartel of white property and privilege.

Yet the same forces that require this concerted disavowal of race lead to its relentless deployment at the same time. Neoliberal policies and social pedagogies promise prosperity but produce austerity. They stoke desires for individual autonomy but deliver collective vulnerability. They preach accountability but promote irresponsibility. Neoliberalism entails a kind of free market fundamentalism that has no falsifiable hypotheses. When it fails, as it does repeatedly, it needs someone to blame. Here race looms large in the neoliberal imagination. Moral panics about the alleged deficiencies of people of color and other designated scapegoats serve to explain and excuse the failures of the system. When tax cuts for the wealthy destroy government's ability to deliver needed services, immigrants and communities of color are blamed. As Pauline Lipman argues, "the cultural politics of race are central to constructing consent for privatizing public goods, including schools" through oppositions between producer and parasite, between public and private, and even between dependency and freedom as racialized metaphors.[15] The neoliberal version of racialized capitalism entails the perpetuation of racist effects but a prohibition against expressing rac-

---

15 Pauline Lipman, *The New Political Economy of Urban Education: Neoliberalism, Race and the Right to the City* (New York: Routledge, 2012), 12.

ist intent. The collective subordination of communities of color becomes explained as the result of the personal deficiencies of members of those groups. People with problems are treated as if they are problems. In Kalamu ya Salaam's apt formulation, people who control nothing are blamed for everything.[16] Black, Latinx, Asian, and Indigenous identities become synonymous with risk, dependency, and illegality.

The simultaneous disavowal and deployment of race functions to make the entire public sphere seem degraded and unclean. The key to securing and solidifying capitalist power over the past four decades has been what Ian Haney Lopez terms "anti-statist whiteness."[17] For the white working and middle classes, downward mobility is not experienced as a class injury, but instead as a register of the diminishing rewards of whiteness. Because they lack an understanding of capitalism as always already a racialized system, trade unions, professional organizations, political parties, and environmental and feminist organizations have been largely unsuccessful in challenging the logic of neoliberalism. It thus falls to race-based but not race-bound social movement organizations such as LACAN, SAC, EHC, PRH, and AIWA to construct a critique and mobilize a constituency for meaningful social change. Race-based but not race-bound movements challenge the social warrant of neoliberalism by promoting plans, programs, and policies grounded in the needs of those in greatest need, by deepening democratic capacity through creating new arenas for face to face deliberation and collective decision making, by developing new leaders and new understandings of leadership, by finding value in undervalued places and undervalued people, and by creating cultures of mutual recognition and respect that challenge neoliberalism's relentless division of society into an ever increasingly small group

---

16 Kalamu ya Salaam, "Poetic Visions," conference presentation, Annual Meeting of the American Studies Association, Washington, DC, November 5, 2009.

17 Ian Haney Lopez, "Post-Racial Racism: Racial Stratification and Mass Incarceration in the Age of Obama," *California Law Review* 98, no. 3 (June 2010): 1023–74, https://doi.org/10.15779/Z38H696.

considered to be and treated as exceptional and an ever increasingly large group relegated to status and treatment as disposable. In attempting to free themselves, their critiques and campaigns identify ways of knowing and ways of being capable of bringing about broader social change and deepening our collective capacity for democracy.

18

Akira

Colin Masashi Ehara

Last night I had a bad dream:
I was taken away
To a home in Hiroshima
And madness swept it away.
My mother's flesh was decayed by radiation from hatred,
Complacency in the matrix,
And fire burning our faces.
Hell became reality
We got over-seized
Hair and skin began to vanish:
7,000 degrees
Satan stripped our bodies when my family learned
The violence of apocalypse:
Uranium hurts.
And it was blinding like the light when some magnesium burns
Crying to the sky
As human freedom adjourned.
Damn.
I watched my little brother hold intestines in his left hand
Frail from fear while wailing the tears invested in our homeland.
The roof collapsed upon my father
Ruthless acts of plunder brought up
The fact our slumber costs us human family…

DOI: 10.21983/P3.0250.1.21

Sons and Daughters.
I dreamt that certain people's suffering meant far less than oth-
ers
And awoke to find cold design
Oppressive to the youngsters.
Connected the dots
Between today
and that of my dreams talking
Suspecting they were telling me
To quit all my sleepwalking.

My people were dehumanized,
Rehumanized,
Then reinstated(?)
A "model" for minorities
To give consent:
Emasculated.
Concerned in evil wars
As an abomination:
"Jap."
Interned for being "foreign"
In some concentration camps.
Linked with fascists racially
I think the facts seem make-believe
But I'm in sync with raps that grace the scene
To shrink the tragic
Faithfully.
But this narrative ain't dominant.
The consequence of "common sense" is sometimes Colin calls
it quits
When trauma gets to callin' him.
But at least for now I will not say "Shikata ga nai."
Gaman is strong
My word is bond
When hollering rhymes:
Hai!
Step inside the Dojo

Douzou:
Go…go…
Rectify the meaningful and
Flow.
So.
Slow…Mo.
Never let the world tell you what M-P-H the speed of life is
Men forget our Mothers held us:
Our tendency's to feed the virus.
Patriarchy?
Malarkey.
Blown away by freedom tracks
But I bet you when they hear this
They'll just go and call it "emo crap."

And still my common sense inspired me to make mileage
with a confidence that's quiet…
But that ain't silent
And I'm looking for the answers to the riddles in the rhythm
And it's crooked like the cancer in the liver of a victim
Of the bottle
Just like Masashi
His death was awful
And God,
It haunts me.
That's my great uncle and namesake
For those of you that didn't know
Got drafted from internment camps
When murder called his prison's phone
Post-traumatic stress disorder: USA Today
And I hope that karma bless his soul and all that brave the rain.
Because these fast times echo like high ceilings
And
#BlackLivesMatter
#fuckwhitefeelings
Inclusive of my own
I'll be truthful to the dawn

Of new ages
Youth raising
Movements of their own
Hundreds of hands up from racist police
Numb from the damage
But rockin' for peace
Running the planet
Not walking in sleep
Nothing
Goddammit
Is better

To me.

19

Provisional Strategies for Decolonizing Consciousness

Phia S. Salter and Glenn Adams

In 2012, 17-year-old Trayvon Martin was on his way back from a convenience store when he caught the attention of self-appointed neighborhood watch "leader" George Zimmerman. Zimmerman thought the young man looked "real suspicious," so he called the police and decided to pursue Martin despite police dispatch explicitly instructing him not to do so. According to Zimmerman, he got out of his car, confronted Martin, and a physical altercation ensued. Martin had a bag of skittles and a can of iced tea. Zimmerman had a 9-millimeter handgun, which he used to shoot and kill Martin. The case caused national controversy, as authorities did not arrest Zimmerman for 44 days under Florida's "Stand Your Ground" law, and a jury subsequently acquitted him of any wrongdoing.

Perceptions of the case differed sharply as a function of race. According to national polls, 53 percent of white Americans believed that racial bias was a "minor factor" or "not a factor at all" in the events leading up to Martin's death, and 52 percent believed that race made no difference in the authorities' decision not to arrest Zimmerman at the time of the shooting. In contrast, 72 percent of Black Americans indicated racial bias as a major factor in the events leading up to Martin's death, and 73

DOI: 10.21983/P3.0250.1.22

percent thought that authorities would have arrested Zimmerman if Martin had been white versus Black.[1]

Different reactions to the killing of Trayvon Martin are one example of a broader topic that is the subject of our research and this chapter: specifically, racial group differences in perceptions of racism and racial bias. White Americans tend to see much less racism in contemporary US society more generally — especially in events involving police or other government actors — than do people from many racial minority groups.[2] The different reactions also illustrate the incorporation of antiracism movements that is the topic of this volume as a whole. Many Black Americans perceived Martin's murder and Zimmerman's acquittal as another example of how American society and the modern global order degrade, dehumanize, and devalue Black lives. This perception inspired the initial use of the hashtag #BlackLivesMatter, which has since become a rallying call for

---

1   Frank Newport, "Blacks, Nonblacks Hold Sharply Different Views of Martin Case," *Gallup Politics,* April 5, 2012, http://www.gallup.com/poll/153776/blacks-nonblacks-hold-sharply-different-views-martin-case.aspx.

2   "Two-in-three Critical of Bush's Relief Efforts: Huge Racial Divide Over Katrina and Its Consequences," *Pew Research Center,* September 8, 2005, http://www.people-press.org/2005/09/08/two-in-three-critical-of-bushs-relief-efforts/; "Sharp Racial Divisions in Reactions to Brown, Garner Decisions: Many Blacks Expect Police-Minority Relations to Worsen," *Pew Research Center,* December 8, 2014, http://www.people-press.org/2014/12/08/sharp-racial-divisions-in-reactions-to-brown-garner-decisions/#race-as-a-factor-in-the-cases; "On Views of Race and Inequality, Blacks and Whites Are Worlds Apart," *Pew Research Center,* June 27, 2016, http://www.pewsocialtrends.org/2016/06/27/on-views-of-race-and-inequality-blacks-and-whites-are-worlds-apart/. For additional scholarly examples, see Amy L. Ai et al., "Racial Identity–Related Differential Attributions of Inadequate Responses to Hurricane Katrina: A Social Identity Perspective," *Race and Social Problems* 3, no. 1 (2011): 13–24, https://doi.org/10.1007/s12552-011-9039-1; James Kluegel and Lawrence Bobo, "Perceived Group Discrimination and Policy Attitudes: The Sources and Consequences of the Race and Gender Gaps," in *Urban Inequality: Evidence from Four Cities,* eds. Alice O'Connor, Chris Tilly, and Lawrence Bobo (New York: Russell Sage Foundation, 2001), 163–216; Laurie T. O'Brien et al., "Understanding White Americans' Perceptions of Racism in Hurricane Katrina-related Events," *Group Processes & Intergroup Relations* 12, no. 4 (2009): 431–44, https://doi.org/10.1177/1368430209105047.

broader efforts at racial justice.[3] In response, hegemonic institutions have reacted to such antiracism efforts by co-opting them, transforming calls for social justice into calls for equal treatment (i.e., #AllLivesMatter) that neutralize the revolutionary potential of antiracism efforts and erase the historical and cultural context in which racial violence, exploitation, and discrimination persist.

The Colonization of Perception and Consciousness

At the heart of *Antiracism Inc.* is a struggle over the definition and perception of reality: is the US a place of "liberty and justice for all" (as the Pledge of Allegiance claims), or is it a white supremacist state founded and maintained by racial violence? According to a poll with "millennials" aged 14–24, 91 percent of these teens and young adults "believe in equality" and believe "everyone should be treated equally."[4] Yet, a majority of them also believe "it's never fair to give preferential treatment to one race over another, regardless of historical inequalities" (65 percent for People of Color, 74 percent for white). These young people, operating in a neoliberal individualist mode of the modern global order, aspire to be enlightened citizens of the world, free from chauvinistic prejudice, who live with mutual respect and in peaceful harmony with their fellow human beings. They rail against blatant expressions of racism with genuine outrage, and they will occasionally take forceful measures to resist them. Yet, this is an inherently ambiguous move: how does one call for the elimination of racism from a position within the modern global

---

3   The *herstory* of Alicia Garza, Patrisse Cullors, and Opal Tometi and why they created the hashtag #BlackLivesMatter is available on the Black Lives Matters website at http://blacklivesmatter.com/herstory/.

4   "MTV Bias Survey Summary," April 2014, http://d1fqdnmgwphrky.cloudfront. net/studies/000/000/001/DBR_MTV_Bias_Survey_Executive_Summary. pdf; see Jamelle Bouie, "Why Do Millennials Not Understand Racism?" *Slate*, May 16, 2014, http://www.slate.com/articles/news_and_politics/politics/ 2014/05/millennials_racism_and_mtv_poll_young_people_are_confused_ about_bias_prejudice.html.

order or mainstream US institutions while failing to acknowledge the racist historical foundations for those systems?

On one hand, hegemonic narratives that inform mainstream constructions of American identity (rooted in an epistemic perspective of white Americans) propose that the US is essentially good: a shining beacon of human progress and a place of freedom and equality. These narratives do not necessarily dispute difficult-to-deny facts about racial violence (e.g., slavery, legal segregation, lynching) that might seem to contradict celebratory claims about the essentially good character of US society. Instead, they incorporate this knowledge into celebratory accounts of US identity in a way that does not disrupt the status quo and require drastic/revolutionary action to remedy.[5] According to these narratives, the problem of racism is a relatively circumscribed matter at odds with the defining features of contemporary US society, something that the virtuous majority of present-day citizens routinely repudiate in the rare instances when it occurs.

On the other hand, more critical constructions of American identity, often rooted in everyday experience and epistemic perspectives of marginalized racial and ethnic minority communities, provide a very different understanding of US society. These constructions note how the US is a colonial imposition, created when Europeans informed by notions of racial superiority stole land and resources from Indigenous societies, imported enslaved Africans to work and develop the stolen property, and then declared their independence when European rulers began

---

5   Take, for instance, a textbook discussion of the transatlantic slave trade where the authors refer to enslaved Africans as "workers." In cases such as this, even hard to deny facts about racial violence are reinterpreted and re-imagined to render them less damning. Laura Isensee, "Why Calling Slaves 'Workers' is More than an Editing Error," NPR, October 23, 2015, http://www.npr.org/sections/ed/2015/10/23/450826208/why-calling-slaves-workers-is-more-than-an-editing-error. For a discussion of "interpretive silence," see Tuğçe Kurtiş, Glenn Adams, and Michael Yellow Bird, "Generosity or Genocide? Identity Implications of Silence in American Thanksgiving Commemorations," Memory 18, no. 2 (2010): 208–24, https://doi.org/10.1080/09658210903176478.

to restrain these racial depredations. They founded a new nation rooted in revolutionary liberal ideals of individual freedom and representative government, but they deliberately excluded racialized Others from equal-status participation in this project. After a bloody Civil War and decades of struggle, this status quo rooted in racist violence persists. From this perspective, the problem of racism is a defining feature of the American project, something that requires a revolutionary intervention if American society is to achieve the lofty ideals to which it claims to aspire.

These different constructions of American history and identity likely inform the profound gap in perception of racism in US society that we mentioned in the introduction. In our contribution for the *Antiracism, Inc.* collection, we take this ubiquitous gap in perception of reality — whereby white Americans tend to perceive less racism in everyday life and foundational institutions of US society than do people from a variety of racialized ethnic minority groups — as a way to discuss the colonization of consciousness. Discussions of this idea emphasize that conventional or hegemonic understandings are not neutral reflections on objective reality from disinterested observers with a view from nowhere in particular. Rather, they are situated understandings from an epistemic perspective of whiteness that have become common sense via the projection of racial and colonial power. Regardless of one's social identities, participation in mainstream knowledge forms tends to colonize perception, affording understandings of everyday reality that reflect white epistemic perspectives (and affective sensibilities) and promote interests of white racial power.

How is one to understand racial group differences in perception of racism? Prevailing accounts in hegemonic psychological science typically focus on claims of racism by people in ethnic minority communities as the deviant phenomenon that requires explanation.[6] Direct or blatant expressions of this orientation are incredulous reactions to claims of racism and dismissal of

6   For discussion of "effect to be explained," see Peter Hegarty and Felicia Pratto, "The Effects of Social Category Norms and Stereotypes on Explanations

claims as an example of "playing the race card": a purportedly strategic move to exaggerate racial grievance.[7] A more subtle expression of this orientation is the tendency for journalists, scientists, and pollsters to report on group differences in ways that set up white patterns as the unremarkable standard from which racial Others deviate. In particular, such reports are likely to frame differences in perception of racism as "Blacks more likely to say race is a factor"[8] when an equally accurate description of results is that Whites are *less likely* to say that race is a factor.

This typical mode of interpretation constructs white American perceptions of limited racism as an unremarkable standard of rational objectivity. Measured against this standard, the tendency in mainstream institutions is to pathologize perception of racism. Mild versions construct Black American perception of racism as a form of "perceptual baggage":[9] excessive stigma consciousness, racial rejection sensitivity, or a willingness to believe in conspiracy theories.[10] Historically, more extreme ver-

for Intergroup Differences," *Journal of Personality and Social Psychology* 80, no. 5 (2001): 723–35, https://doi.org/10.1037/0022-3514.80.5.723.

7   Tim Wise, "What Kind of Card is Race? The Absurdity (and Consistency) of White Denial," *Counterpunch,* April 24, 2006, http://www.counterpunch.org/2006/04/24/what-kind-of-card-is-race; Rachel Weiner, "Herman Cain and the 'Race Card,'" *Washington Post,* October 10, 2011, http://www.washingtonpost.com/blogs/the-fix/post/herman-cain-and-the-race-card/2011/10/10/gIQAVJsRaLblog.html.

8   "Sharp Racial Divisions in Reactions to Brown, Garner Decisions."

9   James D. Johnson et al., "Variation in Black Anti-White Bias and Target Distancing Cues: Factors that Influence Perceptions of 'Ambiguously Racist' Behavior," *Personality and Social Psychology Bulletin* 29, no. 5 (2003): 609–22, at 621, https://doi.org/10.1177/0146167203029005006.

10 Elizabeth C. Pinel, "Stigma Consciousness: the Psychological Legacy of Social Stereotypes," *Journal of Personality and Social Psychology* 76, no. 1 (1999): 114–28, https://doi.org/10.1037/0022-3514.76.1.114; Rodolfo Mendoza-Denton et al., "Sensitivity to Status-based Rejection: Implications for African American Students' College Experience," *Journal of Personality and Social Psychology* 83, no. 4 (2002): 896–918, https://doi.org/10.1037/0022-3514.83.4.896; Jennifer Crocker et al., "Belief in US Government Conspiracies Against Blacks Among Black and White College Students: Powerlessness or System Blame?" *Personality and Social Psychology Bulletin* 25, no. 8 (1999): 941–53.

sions have linked Black American perceptions of racism with irrational fear and akin to paranoia. Black Americans who expressed a general mistrust of white society (i.e., cultural mistrust) were more likely to be misdiagnosed as schizophrenic or otherwise disturbed.[11] These constructions of racism perception as paranoia or exaggeration imply that Black communities are somewhat out of touch with reality in ways that white communities are not.

In summary, hegemonic knowledge systems obscure the operation of racial power and enable otherwise civic-minded people to insulate themselves from knowledge of their participation in the ongoing subordination of global humanity. Social justice advocates seek to illuminate the everyday racism of modern society in order to resist it. In response, defenders of social order seek to incorporate, domesticate, and assimilate understandings about racism — primarily considering it as individual bias and hostile racial animus — in ways that do not fundamentally disrupt the status quo. In this way, the definition and perception of racism becomes a central site of social struggle.

Decolonizing Perception and Consciousness

Resistance to the incorporation of antiracism requires strategies for decolonizing consciousness. The activity of intellectual decolonization is necessary both to counteract the (often apparently progressive) forms of knowledge that promote ignorance about ongoing racial domination and to illuminate ways of being that ensure a more just and sustainable existence for the im-

---

11 Arthur L. Whaley, "Cultural Mistrust and Mental Health Services for African Americans: A Review and Meta-Analysis," *Counseling Psychologist* 29, no. 4 (2001): 513–31, https://doi.org/ 10.1177/0011000001294003; Arthur L. Whaley, "A Two-stage Method for the Study of Cultural Bias in the Diagnosis of Schizophrenia in African Americans," *Journal of Black Psychology* 30, no. 2 (2004): 167–86, https://doi.org/10.1177/0095798403262062; Steven J. Trierweiler et al., "Clinician Attributions Associated with the Diagnosis of Schizophrenia in African American and Non-African American Patients," *Journal of Consulting and Clinical Psychology* 68, no. 1 (2000): 171–75, https://doi.org/10.1037/0022-006X.68.1.171.

poverished global majority. Although very much a theoretical exercise, the task of intellectual decolonization is a key element of the practical struggle against racism and injustice. This imperative task of resistance has commonalities across a variety of liberatory thought traditions (e.g., decolonial, critical race, and liberation theology/philosophy)[12] and global social movements (e.g., Black Power, Chicanx, American Indian, Négritude, Pan-African, and Indian Independence Movements).[13] Though the idea of decolonizing consciousness itself does not reflect a single genealogy, it takes inspiration from several twentieth century scholars and activists including W.E.B. Du Bois, Mahatma Ghandi, Aimé Césaire, Frantz Fanon, and Gloria Anzaldúa among many others.[14] In writing about colonial resistance, they each illuminate the epistemic violence by which global institutions forcefully impose understandings and practices from powerful geopolitical centers to relatively powerless peripheries in ways that maintain systems of exploitation and domination. Intellectual frameworks derived from these thought traditions

---

12 For example: Kimberlé Williams Crenshaw, "Twenty Years of Critical Race Theory: Looking Back to Move Forward," *Connecticut Law Review* 43, no. 5 (2010): 12–53; Frantz Fanon, *The Wretched of the Earth,* trans. Constance Farrington (New York: Grove Press, 1963); Ignacio Martín-Baró, *Writings for a Liberation Psychology* (Cambridge: Harvard University Press, 1994); Walter D. Mignolo, "Decolonizing Western Epistemology / Building Decolonial Epistemologies," in *Decolonizing Epistemologies: Latina/o Theology and Philosophy,* eds. Ada María Isasi-Díaz and Eduardo Mendieta (New York: Fordham University Press, 2011), 19–43.

13 Penny M. Von Eschen, *Race against Empire: Black Americans and Anticolonialism* (Ithaca: Cornell University Press, 1997); Teresa Cordova, "Anti-Colonial Chicana Feminism," in *Latino Social Movements: Historical and Theoretical Perspectives,* eds. Rodolfo D. Torres and George Katsiaficas (New York: Routledge, 1999), 11–41; Vine Deloria, *Custer Died for Your Sins: An Indian Manifesto* (Norman: University of Oklahoma Press, 1969); Reiland Rabaka, *The Negritude Movement: W.E.B. Du Bois, Leon Damas, Aimé Césaire, Leopold Senghor, Frantz Fanon, and the Evolution of an Insurgent Idea* (Lanham: Lexington, 2015).

14 Nelson Maldonado-Torres, "Thinking Through the Decolonial Turn: Post-Continental Interventions in Theory, Philosophy, and Critique — An Introduction," *Transmodernity: Journal of Peripheral Cultural Production of the Luso-Hispanic World* 1, no. 2 (2011): 1–15.

advocate preferential consideration for epistemic perspectives of oppressed peoples as a privileged standpoint from which to understand everyday life in modern global order.[15]

Applied to the present case of differences in perception of racism, the idea of a preferential epistemic option implies taking subordinated group experience as a standpoint for understanding everyday events. Associated with this approach are two provisional strategies for decolonizing consciousness: *normalizing* racism perception and *denaturalizing* racism denial. We refer to these strategies as *provisional* in two senses of the word: both (a) something in process awaiting refinement, and (b) something useful to bring on a journey.[16] In similar fashion, the idea of *decolonizing consciousness* refers both to the process of interrogating existing tools for the production of particular kinds of (un) consciousness and the production of knowledge tools that are useful for this purpose.

The first strategy for decolonization of consciousness is to provide a context-sensitive, normalizing account of Other patterns that hegemonic accounts and psychological science regard as abnormal.[17] Rather than lack of contact with reality, this normalizing strategy suggests that one consider how apparently "paranoid" perceptions of racism may reflect engagement with ecologically valid forms of knowledge that promote racial con-

---

15 See contemporaneous scholarship such as Paulo Freire's (1968) *Pedagogy of the Oppressed* (London: Bloomsbury Academic, 2000), Orlando Fals-Borda's work on participatory action research methodologies, "The Application of Participatory Action-Research in Latin America," *International Sociology* 2, no. 4 (1987): 329–47, https://doi.org/10.1177/026858098700200401, and Linda Tuhiwai Smith's *Decolonizing Methodologies: Research and Indigenous Peoples* (New York: Zed Books, 1999) advocate this perspective when decolonizing consciousness in research and practice.

16 Our use of *provisional* follows Alison Reed's discussion of "queer provisionality" during meetings of the Antiracism Inc. group in April 2013. See also Alison Reed, "Queer Provisionality: Mapping the Generative Failures of the 'Transborder Immigrant Tool'," *Lateral* 4 (2015), https://doi.org/10.25158/L4.1.4.

17 Glenn Adams and Phia S. Salter, "Health Psychology in African Settings: A Cultural-Psychological Analysis," *Journal of Health Psychology* 12, no. 3 (2007): 539–51, https://doi.org/10.1177/1359105307076240.

sciousness. As an example of this strategy, consider our work on the *Marley Hypothesis*: the idea that perception of racism in US society reflects accurate knowledge about historically documented instances of past racism.[18] Black and white Americans completed a true-false test of statements about incidents of racism in US history. Black participants performed better on the test — that is, they were more likely than white participants to confidently identify historically documented instances of racism as true, but they were no more likely to incorrectly identify fake/fictional items as true — and this Black-white difference in accurate knowledge of past racism accounted for the Black-white difference in perception of present-day racism. The normalizing implication is that Black American tendencies to perceive racism are not distortions of reality (e.g., strategic exaggeration), but instead constitute realistic concerns about enduring manifestations of racism that are finely attuned to accurate knowledge about American history.

The second strategy for decolonization of consciousness is to "turn the analytic lens" back on hegemonic knowledge forms to denaturalize the patterns that these forms portray as a just-natural standard.[19] In the present case, the hegemonic knowledge form is the unmarked (and unnamed) white norm to minimize or deny racism in US society and the modern global order. Applied to this case, this strategy of denaturalization suggests that white American tendencies are not an unremarkable reflection of objective reality. Instead, they reflect cultural-psychological processes that lead people to minimize or deny the true extent of racism. From this perspective, the phenomenon that requires explanation in not (only) subordinated group perception of racism (i.e., Blacks see *more* racism), but (also) dominant group denial of racism (i.e., whites see *less* racism). Racism denial is

---

18 Jessica C. Nelson, Glenn Adams, and Phia S. Salter, "The Marley Hypothesis: Racism Denial Reflects Ignorance of History," *Psychological Science* 24, no. 2, (2013): 213–18, https://doi.org/ 10.1177/0956797612451466.

19 Adams and Salter, "Health Psychology in African Settings," 542.

not a natural reflection of objective reality but reflects operation of important sociocultural and psychological processes.

Our own and others' research generally points to two sources of white racism denial. One source is motivated perception or wishful thinking. Perception of racism in US society is threatening to white identity because the continuity of past and present-day racism calls into question the merit of whites' advantaged status, the morality of the nation, and the broader legitimacy of the status quo. As a result of these identity threats, white Americans are motivated to deny the pervasiveness of racism in American society.[20] When researchers use experimental techniques (e.g., self-affirmation strategies) to temporarily neutralize these social identity threats, they observe that white Americans perceive greater racism[21] and are more willing to acknowledge systemic forms of racism and privilege.[22]

A second source of white denial of racism is cultural knowledge. Even if people could put aside identity-defensive motivations and weigh questions about racism in an unbiased fashion, a focus on cultural knowledge suggests that white Americans might still deny the extent of racism in the US because they lack information about and experience with racism-relevant realties. In other words, white Americans fail to perceive racism because

20 Nyla R. Branscombe, Michael T. Schmitt, and Kristin Schiffhauer, "Racial Attitudes in Response to Thoughts of White Privilege," *European Journal of Social Psychology* 37, no. 2 (2007): 203–15, https://doi.org/10.1002/ejsp.348; Eric D. Knowles et al., "On the Malleability of Ideology: Motivated Construals of Color Blindness," *Journal of Personality and Social Psychology* 96, no. 4 (2009): 857–69, https://doi.org/10.1037/a0013595; Brian S. Lowery, Eric D. Knowles, and Miguel M. Unzueta, "Framing Inequity Safely: Whites' Motivated Perceptions of Racial Privilege," *Personality and Social Psychology Bulletin* 33, no. 9 (2007): 1237–50, https://doi.org/10.1177/0146167207303016.

21 Glenn Adams, Teceta Thomas Tormala, and Laurie T. O'Brien, "The Effect of Self-Affirmation on Perception of Racism," *Journal of Experimental Social Psychology* 42, no. 5 (2006): 616–26, https://doi.org/10.1016/j.jesp.2005.11.001.

22 Miguel M. Unzueta and Brian S. Lowery, "Defining Racism Safely: The Role of Self-Image Maintenance on White Americans' Conceptions of Racism," *Journal of Experimental Social Psychology* 44, no. 6 (2008): 1491–97, http://doi.org/10.1016/j.jesp.2008.07.011.

they inhabit information ecologies that enable them to remain ignorant about the extent of racism in US society.

One example of relevant cultural knowledge is representations of history. Just as Black American perceptions of racism have roots in greater knowledge of historical racism, white American denials of racism have roots in greater ignorance of historical racism. As we discuss in a subsequent section, representations of history vary in their attention to past racism, and this variation has consequences for perception of present-day racism. Again, as research on the Marley Hypothesis demonstrates, accurate knowledge about incidents of past racism is associated with tendencies to perceive greater racism in present-day society.[23]

Another example of relevant cultural knowledge is definitions of racism. Even when hegemonic representations of history do address past racism, they frequently construct it as the product of "a few bad apples" limited to a few rogue individuals.[24] This construction resonates with white sensibilities. Research suggests that a majority of white Americans endorse a conception of racism as hostile, individual prejudice rather than something embedded in the structure of society.[25] In contrast, Black Americans tend to endorse a more systemic conception of racism, which reflects and promotes a more expansive understanding of the way that racism operates in US society and the modern global order.

---

23 Nelson et al., "The Marley Hypothesis."
24 James W. Loewen, *Lies My Teacher Told Me: Everything Your American History Textbook Got Wrong* (New York: New Press, 2008).
25 Victoria M. Esses and Gordon Hodson, "The Role of Lay Perceptions of Ethnic Prejudice in the Maintenance and Perpetuation of Ethnic Bias," *Journal of Social Issues* 62, no. 3 (2006): 453–68, https://doi.org/10.1111/j.1540-4560.2006.00468.x; O'Brien et al., "Understanding White Americans' Perceptions of Racism"; Samuel R. Sommers and Michael I. Norton, "Lay Theories About White Racists: What Constitutes Racism (and What Doesn't)," *Group Processes & Intergroup Relations* 9, no. 1 (2006): 117–38, https://doi.org/10.1177/1368430206059881.

Contesting Incorporation: Tools for Colonial and Decolonial Consciousness

The problem with classic distinction between motivated and informational sources perceptual bias is that it can treat informational sources as politically neutral or disinterested cultural differences.[26] In other worlds, it fails to understand the extent to which different cultural realities are "intentional worlds," sites of struggle invested with beliefs and desires of people who create and reproduce them.[27] An emphasis on the intentionality of everyday worlds highlights the extent to which hegemonic institutions in US society have evolved in accordance with the imperative to promote white comfort. White racial power exerts pressure on the evolution of cultural forms, as cultural gatekeepers select understandings of history and society that promote white comfort and omit or deselect understandings that promote white discomfort.[28] This is the domain of *Antiracism Inc.*: institutions that have emerged — sometimes intentionally,

---

26 For a related discussion of the constant interaction and overlap between motivated group interests and inference (perception, memory, ideology), see Charles W. Mills, "White Ignorance," in *Race and Epistemologies of Ignorance*, eds. Shannon Sullivan and Nancy Tuana (Albany: SUNY Press, 2007), 11–38.

27 See Richard A. Shweder, "Cultural Psychology: What Is It?" in *Cultural Psychology: Essays on Comparative Human Development,* eds. James Stigler, Richard Shweder, and Gilbert Herdt (Cambridge: Cambridge University Press, 1990): 1–44. For a more recent articulation, see Glenn Adams, "Context in Person, Person in Context: A Cultural Psychology Approach to Social-Personality Psychology," in *Oxford Handbook of Personality and Social Psychology,* eds. Kay Deaux and Mark Snyder (New York: Oxford University Press, 2012), 182–208; Phia S. Salter and Glenn Adams, "On the Intentionality of Cultural Products: Representations of Black History as Psychological Affordances," *Frontiers in Psychology* 7, art. 1166 (2016): 1–21, https://doi.org/10.3389/fpsyg.2016.01166; George Lipsitz, *The Possessive Investment in Whiteness: How White People Profit from Identity Politics* (Philadelphia: Temple University Press, 2006).

28 See Zeus Leonardo and Logan Manning, "White Historical Activity Theory: Toward a Critical Understanding of White Zones of Proximal Development," *Race Ethnicity and Education* 20, no. 1 (2017): 15–29; http://doi.org/10.1080/13613324.2015.1100988. See, also, Paula Ioanide, *The Emotional Poli-*

but often unwittingly through acts of barely conscious selection based on unrecognized preferences — because they serve needs of people advantaged by domination to produce constructions of reality that represent and "define racism safely."[29]

Incorporating Black History: Celebrating Diversity or Ignoring Racism?

When Carter G. Woodson created the institution of Black History Month (BHM), he believed that the commemoration practice not only would instill racial pride within the African American community, but also would introduce an antiracist consciousness among white Americans.[30] As mainstream American society increasingly incorporated BHM, this cultural tool evolved to serve a variety of different purposes.[31] Some expressions of BHM — for example, advertisements for Budweiser proclaiming that "this chapter of history brought to you by the king of beer" — are clearly tangential (or even antithetical) to the original purpose of antiracism education.[32] In such cases, BHM becomes another opportunity for corporations to advertise

---

tics of Racism: How Feelings Trump Facts in an Era of Colorblindness (Stanford: Stanford University Press, 2015).

29 Unzueta and Lowery, "Defining Racism Safely."

30 Pero Gaglo Dagbovie, "Making Black History Practical and Popular: Carter G. Woodson, the Proto Black Studies Movement, and the Struggle For Black Liberation," Western Journal of Black Studies 28, no. 2 (2004): 372–83; Carter G. Woodson, The Mis-education of the Negro (San Diego: Book Tree, 2006).

31 Abul Pitre and Ruth Ray, "The Controversy around Black History," Western Journal of Black Studies 26, no. 3 (2002): 149–54.

32 Hailey Persinger, "'Black History' Beer Poster Makes a Stir: Budweiser Sponsored the Commemoration of Kings and Queens of Africa," San Diego Union-Tribune, February 16, 2011, http://www.utsandiego.com/news/2011/feb/16/black-history-beer-poster-makes-a-stir/. See also John Hope Franklin et al., "Black History Month: Serious Truth Telling or a Triumph in Tokenism?" Journal of Blacks in Higher Education 18 (1998): 87–92, https://doi.org/10.2307/2998774; Pero Gaglo Dagbovie, "'Of All Our Studies, History is Best Qualified to Reward our Research': Black History's Relevance to the Hip Hop Generation," Journal of African American History 90, no. 3 (2005): 299–323, https://doi.org/10.1086/JAAHv90n3p299.

products to a niche market and thereby profit at the expense of oppressed communities. However, even expressions of BHM that share the goal of antiracism education can vary in effectiveness. Many institutions have incorporated BHM into school programming and curricula for educational purposes, but it is not clear to what extent these efforts have realized Woodson's original mission of promoting antiracism.

In general, representations of American history tend to glorify the heroic efforts of a few individuals and to sanitize identity-threatening versions of the past.[33] The desire to silence events and reemphasize the good of the nation are amplified in cases where the events under consideration — enslavement, rape and torture, segregation, and terroristic violence — are crimes against humanity. This raises a problem for the incorporation of BHM commemoration practices into mainstream US society, because such violent events are central to the collective narrative identity of Black Americans.[34] Despite its relevance to the topic, research that we conducted in Midwest US high schools revealed that BHM commemorations typically silenced memory of such violence via (at least) two sanitizing strategies. One strategy is to highlight individual Black American achievement — whether inventors, intellectuals or Civil Rights heroes — while minimizing the historical barriers that these individuals faced or the collective struggle to eliminate those barriers.[35] Another strategy is to direct discussions about Black history toward multicultural tolerance and diversity instead of focusing on the ongoing legacy of systemic expropriation, exploitation, and violent oppression.[36] We saw this strategy appear to a greater extent in

---

33 Loewen, *Lies My Teacher Told Me*.

34 Ron Eyerman, "The Past in the Present: Culture and the Transmission of Memory," *Acta Sociologica* 47, no. 2 (2004): 159–69, https://doi.org/10.1177/0001699304043853.

35 Wayne Journell, "When Oppression and Liberation are the Only Choices: The Representation of African Americans Within State Social Studies Standards," *Journal of Social Studies Research* 32, no. 1 (2008): 40–50, at 40. See also Pitre and Ray, "The Controversy Around Black History."

36 Glenn Adams et al., "Beyond Prejudice: Toward a Sociocultural Psychology of Racism and Oppression," in *Commemorating Brown: The Social Psychol-*

predominately white schools, where BHM materials highlighted contemporary issues of multiculturalism and diversity rather than historical events specifically.[37]

Implications for Antiracism Efforts

BHM representations are a tool for the production of both knowledge and ignorance about racism. To illustrate how constructions of history afford reproduction of ignorance, first consider implications for the focus of antiracism efforts. Acceptable antiracism efforts within mainstream US institutions require incorporation of sanitized narratives that maintain an image of the US and its citizens as ultimately good. In the case of BHM, mainstream institutions affirm their dedication to diversity (versus social justice) by celebrating BHM with stories highlighting the many contributions of African Americans to US history. The presence of celebratory narratives helps us remember the events about which we can be proud. At the same time, the silences embedded in historical erasure facilitate collective forgetting of those events that afford shame or guilt. The problem with reproducing sanitized versions of history is that, instead of critically addressing the relationship between historical racism and present-day inequality, silence about racism obscures this relationship. Slavery, Jim Crow, and other forms of state-sanctioned violence are at the foundation of many social-psychological, economic, and structural barriers manifest in current day racial disparities. Silence about these historical realities in BHM commemorations promotes collective forgetting and deflects attention away from structural barriers that continue to impact people of African descent.

---

ogy of Racism and Discrimination, eds. Glenn Adams et al. (Washington, DC: American Psychological Association, 2008), 215–46; Stephen C. Wright and Micah E. Lubensky, "The Struggle for Social Equality: Collective Action Versus Prejudice Reduction," in Intergroup Misunderstandings: Impact of Divergent Social Realities, eds. Stephanie Demoulin, Jacques-Philippe Leyens, and John F Dovidio (New York: Psychology Press, 2009), 291–310.

37 Salter and Adams, "On the Intentionality of Cultural Products."

Like the emphasis on tolerance and diversity, the emphasis on heroic and individual achievement also deflects attention from structural barriers. However, this emphasis has the added advantage of resonating with such dominant group ideologies as colorblindness, meritocracy, and protestant work ethic. These ideologies afford the tendency to blame minority group disadvantage on group characteristics rather than systemic forces embedded in the foundations of American society.[38]

Implications for Perception of Racism

Similar to predominantly white schools, representations of BHM from predominantly Black schools also emphasized Black individual achievement. In contrast, and unlike predominantly white schools, representations of BHM in predominantly Black schools made more explicit references to historical racism.[39] This difference in emphasis has important implications for perception of racism and support for antiracist policy. In particular, empirical evidence from two studies indicated that BHM representations typical of schools where Black students were in the majority were more effective at promoting perceptions of racism in US society compared to BHM representations typical of predominately white schools. In the first study, participants engaged with actual BHM materials sampled from commemoration displays in predominantly Black or white Midwestern high schools. In the second study, participants engaged with BHM narratives inspired by the differences we observed in the materials: celebratory representations of Black history that emphasized past achievements of Black Americans, critical representations

---

38 John T. Jost, Mahzarin R. Banaji, and Brian A. Nosek, "A Decade of System Justification Theory: Accumulated Evidence of Conscious and Unconscious Bolstering of the Status Quo," *Political Psychology* 25, no. 6 (2004): 881–919, https://doi.org/10.1111/j.1467-9221.2004.00402.x; Shana Levin et al., "Ethnic Identity, Legitimizing Ideologies, and Social Status: A Matter of Ideological Asymmetry," *Political Psychology* 19, no. 2 (1998): 373–404, https://doi.org/10.1111/0162-895X.00109.

39 Salter and Adams, "On the Intentionality of Cultural Products."

that emphasized historical instances of racism, or mainstream representations of US history that rendered people of African descent invisible. Participants exposed to critical representations not only perceived greater racism in US society, but also indicated greater support for policies designed to ameliorate racial inequality than did participants in the other two conditions. The impact of critical history knowledge on perception is important because, in both studies, perceptions of racism facilitated support for antiracism policies. This research helps to illuminate how white institutional spaces reproduce racism by promoting constructions of the past that fail to mention instances of racist oppression.[40] Sanitized representations of the past minimize perception of racism in present, which undermines support for antiracism policies.

Defining Racism Safely: The Prejudice Problematic

Another epistemic tool that affords ignorance of racism concerns what scholar Margaret Wetherell has referred to as the "prejudice problematic": a way of understanding racism that locates the foundations of the problem in the stereotypical beliefs, prejudicial evaluations, and learned associations of individual minds.[41] Early theorists of prejudice, most notably Gordon Allport, focused on racial dynamics in terms of individual expressions of antipathy and hostility towards a group or its members

---

40 Salter and Adams, "On the Intentionality of Cultural Products"; Carol Schick and Verna St. Denis, "Troubling National Discourses in Anti-Racist Curricular Planning," *Canadian Journal of Education/Revue Canadienne de L'éducation* 28, no. 3 (2005): 295–317, https://doi.org/10.2307/4126472. For a discussion of white institutional space more broadly, see Wendy Leo Moore, *Reproducing Racism: White Space, Elite Law Schools, and Racial Inequality* (Lanham: Rowman and Littlefield, 2008).

41 Margaret Wetherell, "The Prejudice Problematic," in *Beyond Prejudice: Extending the Social Psychology of Conflict, Inequality, and Social Change,* eds. John Dixon and Mark Levine (Cambridge: Cambridge University Press, 2012): 158–78.

based on (false) generalizations or stereotypes.[42] Though some researchers began to consider broader group-level explanations for racial prejudice in the mid-1960s and early 1970s (because conceptions of individual prejudice failed to account for the institutionalized nature of racism that was the focus of the Civil Rights Movement in the US),[43] the root cause was still largely considered the problem of biased individuals who discriminate. Notably, even today, this individual level understanding of racism is more prominent among white Americans than People of Color[44] and despite efforts to shift academic discourse toward discussions of systemic racism, prejudice models continue to inform contemporary conceptions of racism in mainstream institutions such as law, politics, and hegemonic social science.[45] Indeed, within academia, this understanding of racism is perhaps nowhere more evident than in our home discipline of psychological science.

One problem with the prejudice problematic is its location within the broader, neoliberal individualist ways of being and associated forms of knowledge that inform standard accounts in hegemonic social science. Perspectives of decolonial theory emphasize the extent to which these forms of knowledge are not an objectively neutral or politically innocent understanding of social reality, but instead reflect the racial power of colonial violence.[46] From this perspective, the very possibility of modern/

42 Gordon Allport, *The Nature of Prejudice* (Cambridge: Addison-Wesley, 1954); Todd D. Nelson, *The Psychology of Prejudice* (Boston: Allyn and Bacon, 2006).

43 James M. Jones, *Prejudice and Racism* (New York: McGraw-Hill, 1997); Stokely Carmichael and Charles Hamilton, *Black Power: The Politics of Liberation* (New York: Random House, 1967).

44 "On Views of Race and Inequality."

45 "On Views of Race and Inequality"; Alan David Freeman, "Legitimizing Racial Discrimination Through Antidiscrimination Law: A Critical Review of Supreme Court Doctrine," *Minnesota Law Review* 62 (1977): 1049–19; Leah N. Gordon, *From Power to Prejudice: The Rise of Racial Individualism in Midcentury America* (Chicago: University of Chicago Press, 2015).

46 Glenn Adams, Sara Estrada-Villalta, and Luis H. Gómez Ordóñez, "The Modernity/Coloniality of Being: Hegemonic Psychology as Intercultural Relations," *International Journal of Intercultural Relations* 62 (2017):

individualist subjectivity/positionality rests upon the colonial violence that provided a privileged few (at the expense of the vast majority) with sufficient affluence to enable the sense of freedom from constraint and independence from context associated with modern individualism. However, the reference to coloniality is not only a comment on the origins of modern individualism in racial violence, but also refers to the consequence of associated knowledge forms for the ongoing *reproduction* of racial violence.

Implications for Antiracism Efforts

To illustrate how individualist constructions of person — and the prejudice problematic in particular — afford reproduction of violence, consider implications for the focus of antiracism efforts. Simply put, a conception of racism as individual prejudice suggests a focus of antiracism efforts on reduction of this prejudice.[47] One problem with this conception of antiracism efforts is that transforms the historically particular problem of white supremacist violence and European global domination into a more general issue of equipotential intergroup intolerance. In other words, it regards anti-white prejudice among people of

---

13–22, https://doi.org/10.1016/j.ijintrel.2017.06.006; Nelson Maldonado-Torres, "On the Coloniality of Being: Contributions to the Development of a Concept," *Cultural Studies* 21, no. 2-3 (2007): 240–70, https://doi.org/10.1080/09502380601162548; Walter Mignolo, *The Darker Side of Western Modernity: Global Futures, Decolonial Options* (Durham: Duke University Press, 2011).

47 Indeed, resonating with a prevailing conception that equates racism with individual prejudice, influential work in social psychology and interventions based on this work have tended to emphasize prejudice reduction and equipotential intergroup tolerance rather than more powerful interventions to disrupt the embedded structural racism of the colonial present. See John Dixon et al., "'Let Them Eat Harmony': Prejudice-Reduction Strategies and Attitudes of Historically Disadvantaged Groups," *Current Directions in Psychological Science* 19, no. 2 (2010): 76–80, https://doi.org/10.1177/0963721410363366. See also Phillip Hammack, *Narrative and the Politics of Identity: The Cultural Psychology of Israeli and Palestinian Youth* (Oxford: Oxford University Press, 2011).

African descent to be just as problematic as anti-Black prejudice among people of European descent.[48] The result of this conception of racism as equipotential prejudice — any endorsement of intergroup bias regardless of power differentials and historical context — is an #AllLivesMatter approach to antiracism action that focuses on equal treatment regardless of race, while conveniently forgetting the downstream effects of differential treatment set in motion by centuries-old colonial violence that continue to reproduce the unjust status quo.

This suggests a second problem with the conception of antiracism efforts as prejudice reduction. It transforms problems of structural injustice into problems of tolerance and interpersonal emotion. In response to people who express indignation about enduring structural racism, this expression of Antiracism, Inc. asks "can't we all just get along?" In response to the masses who express a deep hunger for social justice, this expression of Antiracism, Inc. replies "Let them eat harmony."[49] That is, let the suffering masses be content with knowledge that (most) people bear them no ill feeling or racial animus. This construction of antiracist action delegitimizes and attenuates indignation about historical and ongoing injustice, leads people to trade justice for peace and harmony, and contributes to the reproduction of an unjust status quo by undermining motivation for resistance.

---

48 The prevalent appeal of this idea in US society is evident in the frequency of questions about anti-white racism and the possibility of Black racists. Our response to such questions is to distinguish between prejudice and racism. Although it is possible (and perhaps adaptive) for people of color in the US to harbor a healthy suspicion or even *prejudice* toward white Americans, this is not what we mean by racism. Instead, we reserve the use of *racism* to refer to beliefs or actions that promote white Supremacy. From this perspective, a person of color performs racism not by harboring biases that portray white people in a negative light (e.g., as potential perpetrators of racism), but instead by acting in ways (e.g., engaging in discriminatory hiring practices by declaring a candidate's name too "ghetto") that ultimately serve the interests of white Supremacy.

49 Dixon et al., "'Let Them Eat Harmony.'"

Implications for Perception of Racism

As another illustration of how conceptions of racism as individual bias afford reproduction of violence, consider implications for perception of racism and support for antiracist policy or collective action. By locating the foundations of racism in individual bias, the prejudice problematic understates the extent to which racism causes harm. In particular, it limits the notion of racism to cases where one person engages in differential treatment toward another person, whether as a result of deliberate prejudice or less conscious bias. It does not admit the possibility of racism via disparate impact, whereby the similar treatment results in systematically different outcomes for racially advantaged and disadvantaged targets. Nor does it admit the possibility of racism embedded in the structure of American society.[50] A person who draws upon this conception to make judgments about the extent of racism in American society or about the role of racism in particular events is likely to focus on the beliefs and attitudes of the people involved. Given that a large proportion of people in US society claim non-racist ideology, the person is likely to conclude that racism is not a plausible explanation for differential outcomes, and this conclusion is likely to undermine the person's support for forceful antiracism measures.

It follows from this reasoning that an important intervention to counteract epistemologies of ignorance is to promote conceptions of racism as a force embedded in the structure of American society. Evidence for this assertion comes from two experiments in which researchers exposed social psychology students to either a "sociocultural" tutorial that defined racism in structural terms or a more standard tutorial that defined racism as individual bias (i.e., the prejudice problematic). Results of both experiments confirmed that students not only, (1) tended to perceive greater racism in everyday events, but also, (2) showed greater endorsement of forceful antiracist policy after exposure to the tutorial outlining a sociocultural conception of

---

50 Adams et al., "Beyond Racism."

racism (i.e., as a force embedded in the structure of modern society) than after exposure to a more standard tutorial rooted in the prejudice problematic.[51]

Conclusion: How to (Re)produce Decolonial Consciousness

In this chapter, we presented two provisional strategies to decolonize consciousness. We applied these strategies to consider group differences in perception of racism. The first strategy is to provide a context-sensitive, normalizing account of oppressed group patterns that hegemonic accounts portray as abnormal. The second strategy is to "turn the analytic lens" and denaturalize white American tendencies of racism denial that mainstream accounts portray as unbiased reflection of objective reality.[52] The foundation of these decolonizing strategies lies in a preferential consideration for epistemic perspectives of the oppressed as a privileged standpoint from which to understand everyday life in modern global order.[53] This suggests that an important direction for antiracism action is cultivation of opportunities for people to engage with marginalized epistemic perspectives.

Like other hegemonic institutions in us society, universities have evolved in accordance with the imperative to promote white comfort. This is perhaps especially true in the context of the neoliberal university, in which instructors face increasing pressure to offer the products that consumers (a.k.a. students)

---

51 Glenn Adams et al., "Teaching about Racism: Pernicious Implications of the Standard Portrayal," *Basic and Applied Social Psychology* 30, no. 4 (2008): 349–61, https://doi.org/10.1080/01973530802502309.

52 Ibid.

53 See Glenn Adams et al., "Decolonizing Psychological Science: Introduction to the Special Thematic Section," *Journal of Social and Political Psychology* 3, no. 1 (2015): 213–38, https://doi.org/10.5964/jspp.v3i1.564; Jean Comaroff and John L. Comaroff, "Theory from the South: Or, How Euro-America is Evolving Toward Africa," *Anthropological Forum: A Journal of Social Anthropology and Comparative Sociology* 22, no. 2 (2011): 113–31, https://doi.org/10.1080/00664677.2012.694169; Boaventura de Sousa Santos, *Epistemologies of the South: Justice Against Epistemicide* (New York: Routledge, 2014).

demand.[54] When those consumers are the modal, middle-class white students who disproportionately constitute many university settings, there are strong pressures to offer products that provide credentials for the market rather than critical thinking skills to prepare people for civic engagement. There are pressures to offer products that produce positive feeling and reinforce glorifying narratives of American exceptionalism. As a result of these pressures, universities are not neutral sites, but rather racialized corporate entities actively engaged in elevating certain epistemic standpoints over others.

To decolonize consciousness, we must decolonize knowledge institutions by infusing them with epistemic perspectives of racially subordinated groups. Within the US, a key site of this struggle is the conflict over Ethnic Studies courses.[55] Outside the US, key sites of this struggle include the #Rhodesmustfall movement or demands by South African students to "Decolonize the University." Advocates for such interventions rightly note their importance as an antidote for internalized oppression, autocolonialism, or colonial mentality[56] among people from racially

---

54 Barbara Tomlinson and George Lipsitz, "Insubordinate Spaces for Intemperate Times: Countering the Pedagogies of Neoliberalism," *Review of Education, Pedagogy, and Cultural Studies* 35, no. 1 (2013): 3–26, https://doi.org/10.1080/10714413.2013.753758.

55 As an example, neighboring states Arizona and Nevada have landed on opposite sides of the debate. While Arizona's legislature is pushing to extend a K–12 ban on courses that are "designed primarily for students of a particular ethnic group" to the college level (HB 2120), Nevada's state senate unanimously passed a bill to create and authorize ethnic studies in public high schools (SB 107). Arizona House Bill 2120, Section 15-112, January 17, 2017, *LegiScan*, https://legiscan.com/AZ/bill/HB2120/2017. Nevada State Bill 107, February 8, 2017, *LegiScan*, http://www.leg.state.nv.us/Session/79th2017/Bills/SB/SB107.pdf.

56 David and Okazaki define colonial mentality as "internalized oppression, characterized by a perception of ethnic or cultural inferiority...that involves an automatic and uncritical rejection of [colonized ways of being] and uncritical preference for [colonizer ways of being]." See Eric John Ramos David and Sumie Okazaki, "The Colonial Mentality Scale (CMS) for Filipino Americans: Scale Construction and Psychological Implications," *Journal of Counseling Psychology* 53, no. 2 (2006): 241–52, at 241, https://doi.org/10.1037/0022-0167.53.2.241. See also Hussein Abdilahi Bulhan, *Frantz*

subordinated groups.[57] Here we emphasize their importance as an antidote to epistemologies of white ignorance that promote denial of racism and opposition to antiracist policy. The fierce resistance to these epistemic interventions serves as a reminder that white racial power has a strong interest in the production of sanitized knowledge and suppression of potentially transformative knowledge. As the case of BHM and other contributions to this book suggest, this resistance and suppression sometimes come in the form of incorporation rather than explicit resistance.

Fanon and the Psychology of Oppression (New York: Plenum Press, 1985); Shawn Utsey et al., "Assessing the Psychological Consequences of Internalized Colonialism on the Psychological Well-Being of Young Adults in Ghana," *Journal of Black Psychology* 41, no. 3 (2015): 195–220, https://doi.org/10.1177/0095798414537935.

57 As an example, educational researchers Thomas S. Dee and Emily K. Penner found significant gains in GPA and attendance rates for at-risk students of color who were enrolled in ethnic studies courses. Thomas S. Dee and Emily K. Penner, "The Causal Effects of Cultural Relevance: Evidence from an Ethnic Studies Curriculum," *American Educational Research Journal* 54, no. 1 (2017): 127–66, https://doi.org.10.3102/0002831216677002.

20

November 5, 2016

Corinne Contreras

This night
Two bodies meet on a public street
Pulling each other in
Ways synonymous with authenticity

Streetlight turned spotlight on
This juncture of histories unknown to one another
Fearing the worst
Had become   customary
Yet an agreeable unspoken arrangement
Between
ourselves,
each other and
trauma
Pushed away to the point of satisfaction
Allowing a pocket of self-gratification to manifest
Just this once
Please

It's always unsettling how a sound as common as a car slowly
driving by can deflate
a moment's charm

DOI: 10.21983/P3.0250.1.23

Tension presents itself to this once peaceful arrangement
A woman's laughter and drunken banter puts peace in question

Why had this been expected to be safe?

Even here in California
Anyone can be a formidable opponent

So certain bad was coming
I pushed myself into a stance
I was taught meant protection

You know
We still talk about that night
How this person
Was so drunk
On their freedom of speech that they
Burst with words they knew we deserved to feel
Yaas queen!
Girl power

21

Our City, Our Solutions: Interview with Gaby Hernandez and Marissa Garcia of PODER

Alison Reed

> *Gang injunctions are modern day apartheid.*
> — Babatunde Folayemi[1]

People Organizing for the Defense and Equal Rights of Santa Barbara Youth (PODER) is a broad coalition of Santa Barbara community residents, students, parents, laborers, and professionals dedicated to social justice and collective empowerment. PODER organizers led a grassroots campaign for three years (2011–14) against a gang injunction civil law proposal. This historic victory continues to reverberate across the country as a sign of what can happen when people fight to replace criminalization of youth with opportunities for their physical, educational, professional, and spiritual flourishing. Through a series of community forums, public safety surveys, media campaigns, pro-youth initiatives, direct actions, and other grassroots mobilizations, PODER put pressure on politicians and exposed the

---

1   Babatunde Folayemi, cited in Kathy Swift, "The People's Voice: Introducing a New Column by PODER," *The Santa Barbara Independent,* February 6, 2015, https://www.independent.com/news/2015/feb/06/peoples-voice/.

gang injunction's proposed "Safety Zones" as open-air prisons that further criminalize and contain people of color. Gang injunctions perpetuate racial profiling while protecting vested interests in gentrification, the denial of civil rights, and interlocking systems of policing, surveillance, and imprisonment.

Understanding how gang injunctions fuel the prison industrial complex, Antiracism Inc. joined PODER's struggle in the wake of a series of "Activist Encounters" we facilitated on the UC Santa Barbara campus during the 2013–14 programming year. This second year of the program featured the subheading *Antiracism Works* and sought to extend the critical frames for addressing issues central to *Antiracism Inc.* by bridging intellectual work with community connection and engagement. For example, we hosted an organizing meeting on "How to Stop Prison Expansion" facilitated by Diana Zuñiga, former statewide coordinator at Californians United for a Responsible Budget (CURB) in Los Angeles. This event organically prompted the Coalition for Sustainable Communities (CSC) to form and mobilize against the jail and ICE detention center projects in North Santa Barbara County. CSC was initially invited to present on the proposed jail at a PODER community forum on 27 March 2014. Then, CSC continued to operate in solidarity with PODER, who successfully defeated the proposed gang injunction in the summer of 2014. Like PODER, CSC was committed to building life-affirming relations that support and sustain the physical, mental, spiritual, and social health of our communities. From light brigades to town halls and court hearings, we collectively fought for recognition of how the wars on drugs and terror, racial profiling, and policing impact our communities, and further, for acknowledgment of the difference between people *with* problems and people *as* problems — seeking new visions of security and accountability without cages.

Alison Reed served as Graduate Fellow of the Antiracism Inc. program series at UC Santa Barbara. She met two key organizers of PODER, Gaby Hernandez and Marissa Garcia, during a community forum at which the Coalition for Sustainable Communi-

ties was invited to speak on prison expansion projects in North Santa Barbara County. This interview was conducted via email in March 2017 and is edited for length and clarity.

Gabriela "Gaby" Hernandez, *Licensed Clinical Social Worker in Orange County Mental Health, grew up on the east side neighborhood of Santa Barbara. She was raised in poverty by a single mother of three. At the young age of 12, Gaby got involved with gangs, the juvenile criminal justice system, and began a cycle of self-destructive behaviors. With the support of her family, community-based mentors, social workers, probation officers, educators, and effective community-based programs, Gaby was able to transition from offender to student. Gaby received her bachelor's degree in Criminal Justice from Long Beach State University and her master's in Social Work from the University of Southern California. She now works as a therapist/social worker with Orange County's most vulnerable children, youth, and their families. Gaby is also an active member of several grassroot organizations that focus on issues of social justice. Gaby is an advocate for community-based programs that are effective and opposes punitive/oppressive measures that only limit the possibilities for youth of color.*

Marissa Garcia *was born and raised in Santa Barbara. She is involved with several organizations and has worked on campaigns including the mail ban at the Santa Barbara County Jail. She dedicates most of her time to prison advocacy and is currently working on the national movement to amend the 13th Amendment.*

Reed: Thank y'all so much for agreeing to discuss your crucial work with PODER (People Organizing for the Defense and Equal Rights of Santa Barbara Youth) defeating the gang injunction in Santa Barbara. To begin, would you describe how folks started mobilizing when it was proposed in 2011? What were the first steps?

Hernandez: I was not around for the initial mobilization, but my mentor Babatunde Folayemi, a former city council member and youth advocate, had begun contesting the injunction and holding forums to inform community members about its impact. Osiris Castaneda as well as some (paid) activists — Jacqueline Inda and JP Herreda — quickly got attorneys for some of the defendants. They also worked on the beginning stages of mobilizing, such as holding forums and getting the word out. Osiris Castaneda made some documentaries through Youth-CineMedia to show the face of those accused. So, the first steps were getting legal representation, community education, and mobilizing people to get involved.

I got involved after Babatunde passed away in March 2012. I ran into some of Babatunde's mentees and we talked about his work with the injunction, and how he had asked us to get involved, but we were always too busy. On the day of his candle-light vigil we agreed to meet up and see how we could help. We researched who was involved, what steps were taken, and what still had to be done. The paid activists had stopped organizing because their funds had dried up. When we expressed commitment regardless of funding they pretty much handed their information over to us. Within two months we had linked up with several other folks interested in fighting the injunction. Within six months we started bringing our resources together, brainstorming, power mapping, and putting on presentations for anyone who was interested. We began to challenge the status quo, specifically the Democratic liberals who claimed to care about community but were allowing this to happen. We agreed that a direct and indirect approach would be most important to challenge the system that was pushing this injustice.

Garcia: To add to what Gaby mentioned, I too was not involved in the beginning stages of bringing [the gang injunction] to light or mobilizing any efforts when it was initially proposed in 2011. I remember reading the *Santa Barbara News Press* one day and seeing an article about it that listed 30 names of people. That is how I found out my boyfriend (now husband) Marcial was even targeted. He was still incarcerated in Mississippi when the gang injunction (GI) was proposed in 2011, and at that time — like most folks in the system — he had received a letter from the city, and not understanding what it meant, disregarded it. I remember not too long after, I saw a post on Facebook by Osiris Castaneda about holding a meeting at the Westside Community Center. I met Osiris back when I was 15 years old; he made a presentation at La Cuesta for "at-risk" youth, and he became my mentor. I guess you can say he planted the seed. He exposed me to everything schools never taught me.

So, when I saw his post, I was curious about what this gang injunction was and why my boyfriend's name was on it — it seemed scary. I attended the meeting, and the majority of the people there were people from the neighborhood — kids, gang members, family members, etc. I think back on that meeting now, and for someone in the community to actually gather a group of people from the neighborhood like that — who had no idea what activism was, or rights and law, anything like that — was pretty damn amazing. I remember he put up a large screen and started his presentation; he was so passionate that day he was sweating, but it seemed like he was acting out of desperation to inform us something bad was going to happen. Of course, most of the people from the neighborhood took off halfway through, saying that this was too much information and they didn't understand what the words meant, but thanked him anyways. There were just a few people left at the end, and I remember putting my name and number down on a piece of paper.

Some time went by, and my man was released in July 2011. Within three weeks he had been arrested. Somewhere between the release and arrest, Osiris reached out to me and asked to meet Marcial, saying that it was important for him to understand what was happening to him. I was for it. Marcial wasn't so sure, but I convinced him and the two met. Osiris found Marcial legal representation through Juan Huerta. I remember how hard Osiris tried to motivate Marcial about it, offering him trips to Los Angeles to get involved with projects. I remember after we left the attorney's office, Osiris pulled me aside, and warned me. He knew at the time Marcial and I were still living that life, and he was concerned I made a bad choice being with him. He told us to be careful, because we would be targeted everywhere we went. And we were. Marcial was arrested during a "gang raid" in October 2012. We were both homeless and strung out on drugs at the time. I found out right away about his arrest and ran down to the police station demanding what his charges were. Refusing to leave, the now-retired police chief Cam Sanchez pulled me aside, and convinced me it was nothing serious, but if I helped them Marcial would be okay.

I had no idea at the time how serious his charges were going to become, and I was so fearful of his parole officer giving him a violation, that I agreed to let them search my garage. Cam Sanchez drove me in his car with parole officer Alvarez, convincing me this was nothing bad, but they just had to show for the record that parole searched his property. (We were homeless, so I told him all we had was stored in my parents' garage.) To protect Marcial, I agreed to let them search, and again they kept telling me it would just be a few minutes and no big deal. I remember I was high, but all I kept thinking was, *What did Marcial do?* I knew if it had been bad, he would have told me, and we would have bounced. Cam Sanchez pulled up in front of my house, and I asked him if he wouldn't mind knocking on my door and talking to my mom first, as she was going to freak out over seeing a police officer at home.

Instead, he pulled out a walkie talkie, said some code words and within 30 seconds, 12–16 swat officers ran up to my house. I guess they had all parked just blocks away. They were suited up head to toe with rifles, shotguns, the vests, everything. By the time I got to the door to tell my mom what was going on, KEYT had posted up on my front lawn and recorded my house being raided, my mom and me trying to hide, and they interviewed Cam Sanchez. He had lied to me about everything. I still have those pictures of all the police officers in my garage tearing everything apart. My mom was having a nervous breakdown in the backyard, and I was sweating and crying — wondering, *What the hell did my husband just do?* They were treating my house like a murder had happened. Of course, they walked away with nothing but my letters and pictures of my twenty-first birthday party, pictures they used as evidence in the gang injunction trial. I couldn't believe what I was seeing, and to top it off, I had the police chief trying to convince me to give him information in return for a softening of Marcial's charges. I of course knew better, and as they all started to leave, sobbing I went to his parole officer pleading with him to tell me what was going on, what he did, what his charges were, and why did you guys do this to my family. He just walked away and said, "Marcial will probably never come home."

The raid was aired on the 6 o'clock news, with an anchor reporting live, and I remember sitting down watching myself trying to get in my house, and the police raiding it, and watching the direct lies the police chief gave to the news about what happened at my house. I spent the next few months out in the streets, trying to escape everything. I had left Marcial, and was lost and confused, until I started researching his case. As I read things in the paper about this "gang injunction," I put two and two together and realized something was very wrong about everything. Not just his criminal case, but this civil case. I sobered up and decided to try looking for answers as to why this was happening to him. I remember telling my mom — something is wrong, and I need to save him. In January 2013 I attended a meeting and was told to reach out to PODER. I didn't even know what an "activist" was, what city council people do. The big fancy words: protests, legislation... all that stuff was foreign to me. I used to think the people who stood on corners with signs shouting and protesting were crazy people. And then I guess, I became one.

Gonzalo Rios, who was also a student of Osiris, asked me to come to meetings, and I started to volunteer and help in any way I could, and that's all I remember. From that point on in early 2013, PODER and the gang injunction became my life. Meetings, community walks, speaking out publicly, are what I remember the most. We had to educate people; it was crazy how many people had no idea what was going on. Lots of reading, staying up late, and constantly strategizing. When you ask about first steps,

I don't think there is one that could clearly be defined. There were so many steps, so many people, so much work, so much learning, so much trying to tell strangers about something that was taboo, or controversial… I wouldn't have known where to start without PODER.

Reed: That definitely speaks to the power of collective action. Social justice victories require deep commitment to a vision of liberation for everyone. It was a three-year fight until the gang injunction was declared unconstitutional, yes? But of course, the struggle is ongoing. What means of community nourishment did y'all cultivate during that time, to sustain the work?

Garcia: What first started as a quest to find answers for my husband became an act of desperation to save him. I believed in my heart that he was being used as a tool to pass the gang injunction, and I believed his criminal case was one of the poster examples used to try to scare the community. Until you witness with your own two eyes, and hear with your own two ears, direct lies by the people you grow up thinking are supposed to protect you and tell the truth, but do the exact opposite — with the person you love, your family, your everything — unfortunately, you will never quite understand how traumatic and life-altering it becomes. I started this commitment with an intent of liberation for him, my husband, and as time went on, the more I learned, the more I was exposed to, the more angry and sad I became; it was like an explosion went off in my head when I realized what was really happening not only in my community, but the rest of this country, and it evolved into a vision of liberation and love for everyone.

I was determined to find the truth behind what was happening to him, and in the process, learned more than what I signed up for. When you ask about community nourishment, what sustained the work was *love*. Everyone who worked on the GI — from the lead organizers to the neighbors who just showed up to eat our food — operated from a sense of love. There was something very unique about this fight. I was never exposed to any of this before, but everyone I worked with and met along the way, taught me something, forced me to rethink my attitudes and beliefs, pushed me out of my comfort zone — everyone brought something to the table. The work was never-ending, and at times, we overcommitted; I remember instances when we were beyond exhaustion. I remember being told to take care of myself. I was literally rolling out of bed, throwing my hair up in a bun, with no makeup on and dirty clothes from the day before — running late to lead some protest or some meeting. I remember everyone sacrificing something significant — lots of missed family events, job opportunities, trips, sleep. This "nourishment" I experienced while working for something, something I had no idea how huge it would be, is probably what saved my life.

I remember the first time a stranger came up to me and genuinely thanked me for everything PODER was doing, and thinking *why?* I thought what we were doing was normal. Or, the time I was told that what I was doing inspired someone else to do the same… I felt weird. The bond created with PODER — I can't explain it other than as family. PODER will always be in my heart; they were there for me in ways no one had been before, and in return, they have my loyalty for life. Before PODER, the GI, and all the work put into it, I had never felt accepted for who I was, loved for just me, and through this experience, I felt like I finally found a place where I belonged. I found a purpose. The nourishment the community gave to me while in my quest and determination to liberate them, I believe, though not realizing it then, ultimately liberated me.

Hernandez: We became a family, and our closeness is what helped me survive. I have never been involved in a fight so time-consuming and emotional. My cousin was named on the injunction; it was my neighborhood and a lot of people I grew up with. This was a personal fight for me and many of the other organizers. So we would eat, drink, and hang out together as much as we could. We had working parties where we would work together and chill at the same time. We all remain like brothers and sisters because we spent so much time together. I also relied on emotional support and guidance from experienced organizers with Chicanxs Unidxs, which I am a part of. Babatundes' wife provided emotional healing when I felt like a victory was so far away. She would compare our struggle to past struggles and motivate us. Seeing people come out to events and support us also motivated me to keep going. Towards the end we were so exhausted and burnt-out that I didn't have energy to plan a win or loss. When we found out we had won, I remember crying, because, 1) I was in disbelief, and, 2) we were utterly drained after having fought so hard for so long.

I worked fulltime while raising my two daughters who are active in sports and community activities. I was also running a Girl Scout troop, organizing in Orange County, and traveling back and forth to Santa Barbara for sometimes weekly events or meetings. I would stay up until two in the morning finishing up projects for the next day. I tried to help as much as I could from here because folks in Santa Barbara were on the ground pretty much every day. Just thinking about it now brings tears to my eyes because of those same reasons.

Reed: I love how you both express the struggle itself as being spiritually sustaining, even when (at times) draining. What was the greatest resistance y'all faced in convincing people that gang injunctions are so obviously racist? What were strategies you used to bring folks into an understanding of the relationship between race and space?

Hernandez: We were strategic in how we approached folks; of course, some people didn't care about race issues but did care about Santa Barbara's image or their property values. It is really hard to organize around injunctions, because the majority of the community does not care about alleged gang members. They didn't care if it was racist or classist — they just didn't want "those people in their neighborhood." You realized just how marginalized they were. With folks from the neighborhoods we were able to talk about race and how it affected people in the criminal injustice system and they quickly got it because they had either been affected by the system or had a loved one affected. We made sure to have statistics with us and stories of unjust sentences or charges.

Garcia: I felt surprisingly enough, at times, some of the greatest resistance we faced was from the same people who had started working on the issue. We operated with no fear, and donated our time; we were never paid, until a small emergency grant towards the end to help us during the trial. I feel PODER challenged everyone, on both sides. Even the ones against the injunctions were hesitant to be as outspoken or involved. The most resistance I felt in terms of blatant racism was the comments on *Edhat* — you never saw anyone say anything like that publicly. I remember one time doing a door-to-door walk to businesses on State Street. There was a tattoo parlor, and I went in and started talking it up, and it turned out one of the guys I was talking to was deputy at the jail and knew my husband. It hurt to hear the hate in his voice, but I stood there and listened to him, so I could learn and try to see from their point of view. I knew I couldn't change his mind, but it helped me prepare for another encounter — perhaps better lingo for the next person. Perhaps a new approach PODER hadn't tried before.

Like Gaby mentioned, in the beginning no one talked about the value of homes going down in affected areas. As soon as that approach was discussed by Gregg Hart, the Santa Barbara Association of Realtors signed on real quick in opposition to the GI. Strategy was crucial when it came to race, or when to pull the "race card." With statistics and proof to back up our claims, we always had to be one step ahead of the opposition, and we were. There were times I feel we had to negotiate our usage of words to unite folks, which shouldn't have to happen to begin with... but the facts didn't lie, and people couldn't deny that race was and is an issue. Race was crucial in strategy as well as in the discussion and implementation of solutions.

Reed: It still makes me feel physically ill when I go to the jail every week and the sign out front reads "Jail/Public Safety." So-called safety for some means brutality for many. It's soulless, I think — that people actively support the prison industrial complex when seduced by the misguided popular notion that cops and cages protect communities from harm. The US carceral state relies on notions of "safety" to protect white interests and property while criminalizing people of color. What other code words did your opponents deploy to champion surveillance, policing, and imprisonment?

Hernandez: The Milpas Community Association (our #1 nemesis) had a March for Public Safety in October 2010, which we believe led to the push of the injunction in January 2011. Public safety was clearly a way to target Brown youth. We continue to see organizations like the MCA and other wannabe community groups that want to keep Brown folks in the shadow for the sake of racism, classism, or both. We were often accused of being pro-gangs or pro-crime to harm our efforts. They would also ask "if not injunctions, then what" and we would turn the question on them: What else is the city doing to address gang issues since they say they have exhausted all other remedies? We expect that from white nationalist groups; however, one might expect more from the Democrats who use the same verbiage of "Safety First" when they run for office. The lack of knowledge about why police and prisons even exist blinds their ability to fully understand the root causes of crime, violence, or gangs. They all want a scapegoat to look like the heroes.

Garcia: I agree with everything Gaby stated. We noticed the city attempted to validate the issue by overpublicizing outdated information — basically, relying on one to two instances where a crime had been committed in the neighborhood, and using cases that were ten years old. I felt out of desperation they started to use fear tactics. I remember watching a report on KEYT right before the trial, where they aired a news special about the Mexican mafia taking over SB and showed a picture of Marcial (my husband), claiming he was taxing vendors on the Westside. All I could do was laugh. I became used to the blatant lies. All they had was his face full of tattoos, and an ongoing criminal case — so they blew it out of proportion to scare people. "Pro-gangs" we heard a lot. When you speak on public safety crimi-nalizing people of color, even with the facts, that is still an on-going fight in Santa Barbara. People who have experienced it believe it, and those who haven't don't want to see it. Comparing cases helped, but tackling the criminal court injustice system in Santa Barbara was, and still will be, difficult.

Reed: As a follow-up question, did you find it useful to strategi-cally reclaim and empower these code words, such as "safety" and "security"? If so, how? And/or did you create new language to address issues?

Hernandez: Yes, we definitely had to reclaim those code words and align with the same goals that we all want safety and securi-ty in our city. But we stressed how injunctions were not the solu-tion and that we needed to address these issues from the bottom up. "Our City, Our Solutions" became our motto. Some of our members were gifted in creating confrontational language as well as language to unite. They were not used to folks using their terms against them such as "democratic process," "fiscally re-sponsible," or "proactive approach." "Safety" and "security" also meant loving, helping, and healing our community, and people seemed to unite in that sense.

Reed: While I would never conflate people directly and indi-rectly affected by state violence, I wonder if in building alliances and broad-based coalitions, it's important to remember that this thing — whether we name the gang injunction, white su-premacy, global racial capitalism, the prison industrial complex, etc. — is killing *all* of us. Have you found it effective convincing people that what they think helps them actually harms them?

Hernandez: Working on the injunction helped shed light on so many other issues in Santa Barbara. It took so much more energy because we couldn't ignore those issues and had to call them out. From gentrification, unjust sentences for Brown youth, political cowardice, homelessness, mail being banned in jail, privileged youth taking Brown youth's funding, police abuse... the list went on and on. We attempted to intersect the injunction with other issues; when we had forums, we didn't just focus on the injunction but how other factors led to the injunction being seen as the only alternative. With as much information as we gave at those forums, I think we began to create mass consciousness about these issues. Pretty soon other organizations started using our terms in their language, especially nonprofits.

Garcia: There was no other way to convince people than to at times overload them with the truth; sometimes we crammed too much in at once. But I saw everyday people, my neighbors, start connecting the dots, thinking for themselves, and even if they didn't fully agree with the messaging, they brought up an issue to address, and we did our best to follow up. To me, PODER was more successful in creating alliances with our people, versus other nonprofits and orgs. People who never came to meetings before would come, and they would raise an issue, and someone else would agree, and the discussion would begin about ideas for solutions. People started to plug into their area of interest, or passion. We didn't use terms or money to make that happen.

Reed: Yes, against a monetized version of social justice, people find themselves by showing up and doing the work. What organizing strategies, testimonies, events, and evidence do you think helped convince people that the gang injunction was part of the problem, not the solution?

Hernandez: Media was a critical component of our efforts. It was a quick way to get our message out and capture people's interest. We held forums on a monthly basis with the intent to present whether ten people or 300 people showed up. Those numbers scared politicians who saw our audience grow and grow, as well as the diversity of people attending. We held fundraisers to hang out with supporters while showcasing local talent and demonstrating that efforts could run on hardly any money. Our light brigades became popular and got a lot of attention; they also became a place to gather. We held protests and showed fearlessness of criticism and being ostracized by "power holders." We began to take up space at city council meetings while at the same time respecting people's time and hunger — so we made sure to have food outside of City Hall, so people could eat before and during meetings. We held space at tourist attractions with signs that cautioned against gang war zones: "Be aware you are now entering a gang war zone." We posted advisory notices to tourists all over beach areas and downtown.

We got people of different ages, races, and classes standing to write declarations stating they were not afraid of their neighborhood and did not feel an injunction was necessary. We had experts and white folks who were respected in the community speak out against the injunction, which shifted the political climate. Once we got the Democratic Party to support our efforts and the Homeowners Association to express opposition to the GI, many people started to change their minds. I think most people were just tired of hearing about the injunction and wanted it gone; it brought a lot of negative publicity to the city.

Garcia: Yes, to be honest, the city was so tired of it all. We literally operated on the strategy of one step ahead: if we got hit with something, we had to come right back harder, whether staging a press conference inside the police department, lawsuits, or memes. We just kept going and going — open to new ideas and opportunities. People supported and helped from all races, backgrounds, educational levels, etc. It was beautiful. The leaders did not know what else to do.

Reed: What pro-youth alternatives did you present in redirecting resources away from policing and punishment to programs that support the collective health and healing of communities impacted by state violence?

Hernandez: We conducted our own research, which we always do when addressing an issue, and explained in the Solutions Proposals how tons of research had already been done to outline what kind of services were needed and did not exist in Santa Barbara. This clearly showed that we were interested in addressing the issue, that we knew what we were talking about, and that Santa Barbara was being sneaky about the GI.

Garcia: And some of those proposals are currently being implemented today!

Reed: Beautiful. I see in the PODER Solutions Proposals recommendations such as reentry, mentorship, and afterschool programs; community collaboratives and support services; funding for youth sports; and spaces for collective study of pressing issues such as incarceration and immigration policy. Which movement legacies, ancestors, chosen family, and stories empower you in the struggle?

Hernandez: Of course, Assata Shakur's famous chant was used repeatedly in events: "It is our duty to fight for our freedom. It is our duty to win. We must love each other and support each other. We have nothing to lose but our chains!"

Babatunde's legacy kept me going: "Gang injunctions are modern day apartheid."

My ancestors "Los Chupes" who were not conquered by the Aztecs and had women in the front lines with men. Learning from the Black Panther Party and Los Zapatistas. Looking back at myself being a young girl who had been harmed and grew up to be tough just to survive and how I could have easily been included in an injunction had that happened when I was a kid. I see myself in all the youngsters; I see my friends and family members who were able to change their lives because we were given a second chance at life.

Garcia: Angela Davis, and the ongoing battle for this world to finally see peace.

Reed: What was the greatest lesson you learned in defeating the injunction?

Hernandez: That people power is important and that you can win as long as you are more committed than the system. Any opposition is a win.

Garcia: The power really is with the people. The truth, no matter how ugly, will set you free, and as long as you operate out of the love in your heart, with no personal agenda, love will always win. It was *love* that defeated the injunction.

Reed: What advice would you give young community organizers starting out their journey?

Garcia: Take constructive criticism as a blessing, and as you learn your strengths, always seek opportunities to grow and learn from others; don't feel discouraged or stupid because you never graduated from high school and are sitting in a room with politicians and college graduates trying to put in work. Shine; be you. Take care of yourself or you will burn out.

Hernandez: Do not reinvent the wheel; use other organizations and their efforts. Many orgs including PODER are willing to share media, research, and documents to fight back. Create a system where self-care is encouraged and one day a week of connecting (no work) is promoted. Too often that is the last thing that one feels like one can do because of deadlines and fast-paced organizing, but it pays off. Keep building and training new people. Do not spread yourselves thin.

Reed: What are y'all working on now? How does your past work with PODER inform and inspire you today?

Hernandez: PODER is my baby; I helped start and sustain it. It was a long time coming. The last organization that existed was in the 1970s and 80s — Concilio de la Raza, which was super organized and funded to fight against issues affecting people of color in Santa Barbara. When I think of PODER, I think of a pure form of people power: we didn't have a hidden agenda, we didn't have funding to check us, we didn't care if the Dems liked us, and we didn't care if we made people uncomfortable. We stayed loyal to our efforts and the people.

At this time, we are working on several issues from gentrification to youth in the criminal injustice system. Some of our members are active with the Ethnic Studies Now Coalition and building El Centro. We are in the midst of training new folks to sustain our efforts as we have had many members move out of the area. We continue to be successful at calling out the system in Santa Barbara and pushing national issues like increasing rents and police abuse.

Garcia: After the GI, I focused on my husband's trial. I held it together. It was my goal that perhaps if I got his name in the paper enough in opposition to the GI, that maybe the judge would remember him and give him leniency. I found an investigative reporter who followed us for two years on his story; her hope is to publish it nationally in a few months. Marcial was found guilty of second-degree robbery, false imprisonment, street terrorism, and gang enhancements. He was a two-striker, and his convictions should have given him a life sentence. I humbly believe my tireless efforts, and unwillingness to trust our attorneys, is what spared Marcial a life sentence. I prepared, edited, and filed a Romero Motion with our attorney's assistant. A Romero Motion in California is rarely granted. Because of that Marcial received a 35-year sentence. We are still in the appellate process and have successfully gotten ten years reduced so far. After he was sentenced and transferred I relapsed hard, ended up homeless, and lost everything. Losing him hurt, but in the process, issues I experienced growing up I could no longer hide and started to come out, so it was a blessing in disguise that I was introduced to activism — I never would have known my worth without it. I am a survivor of sexual, physical, and emotional abuse. Fighting to survive is all I know how to do. I am currently working on healing and trying my best to be as involved as I can with the prisons and amending the 13th. Marcial and I are currently separated, but my promise stays the same, and I will never stop fighting until he is home, and everyone is free.

Contested Language of Freedom

Daniel Hershel Silber-Baker

If antiracism has been incorporated into the state discourses of liberal democracies, the presumptions of neoliberalism, neo-conservative agendas, and the sound bites of transnational commercialism, what language do we use to contest the marginalization of people historically colonized or impacted by European and US racism and imperialism?

The meaning of words is this elusive thing
A contested territory in which material meaning is made
Most often, most voices, are left
Out
Of the *'room where it happens'*
the kept out-side voices
turned to screams and cries
which are answered with a violent
silence
The volatile language of freedom
Emerges beneath the tongues of those most
Left-Kept out
The Red-Lined choir sings of home
So beautifully

DOI: 10.21983/P3.0250.1.25   347

we might all end up with places to live
The Women of Okinawa say safety
And mean all of us,
In the language of the emerging horizons of possibility,
Me transforms into We
And the truth of our words erupt
Into the marvelous contours of a new world
A Phoenix from no ash

Selective Bibliography

Adams, Glenn, Sara Estrada-Villalta, and Luis H. Gómez
Ordóñez. "The Modernity/Coloniality of Being: Hegemonic
Psychology as Intercultural Relations." *International Journal of Intercultural Relations* 62 (2017): 13–22. https://doi.
org/10.1016/j.ijintrel.2017.06.006.

Adams, Glenn, and Phia S. Salter. "Health Psychology in African Settings: A Cultural-Psychological Analysis." *Journal
of Health Psychology* 12, no. 3 (2007): 539–51. https://doi.
org/10.1177/1359105307076240.

Adams, Glenn, Teceta Thomas Tormala, and Laurie T. O'Brien.
"The Effect of Self-Affirmation on Perception of Racism."
Journal of Experimental Social Psychology 42, no. 5 (2006):
616–26. https://doi.org/10.1016/j.jesp.2005.11.001.

Adams, Glenn, et al., eds. *Commemorating Brown: The Social
Psychology of Racism and Discrimination.* Washington, DC:
American Psychological Association, 2008.

———. "Teaching about Racism: Pernicious Implications of the Standard Portrayal." *Basic and Applied Social Psychology* 30, no. 4 (2008): 349–61. https://doi.
org/10.1080/01973530802502309.

———. "Decolonizing Psychological Science: Introduction to
the Special Thematic Section." *Journal of Social and Political*

Psychology 3, no. 1 (2015): 213–38. https://doi.org/10.5964/jspp.v3i1.564.

Ahmed, Sara. *The Cultural Politics of Emotion*. New York: Routledge, 2004.

———. *On Being Included: Racism and Diversity in Institutional Life*. Durham: Duke University Press, 2012.

Ai, Amy L., et al. "Racial Identity–Related Differential Attributions of Inadequate Responses to Hurricane Katrina: A Social Identity Perspective." *Race and Social Problems* 3, no. 1 (2011): 13–24. https://doi.org/ 10.1007/s12552-011-9039-1.

Alexander-Floyd, Nikol. "Disappearing Acts: Reclaiming Intersectionality in the Social Sciences in a Post-Black Feminist Era." *Feminist Formations* 24, no. 1 (2012): 1–25. https://doi.org/10.1353/ff.2012.0003.

Allport, Gordon. *The Nature of Prejudice*. Cambridge: Addison-Wesley, 1954.

Anderson, Carol. *White Rage: The Unspoken Truth of Our Racial Divide*. New York: Bloomsbury, 2016.

Anthias, Floya, and Nira Yuval-Davis. "Contextualizing Feminism: Gender, Ethnic, and Class Divisions." *Feminist Review* 15 (1983): 62–75. https://www.jstor.org/stable/1394792.

Anzaldua, Gloria, and Cherrie A. Moraga, eds. *This Bridge Called My Back*. New York: Kitchen Table: Women of Color Press, 1983.

Attali, Jacques. *Noise: The Political Economy of Music,* trans. Brian Massumi. Minneapolis: University of Minnesota Press, 1985.

Bilge, Sirma. "Intersectionality Undone: Saving Intersectionality from Feminist Intersectionality Studies." *Du Bois Review* 10, no. 2 (2013): 405–24. https://doi.org/10.1017/S1742058X13000283.

———. "Whitening Intersectionality: Evanescence of Race in Current Intersectionality Scholarship." In *Racism and Sociology,* edited by Wulf D. Hund and Alana Lentin, 175–205. Berlin: Lit Verlag, 2014.

Blee, Kathleen M. *Inside Organized Racism: Women in the Hate Movement*. Berkeley: University of California Press, 2003.

Boggs, Grace Lee. *The Next American Revolution: Sustainable Activism for the 21st Century.* Berkeley: University of California Press, 2012.

Baldwin, James. *Notes of a Native Son.* Boston: Beacon, 1955.

———. *Going to Meet the Man.* New York: Dell, 1988.

———. *No Name in the Street.* New York: Vintage, 2007.

Banet-Weiser, Sarah. *Authentic™: The Politics of Ambivalence in a Brand Culture.* New York: New York University Press, 2012.

Black Lives Matter. "Herstory." [n.d.] https://blacklivesmatter.com/herstory.

Blackwell, Maylei, and Nadine Naber. "Intersectionality in an Era of Globalization: The Implications of the UN World Conference Against Racism for Transnational Feminist Practices—A Conference Report." *Meridians: Feminism, Race, Transnationalism* 2, no. 2 (2002): 237–48. https://www.jstor.org/stable/40338519.

Blake, Felice. "Global Mass Violence: Examining Racial and Gendered Violence in the Twilight of Multiculturalism." *Ethnic and Racial Studies* 40, no. 14 (2017): 2615–33. https://doi.org/10.1080/01419870.2016.1237669.

Bonilla-Silva, Eduardo. *Racism without Racists: Color-Blind Racism and the Persistence of Racial Inequality in the United States.* 2nd edn. Lanham: Rowman & Littlefield, 2006.

———. *White Supremacy and Racism in the Post-Civil Rights Era.* Boulder: Lynne Rienner, 2001.

Bouie, Jamelle. "Why Do Millennials Not Understand Racism?" *Slate,* May 16, 2014. http://www.slate.com/articles/news_and_politics/politics/2014/05/millennials_racism_and_mtv_poll_young_people_are_confused_about_bias_prejudice.html.

Branscombe, Nyla R., Michael T. Schmitt, and Kristin Schiffhauer. "Racial Attitudes in Response to Thoughts of White Privilege." *European Journal of Social Psychology* 37, no. 2 (2007): 203–15. https://doi.org/10.1002/ejsp.348.

Breitman, George, ed. *Malcolm X Speaks.* New York: Pathfinder Press, 2017.

Buck, Elizabeth. *Paradise Remade: The Politics of Culture and History in Hawai'i.* Philadelphia: Temple University Press, 1993.

Bulhan, Hussein Abdilahi. *Frantz Fanon and the Psychology of Oppression.* New York: Plenum Press, 1985.

Cacho, Lisa Marie. *Social Death: Racialized Rightlessness and the Criminalization of the Unprotected.* New York: New York University Press, 2012.

Carastathis, Anna. *Intersectionality: Origins, Contestations, Horizons.* Lincoln: University of Nebraska Press, 2016.

Carbado, Devon. "Colorblind Intersectionality." *Signs: A Journal of Women in Culture and Society* 38, no. 4 (2013): 811–45. https://doi.org/10.1086/669666.

Carmichael, Stokely, and Charles Hamilton. *Black Power: The Politics of Liberation.* New York: Random House, 1967.

Césaire, Aimé. *Discourse on Colonialism.* Translated by Joan Pinkham. New York: New York University Press, 2001.

Chan-Tiberghien, Jennifer. "Gender-Skepticism or Gender Boom? Poststructural Feminists, Transnational Feminisms and the World Conference Against Racism." *International Feminist Journal of Politics* 6, no. 3 (2004): 454–84. https://doi.org/10.1080/1461674042000235618.

Cho, Sumi, Kimberlé Williams Crenshaw, and Leslie McCall, eds. *Intersectionality: Theorizing Power, Empowering Theory* [special journal issue]. *Signs* 38, no. 4 (Summer 2013): 785–1055. https://www.jstor.org/stable/10.1086/669610.

Churchill, Ward, and Sharon H. Venne, eds. *Islands in Captivity: The Record of the International Tribunal on the Rights of Native Hawaiians.* Hawaiian language edn. Cambridge: South End, 2004.

Cobb, Daniel, ed. *Say We Are Nations: Documents of Politics and Protest in Indigenous America since 1887.* Chapel Hill: University of North Carolina Press, 2015.

Cohen, Cathy. *The Boundaries of Blackness: AIDS and the Breakdown of Black Politics.* Chicago: University of Chicago Press, 1999.

Collins, Patricia Hill. *Black Feminist Thought.* New York: Routledge, 1990.

———— and Sirma Bilge. *Intersectionality.* Malden: Polity, 2016.

Comaroff, Jean, and John L. Comaroff. "Theory from the South: Or, How Euro-America is Evolving Toward Africa." *Anthropological Forum: A Journal of Social Anthropology and Comparative Sociology* 22, no. 2 (2011): 113–31. https://doi.org/10.1080/00664677.2012.694169.

Crenshaw, Kimberlé Williams. "Demarginalizing the Intersection of Race and Sex: A Black Feminist Critique of Antidiscrimination Doctrine." *University of Chicago Legal Forum,* no. 1, art. 8 (1989): 139–67. https://chicagounbound.uchicago.edu/uclf/vol1989/iss1/8.

————. "Mapping the Margins: Intersectionality, Identity Politics, and Violence Against Women of Color." *Stanford Law Review* 43, no. 6 (1991): 1241–99. https://www.jstor.org/stable/1229039.

————. "Twenty Years of Critical Race Theory: Looking Back to Move Forward." *Connecticut Law Review* 43, no. 5 (2010): 12–53.

————. "From Private Violence to Mass Incarceration: Thinking Intersectionally about Women, Race, and Social Control." *UCLA Law Review* 59 (2012): 1418–17. https://escholarship.org/uc/item/7mp3k6m3.

————, Neil Gotanda, Gary Peller, and Kendall Thomas, eds. *Critical Race Theory: The Key Writings That Formed the Movement.* New York: The New Press, 1995.

Crocker, Jennifer, et al. "Belief in US Government Conspiracies Against Blacks Among Black and White College Students: Powerlessness or System Blame?" *Personality and Social Psychology Bulletin* 25, no. 8 (1999): 941–53.

Dagbovie, Pero Gaglo. "Making Black History Practical and Popular: Carter G. Woodson, the Proto Black Studies Movement, and the Struggle For Black Liberation." *Western Journal of Black Studies* 28, no. 2 (2004): 372–83.

————. "'Of All Our Studies, History is Best Qualified to Reward our Research': Black History's Relevance to the

Hip Hop Generation." *Journal of African American History* 90, no. 3 (2005): 299–323. https://doi.org/10.1086/JAAH-v90n3p299.

David, Eric John Ramos, and Sumie Okazaki. "The Colonial Mentality Scale (CMS) for Filipino Americans: Scale Construction and Psychological Implications." *Journal of Counseling Psychology* 53, no. 2 (2006): 241–52. https://doi.org/10.1037/0022-0167.53.2.241.

Davis, Angela Y. "From the Prison of Slavery to the Slavery of Prison: Frederick Douglass and the Convict Lease System." In *The Angela Y. Davis Reader,* edited by Joy James, 74–96. Oxford: Blackwell, 1998.

Dee, Thomas S., and Emily K. Penner. "The Causal Effects of Cultural Relevance: Evidence from an Ethnic Studies Curriculum." *American Educational Research Journal* 54, no. 1 (2017): 127–66. https://doi.org.10.3102/0002831216677002.

Diamond, Heather A. *American Aloha: Cultural Tourism and the Negotiation of Tradition.* Honolulu: University of Hawai'i Press, 2008.

Dixon, John, et al. "'Let Them Eat Harmony': Prejudice-Reduction Strategies and Attitudes of Historically Disadvantaged Groups." *Current Directions in Psychological Science* 19, no. 2 (2010): 76–80. https://doi.org/10.1177/0963721410363366.

Dixon, John, and Mark Levine, eds. *Beyond Prejudice: Extending the Social Psychology of Conflict, Inequality, and Social Change.* Cambridge: Cambridge University Press, 2012.

Du Bois, W.E.B. *Black Reconstruction in America: 1860–1880.* New York: Free Press, 1998.

Dunbar-Ortiz, Roxanne. *An Indigenous People's History of the United States.* Boston: Beacon, 2015.

Esses, Victoria M., and Gordon Hodson. "The Role of Lay Perceptions of Ethnic Prejudice in the Maintenance and Perpetuation of Ethnic Bias." *Journal of Social Issues* 62, no. 3 (2006): 453–68. https://doi.org/10.1111/j.1540-4560.2006.00468.x.

Eyerman, Ron. "The Past in the Present: Culture and the Transmission of Memory." *Acta Sociologica* 47, no. 2 (2004): 159–69. https://doi.org/10.1177/0001699304043853.

Falcón, Sylvanna M. *Power Interrupted: Antiracist and Feminist Activism inside the United Nations.* Seattle: University of Washington Press, 2016.

Fanon, Frantz. *The Wretched of the Earth.* Translated by Constance Farrington. New York: Grove Press, 1963.

Fast, Susan, and Kip Pegley, eds. *Music, Politics, and Violence.* Middleton: Wesleyan University Press, 2012.

Feagin, Joe R. *Racist America: Roots, Current Realities, and Future Reparations.* New York: Routledge, 2001.

Ferguson, Roderick. *The Reorder of Things: The University and Its Pedagogies of Minority Difference.* Minneapolis: University of Minnesota Press, 2012.

Frankenberg, Ruth. *White Women, Race Matters: The Social Construction of Whiteness.* Minneapolis: University of Minnesota Press, 1993.

Franklin, John Hope, et al. "Black History Month: Serious Truth Telling or a Triumph in Tokenism?" *Journal of Blacks in Higher Education* 18 (1998): 87–92. https://doi.org/10.2307/2998774.

Fraser, Nancy. "Social Justice in the Age of Identity Politics: Redistribution, Recognition and Participation." In Nancy Fraser and Axel Honneth, *Redistribution or Recognition? A Political Philosophical Exchange,* 7–109. New York: Verso, 2003.

Freeman, Alan David. "Legitimizing Racial Discrimination Through Antidiscrimination Law: A Critical Review of Supreme Court Doctrine." *Minnesota Law Review* 62 (1977): 1049–19.

Fujikane, Candace, and Jonathan Y. Okamura, eds. *Asian Settler Colonialism: From Local Governance to the Habits of Everyday Life in Hawai'i.* Honolulu: University of Hawai'i Press, 2008.

Gallagher, Charles A., ed. *Rethinking the Color Line.* New York: McGraw-Hill, 1999.

Garrett, Charles Hiroshi. *Struggling to Define a Nation: American Music and the Twentieth Century.* Berkeley: University of California Press, 2008.

Gilmore, Ruth Wilson. *Golden Gulag: Prisons, Surplus, Crisis, and Opposition in Globalizing California.* Berkeley: University of California Press, 2007.

Gordon, Leah N. *From Power to Prejudice: The Rise of Racial Individualism in Midcentury America.* Chicago: University of Chicago Press, 2015.

Gray, Herman. *Cultural Moves: African Americans and the Politics of Representation.* Berkeley: University of California Press, 2005.

Hall, Lisa Kahaleole. "'Hawaiian at Heart' and Other Fictions." *Contemporary Pacific* 17, no. 2 (2005): 404–13. https://doi.org/10.1353/cp.2005.0051.

Hall, Stuart. "What is This 'Black' in Black Popular Culture?" In *Black Popular Culture,* edited by Gina Dent, 21–37. Seattle, WA: Bey Press, 1992.

———, Chas Critcher, Tony Jefferson, John Clarke, and Brian Roberts. *Policing the Crisis: Mugging, the State, and Law and Order.* London: Palgrave Macmillan, 1978.

Hammack, Phillip. *Narrative and the Politics of Identity: The Cultural Psychology of Israeli and Palestinian Youth.* Oxford: Oxford University Press, 2011.

Hancock, Ange-Marie. *Intersectionality: An Intellectual History.* New York: Oxford University Press, 2016.

Hanhardt, Christina B. *Safe Space: Gay Neighborhood History and the Politics of Violence.* Durham: Duke University Press, 2013.

Harding, Vincent. *Martin Luther King: The Inconvenient Hero.* Ossining: Orbis, 2008.

Harney, Stefano, and Fred Moten. *The Undercommons: Fugitive Planning & Black Study.* New York: Autonomedia, 2013.

Harris, Cheryl. "Whiteness as Property." *Harvard Law Review* 106, no. 8 (1993): 1707–91. https://doi.orgs/10.2307/1341787.

Hegarty, Peter, and Felicia Pratto. "The Effects of Social Category Norms and Stereotypes on Explanations for Intergroup

Differences." *Journal of Personality and Social Psychology* 80, no. 5 (2001): 723–35. https://doi.org/10.1037/0022-3514.80.5.723

Hong, Grace Kyungwon. "'The Future of Our Worlds': Black Feminism and the Politics of Knowledge in the University under Globalization." *Meridians: Feminism, Race, Transnationalism* 8, no. 2 (2008): 95–115. https://www.jstor.org/stable/40338753.

Hughey, Matthew W. *White Bound: Nationalists, Antiracists, and the Shared Meanings of Race.* Stanford: Stanford University Press, 2012.

Ignatiev, Noel. *How the Irish Became White.* New York: Routledge, 1995.

Ioanide, Paula. *The Emotional Politics of Racism: How Feelings Trump Facts in an Era of Colorblindness.* Stanford: Stanford University Press, 2015.

Isasi-Díaz, Ada María, and Eduardo Mendieta, eds. *Decolonizing Epistemologies: Latina/o Theology and Philosophy.* New York: Fordham University Press, 2011.

James, C.L.R. *A History of Pan-African Revolt.* Oakland: PM Press, 2012.

Jibrin, Rekia, and Sara Salem. "Revisiting Intersectionality: Reflections on Theory and Praxis." *Trans-Scripts* 5 (2015): 7–24. http://sites.uci.edu/transscripts/files/2014/10/2015_5_salem.pdf.

Johnson, Bruce, Martin Cloonan, and Derek B. Scott, eds. *Dark Side of the Tune: Popular Music and Violence.* Burlington: Ashgate, 2013.

Johnson, James D., et al. "Variation in Black Anti-White Bias and Target Distancing Cues: Factors that Influence Perceptions of 'Ambiguously Racist' Behavior." *Personality and Social Psychology Bulletin* 29, no. 5 (2003): 609–22. https://doi.org/10.1177/0146167203029005006.

Jones, James M. *Prejudice and Racism.* New York: McGraw-Hill, 1997.

Jost, John T., Mahzarin R. Banaji, and Brian A. Nosek. "A Decade of System Justification Theory: Accumulated Evidence of Conscious and Unconscious Bolstering of the Status Quo." *Political Psychology* 25, no. 6 (2004): 881–919. https://doi.org/10.1111/j.1467-9221.2004.00402.x.

Journell, Wayne. "When Oppression and Liberation are the Only Choices: The Representation of African Americans Within State Social Studies Standards." *Journal of Social Studies Research* 32, no. 1 (2008): 40–50.

Kelley, Robin D.G. *Freedom Dreams: The Black Radical Imagination.* New edn. Boston: Beacon Press, 2003.

Klopotek, Brian. *Recognition Odysseys: Indigeneity, Race, and Federal Tribal Recognition Policy in Three Louisiana Indian Communities.* Durham: Duke University Press, 2011.

Knowles, Eric D., et al. "On the Malleability of Ideology: Motivated Construals of Color Blindness." *Journal of Personality and Social Psychology* 96, no. 4 (2009): 857–69. https://doi.org/10.1037/a0013595.

Kurtiş, Tuğçe, Glenn Adams, and Michael Yellow Bird. "Generosity or Genocide? Identity Implications of Silence in American Thanksgiving Commemorations." *Memory* 18, no. 2 (2010): 208–24. https://doi.org/10.1080/09658210903176478.

Lee, James Kyung-Jin. *Urban Triage: Race and the Fictions of Multiculturalism.* Minneapolis: University of Minnesota Press, 2004.

Leonardo, Zeus, and Logan Manning. "White Historical Activity Theory: Toward a Critical Understanding of White Zones of Proximal Development." *Race Ethnicity and Education* 20, no. 1 (2017): 15–29. http://doi.org/10.1080/13613324.2015.1100988.

Levin, Shana, et al. "Ethnic Identity, Legitimizing Ideologies, and Social Status: A Matter of Ideological Asymmetry." *Political Psychology* 19, no. 2 (1998): 373–404. https://doi.org/10.1111/0162-895X.00109.

Lewis, George H. "The Role of Music in Popular Social Movements: A Theory and Case Study of the Island State of Hawaii, USA." *International Review of the Aesthetics and Sociology of Music* 16, no. 2 (1985): 153–62. https://doi.org/10.2307/836774.

Lilikalā, Kameʻeleihiwa. *Native Land and Foreign Desires: Pehea La E Pono Ai?* Honolulu: Bishop Museum Press, 1992.

Linebaugh, Peter. *The Many-Headed Hydra: Sailors, Slaves, Commoners, and the Hidden History of the Revolutionary Atlantic.* Boston: Beacon Press, 2000.

Linnekin, Jocelyn S. "Cultural Invention and the Dilemma of Authenticity." *American Anthropologist* 93, no. 2 (1991): 446–49. https://doi.org/10.1525/aa.1991.93.2.02a00120.

Lipman, Pauline. *The New Political Economy of Urban Education: Neoliberalism, Race and the Right to the City.* New York: Routledge, 2012.

Lipsitz, George. *Dangerous Crossroads: Popular Music, Postmodernism and the Poetics of Place.* New York: Verso, 1994.

———. "Learning from New Orleans: The Social Warrant of Hostile Privatism and Competitive Consumer Citizenship." *Cultural Anthropology* 21, no. 3 (2006): 451–68. https://doi.org/10.1525/can.200621.3.451.

———. *The Possessive Investment in Whiteness: How White People Profit from Identity Politics.* Rev. and expanded edn. Philadelphia: Temple University Press, 2006.

———. *Footsteps in the Dark: The Hidden Histories of Popular Music.* Minneapolis: University of Minnesota Press, 2007.

———. "Breaking the Chains and Steering the Ship: How Activism Can Help Change Teaching and Scholarship." In *Engaging Contradictions: Theory, Politics, and Methods of Activist Scholarship,* edited by Charles R. Hale, 88–111. Berkeley: University of California Press, 2008.

Loewen, James W. *Lies My Teacher Told Me: Everything Your American History Textbook Got Wrong.* New York: New Press, 2008.

López, Ian Haney. *White by Law: The Legal Construction of Race.* New York: New York University Press, 1996.

———. "Post-Racial Racism: Racial Stratification and Mass Incarceration in the Age of Obama." *California Law Review* 98, no. 3 (June 2010): 1023–74. https://doi.org/10.15779/Z38H696.

Lorde, Audre. *Sister Outsider: Essays and Speeches by Audre Lorde.* Berkeley: Crossing Press, 2007.

Lowery, Brian S., Eric D. Knowles, and Miguel M. Unzueta. "Framing Inequity Safely: Whites' Motivated Perceptions of Racial Privilege." *Personality and Social Psychology Bulletin* 33, no. 9 (2007): 1237–50. https://doi.org/10.1177/0146167207303016.

Lutz, Helma, Maria Teresa Herrera Vivar, and Linda Supik, eds. *Framing Intersectionality: Debates on a Multi-faceted Concept in Gender Studies.* Burlington: Ashgate, 2011.

Mackey, Nathaniel. "Other: From Noun to Verb." In *Jazz Among the Discourses,* edited by Krin Gabbard, 76–99. Durham: Duke University Press, 1995.

Madsen, Deborah L., ed. *Native Authenticity: Transnational Perspectives on Native American Literary Studies.* Albany: State University of New York Press, 2010.

Maira, Sunaina. "Henna and Hip Hop: The Politics of Cultural Production and the Work of Cultural Studies." *Journal of Asian American Studies* 3, no. 3 (October 2000): 329–69. https://doi.org/10.1353/jaas.2000.0038.

Maldonado-Torres, Nelson. "On the Coloniality of Being: Contributions to the Development of a Concept." *Cultural Studies* 21, no. 2-3 (2007): 240–70. https://doi.org/10.1080/09502380601162548.

———. "Thinking Through the Decolonial Turn: Post-Continental Interventions in Theory, Philosophy, and Critique— An Introduction." *Transmodernity: Journal of Peripheral Cultural Production of the Luso-Hispanic World* 1, no. 2 (2011): 1–15. https://escholarship.org/uc/item/59w8jo2x.

Martín-Baró, Ignacio. *Writings for a Liberation Psychology.* Cambridge: Harvard University Press, 1994.

May, Vivian M. "'Speaking into the Void'? Intersectionality Critiques and Epistemic Backlash," *Hypatia* 29, no. 1 (2014): 94–112. https://doi.org/10.1111/hypa.12060.

———. *Pursuing Intersectionality: Unsettling Dominant Imaginaries.* New York, Routledge, 2015.

McAlister, Lelani. *Epic Encounters: Culture, Media, and US Interests in the Middle East Since 1945.* 2nd edn. Berkeley: University of California Press, 2005.

McKinney, Karyn. *Being White: Stories of Race and Racism.* New York: Routledge, 2004.

McClure, Stephanie M., and Cherise A. Harris, eds. *Getting Real About Race.* 2nd edn. Los Angeles: SAGE, 2018.

McLemee, Sott, ed. *C.L.R. James on the "Negro Question."* Jackson: University Press of Mississippi, 1996.

Melamed, Jodi. "The Spirit of Neoliberalism: From Racial Liberalism to Neoliberal Multiculturalism." *Social Text* 24, no. 4 (2006): 1–24. https://doi.org/10.1215/01642472-2006-009.

———. *Represent and Destroy: Rationalizing Violence in the New Racial Capitalism.* Minneapolis: University of Minnesota Press, 2011.

Meller, Norman, and Ann Feder Lee. "Hawaiian Sovereignty." *Publius* 27, no. 2 (1997): 167–85. https://doi.org/10.1093/oxfordjournals.pubjof.a029904.

Mendoza-Denton, Rodolfo, et al. "Sensitivity to Status-based Rejection: Implications for African American Students' College Experience." *Journal of Personality and Social Psychology* 83, no. 4 (2002): 896–918. https://doi.org/10.1037/0022-3514.83.4.896.

Mignolo, Walter. *The Darker Side of Western Modernity: Global Futures, Decolonial Options.* Durham: Duke University Press, 2011.

Mills, Charles W. *The Racial Contract.* Ithaca: Cornell University Press, 1997.

Moore, Wendy Leo. *Reproducing Racism: White Space, Elite Law Schools, and Racial Inequality.* Lanham: Rowman and Littlefield, 2008.

Moten, Fred. "Knowledge of Freedom." *New Centennial Review* 4, no. 2 (Fall 2004): 269–310.

Nandy, Ashis. *The Intimate Enemy: Loss and Recovery of Self Under Colonialism.* Oxford: Oxford University Press, 2009.

Narayan, Uma, and Sandra Harding, eds. *Decentering the Center: Philosophy for a Multicultural, Postcolonial, and Feminist World*. Bloomington: Indiana University Press, 2000.

Nelson, Jessica C., Glenn Adams, and Phia S. Salter. "The Marley Hypothesis: Racism Denial Reflects Ignorance of History." *Psychological Science* 24, no. 2, (2013): 213–18. https://doi.org/ 10.1177/0956797612451466.

Nelson, Todd D. *The Psychology of Prejudice*. Boston: Allyn and Bacon, 2006.

Noble, Safiya. *The Algorithms of Oppression: How Search Engines Reinforce Racism*. New York: New York University Press, 2018.

Norton, Michael I., and Samuel R. Sommers. "Whites See Racism as a Zero-Sum Game That They Are Now Losing." *Perspectives on Psychological Science* 6, no. 3 (2011): 215–18. https://doi.org/10.1177/1745691611406922.

O'Brien, Laurie T., et al. "Understanding White Americans' Perceptions of Racism in Hurricane Katrina-related Events." *Group Processes & Intergroup Relations* 12, no. 4 (2009): 431–44. https://doi.org/10.1177/1368430209105047.

O'Connor, Alice, Chris Tilly, and Lawrence Bobo, eds. *Urban Inequality: Evidence from Four Cities*. New York: Russell Sage Foundation, 2001.

Oliver, Melvin L., and Thomas M. Shapiro. *Black Wealth/White Wealth: A New Perspective on Racial Inequality*. New York: Routledge, 1997.

Pinel, Elizabeth C. "Stigma Consciousness: The Psychological Legacy of Social Stereotypes." *Journal of Personality and Social Psychology* 76, no. 1 (1999): 114–28. https://doi.org/10.1037/0022-3514.76.1.114.

Pitre, Abul, and Ruth Ray. "The Controversy around Black History." *Western Journal of Black Studies* 26, no. 3 (2002): 149–54.

Powell, John A., and Caitlin Watt. "Negotiating the New Political and Racial Environment." *Journal of Law in Society* 31, no. 11 (2010): 31–69.

Pulido, Laura. *Black, Brown, Yellow, and Left: Radical Activism in Los Angeles.* Berkeley: University of California Press, 2006.

Rabaka, Reiland. *The Negritude Movement: W.E.B. Du Bois, Leon Damas, Aimé Césaire, Leopold Senghor, Frantz Fanon, and the Evolution of an Insurgent Idea.* Lanham: Lexington, 2015.

Ransby, Barbara. *Ella Baker and the Black Freedom Movement: A Radical Vision.* Chapel Hill: University of North Carolina Press, 2003.

Ray, Rashawn, Melissa Brown, Neil Fraistat, and Edward Summers. "Ferguson and the Death of Michael Brown on Twitter: #BlackLivesMatter, #TCOT, and the Evolution of Collective Identities." *Ethnic and Racial Studies* 40, no. 11 (2017): 1797–813. https://doi.org/10.1080/01419870.2017.1335422.

Reddy, Chandan. *Freedom with Violence: Race, Sexuality, and the US State.* Durham: Duke University Press, 2011.

Reed, Alison. "Queer Provisionality: Mapping the Generative Failures of the 'Transborder Immigrant Tool.'" *Lateral* 4 (2015). https://doi.org/10.25158/L4.1.4.

Roberts, Dorothy. *Killing the Black Body: Race, Reproduction, and the Meaning of Liberty.* New York: Vintage, 1997.

Robinson, Cedric J. *Black Marxism: The Making of the Black Radical Tradition.* Chapel Hill: University of North Carolina Press, 1983.

———. *Forgeries of Memory and Meaning: Blacks and the Regimes of American Theatre and Film Before World War II.* Chapel Hill: University of North Carolina Press, 2007.

Roediger, David. *The Wages of Whiteness: Race and the Making of the American Working Class.* London: Verso, 1991.

———. *Working Toward Whiteness: How America's Immigrants Became White: The Strange Journey from Ellis Island to the Suburbs.* New York: Basic Books, 2005.

Rogin, Michael Paul. *Fathers and Children: Andrew Jackson and the Subjugation of the American Indian.* New Brunswick: Transaction Publishers, 1991.

Rohrer, Judy. *Haoles in Hawai'i: Race and Ethnicity in Hawai'i.* Honolulu: University of Hawai'i Press, 2010.

———. *Staking Claim: Settler Colonialism and Racialization in Hawai'i.* Tucson: University of Arizona Press, 2016.

Rose, Tricia. *The Hip Hop Wars: What We Talk About When We Talk About Hip Hop.* New York: Basic, 2008.

———. "Hansberry's A Raisin in the Sun and the 'Illegible' Politics of Interpersonal Justice." *Kalfou* 1, no. 1 (2014): 27–60. https://doi.org/10.15367/kf.v1i1.9.

Salter, Phia S., and Glenn Adams. "On the Intentionality of Cultural Products: Representations of Black History as Psychological Affordances." *Frontiers in Psychology* 7, art. 1166 (2016): 1–21. https://doi.org/ 10.3389/fpsyg.2016.01166.

Santos, Boaventura de Sousa. *Epistemologies of the South: Justice Against Epistemicide.* New York: Routledge, 2014.

Schick, Carol, and Verna St. Denis. "Troubling National Discourses in Anti-Racist Curricular Planning." *Canadian Journal of Education/Revue Canadienne de L'éducation* 28, no. 3 (2005): 295–317. https://doi.org/10.2307/4126472.

Shank, Barry. *Political Force of Musical Beauty.* Durham: Duke University Press, 2014.

Sharkey, Patrick. *Stuck in Place: Urban Neighborhoods and the End of Progress Toward Racial Equality.* Chicago: University of Chicago Press, 2013.

Silva, Noenoe K. *Aloha Betrayed: Native Hawaiian Resistance to American Colonialism.* Durham: Duke University Press, 2004.

Simpson, Audra. *Mohawk Interruptus: Political Life Across the Borders of Settler States.* Durham: Duke University Press, 2014.

Simpson, Leanne Betasamosake. *As We Have Always Done: Indigenous Freedom Through Radical Resistance.* Minneapolis: University of Minnesota Press, 2017.

Singh, Nikhil. "A Note on Race and the Left." *Social Text Online,* July 31, 2015. http://www.socialtextjournal.org/a-note-on-race-and-the-left/.

Smith, Barbara. "Toward a Black Feminist Criticism," *Conditions: Two* 1, no. 2 (October 1977): 25–44.

———. *Home Girls: A Black Feminist Anthology.* New York: Kitchen Table: Women of Color Press, 1983.

Smith, Linda Tuhiwai. *Decolonizing Methodologies: Research and Indigenous Peoples.* New York: Zed Books, 1999.

Snow, David A., E. Burke Rochford, Jr., Steven K. Worden, and Robert D. Benford. "Frame Alignment Processes, Micromobilization and Movement Participation." *American Sociological Review* 51, no.4 (1986): 464–81. https://doi.org/10.2307/2095581.

Snow, David, Robert D. Benford, Holly McCammon, Lyndi Hewitt, and Scott Fitzgerald. "The Emergence, Development, and Future of the Framing Perspective: 25+ Years Since 'Frame Alignment.'" *Mobilization* 19, no. 1 (2014): 23–45.

Sommers, Samuel R., and Michael I. Norton. "Lay Theories About White Racists: What Constitutes Racism (and What Doesn't)." *Group Processes & Intergroup Relations* 9, no. 1 (2006): 117–38. https://doi.org/10.1177/1368430206059881.

Sullivan, Shannon, and Nancy Tuana, eds. *Race and Epistemologies of Ignorance.* Albany: SUNY Press, 2007.

Sunkara, Bhashkar. "Let them Eat Diversity: An Interview with Walter Benn Michaels." *Jacobin,* January 1, 2011. http://www.jacobinmag.com/2011/01/let-them-eat-diversity.

Tatar, Elizabeth. *Strains of Change: The Impact of Tourism on Hawaiian Music.* Honolulu: Bishop Museum Press, 2012.

Tomlinson, Barbara. "Category Anxiety and the Invisible White Woman: Managing Intersectionality at the Scene of Argument." *Feminist Theory* 19, no. 1 (2018): 1–20. https://doi.org/10.1177/1464700117734735.

———. *Undermining Intersectionality: The Perils of Powerblind Feminism.* Philadelphia: Temple University Press, 2019.

Tomlinson, Barbara, and George Lipsitz. "American Studies as Accompaniment." *American Quarterly* 65, no. 1 (2013): 1–30. https://doi.org/10.1353/aq.2013.0009.

————. "Insubordinate Spaces for Intemperate Times: Countering the Pedagogies of Neoliberalism." *Review of Education, Pedagogy, and Cultural Studies* 35, no. 1 (2013): 3–26. https://doi.org/10.1080/10714413.2013.753758.

Torres, Rodolfo D., and George Katsiaficas, eds. *Latino Social Movements: Historical and Theoretical Perspectives.* New York: Routledge, 1999.

Trask, Haunani-Kay. *From a Native Daughter: Colonialism and Sovereignty in Hawai'i.* 2nd edn. Honolulu: University of Hawai'i Press, 1999.

Trierweiler, Steven J., et al. "Clinician Attributions Associated with the Diagnosis of Schizophrenia in African American and Non-African American Patients." *Journal of Consulting and Clinical Psychology* 68, no. 1 (2000): 171–75. https://doi.org/10.1037/0022-006X.68.1.171.

Unzueta, Miguel M., and Brian S. Lowery. "Defining Racism Safely: The Role of Self-Image Maintenance on White Americans' Conceptions of Racism." *Journal of Experimental Social Psychology* 44, no. 6 (2008): 1491–97. http://doi.org/10.1016/j.jesp.2008.07.011.

Utsey, Shawn, et al. "Assessing the Psychological Consequences of Internalized Colonialism on the Psychological Well-Being of Young Adults in Ghana." *Journal of Black Psychology* 41, no. 3 (2015): 195–220. https://doi.org/10.1177/0095798414537935.

Von Eschen, Penny M. *Race against Empire: Black Americans and Anticolonialism.* Ithaca: Cornell University Press, 1997.

Wekker, Gloria. *White Innocence: Paradoxes of Colonialism and Race.* Durham: Duke University Press, 2016.

Whaley, Arthur L. "Cultural Mistrust and Mental Health Services for African Americans: A Review and Meta-Analysis." *Counseling Psychologist* 29, no. 4 (2001): 513–31. https://doi.org/ 10.1177/0011000001294003.

————. "A Two-stage Method for the Study of Cultural Bias in the Diagnosis of Schizophrenia in African Americans." *Journal of Black Psychology* 30, no. 2 (2004): 167–86. https://doi.org/10.1177/0095798403262062.

Williams, Patricia J. *Seeing a Color-Blind Future: The Paradox of Race.* New York: Noonday, 1998.

Winant, Howard. *The New Politics of Race: Globalism, Difference, Justice.* Minneapolis: University of Minnesota Press, 2004.

Wise, Tim. "What Kind of Card is Race? The Absurdity (and Consistency) of White Denial." *Counterpunch,* April 24, 2006. http://www.counterpunch.org/2006/04/24/what-kind-of-card-is-race.

Woods, Clyde. *Development Arrested: The Blues and Plantation Power in the Mississippi Delta.* New edn. New York: Verso, 1998.

———. "Do You Know What It Means to Miss New Orleans? Katrina, Trap Economics, and the Rebirth of the Blues." *American Quarterly* 57, no. 4 (2005): 1005–18. https://doi.org/10.1353/aq.2006.0017.

———. "Les Misérables of New Orleans: Trap Economics and the Asset Stripping Blues, Part 1." *American Quarterly* 61, no. 3 (2009): 769–96. https://www.jstor.org/stable/27735018.

Woodson, Carter G. *The Mis-education of the Negro.* San Diego: Book Tree, 2006.

Wright, Stephen C., and Micah E. Lubensky. "The Struggle for Social Equality: Collective Action Versus Prejudice Reduction." In *Intergroup Misunderstandings: Impact of Divergent Social Realities,* edited by Stephanie Demoulin, Jacques-Philippe Leyens, and John F Dovidio, 291–310. New York: Psychology Press, 2009.

Yancy, George, and Judith Butler. "What's Wrong With 'All Lives Matter'?" *New York Times Opinionator,* January 12, 2015. http://www.opinionator.blogs.nytimes.com/2015/01/12/whats-wrong-with-all-lives-matter/.

Yuval-Davis, Nira. "Intersectionality and Feminist Politics." *European Journal of Women's Studies* 13, no. 3 (2006): 193–209. https://doi.org/10.1177/1350506806065752.

———. "Intersectionality, Citizenship and Contemporary Politics of Belonging." *Critical Review of International Social*

and Political Philosophy 10, no. 4 (2007): 561–74. https://doi.
org/10.1080/13698230701660220.

Zinn, Maxine Baca, and Bonnie Thornton Dill, eds. *Women of
Color in US Society.* Philadelphia: Temple University Press,
1994.

Index